Something Ventured

▶IN▲TELE▼COM◀
INTELLIGENT TELECOMMUNICATIONS

Marcy M. Rothenberg
Rothenberg Communications

FOR USE WITH

11TH EDITION

Small Business Management

An Entrepreneurial Emphasis

Longenecker, Moore, and Petty

South-Western College Publishing
Thomson Learning™

Australia • Canada • Denmark • Japan • Mexico • New Zealand • Philippines
Puerto Rico • Singapore • South Africa • Spain • United Kingdom • United States

Something Ventured Telecourse Guide, 4th edition, for use with *Small Business Management: An Entrepreneurial Emphasis*, 11th edition, by Longenecker, Moore, and Petty

Publisher/Team Director: Dave Shaut
Executive Editor: John Szilagyi
Developmental Editor: Judith O'Neill and Lifland et al., Bookmakers
Marketing Manager: Rob Bloom
Production Editor: Barbara Fuller Jacobsen
Manufacturing Coordinator: Dana Began Schwartz
Production: Judy Sullivan/INTELECOM
Cover Design: Ann Small/A Small Design Studio
Cover Photographer: Matulionis Photography
Printer: Transcontinental Printing, Inc., Louiseville, QC

COPYRIGHT ©2000 by INTELECOM Intelligent Telecommunications

Something Ventured is a television-based course produced by INTELECOM Intelligent Telecommunications.

All Rights Reserved. No part of this work covered by the copyright hereon may be reproduced or used in any form or by any means – graphic, electronic, or mechanical, including photocopying, recording, taping, or information storage and retrieval systems – without the written permission of INTELECOM Intelligent Telecommunications, 150 E. Colorado Blvd., Suite 300, Pasadena, CA 91105-1937.

Printed in Canada
1 2 3 4 5 02 01 00 99

ISBN 0-538-89021-5

For more information contact South-Western College Publishing, 5101 Madison Road, Cincinnati, Ohio, 45227 or find us on the Internet at http://www.swcollege.com.

South-Western College Publishing is a division of Thomson Learning. The Thomson Learning logo is a registered trademark used herein under license.

This book is printed on acid-free paper.

Contents

CORRELATION OF COURSE COMPONENTS

Telecourse Guide Lesson Number and Title	Text Chapter Assignment	Video Program Number and Title
1 Small Business in a Big World	Chapter 1 pgs. 14–18	101 Small Business in a Big World
2 On Your Own?	Chapter 1	102 On Your Own?
3 Finding a Niche	Chapter 5	103 Finding a Niche
4 New or Used?	Chapter 4	104 New or Used?
5 The Ties that Bind	Chapter 3	105 The Ties that Bind
6 A Different Look	Chapters 1 & 3–5	6 A Different Look
7 The Business Plan	Chapter 6	NO VIDEO
8 Taking Aim	Chapter 7	107 Taking Aim
9 Where to Hang the Sign	Chapter 9	108 Where to Hang the Sign
10 The Buck Starts Here	Chapter 10 & 11	109 The Buck Starts Here
11 Making it Legal	Chapter 8	110 Making it Legal
12 From the Ground Up	Chapters 6–11	111 From the Ground Up
13 The Right Mix	Chapter 12	112 The Right Mix
14 What the Market Will Bear	Chapter 13	113 What the Market Will Bear
15 Out From the Crowd	Chapter 14	114 Out From the Crowd
16 Going Places	Chapter 15	115 Going Places
17 A Vintage Blend	Chapters 12-15	116 A Vintage Blend
18 Making the Pieces Fit	Chapter 17	117 Making the Pieces Fit
19 The Human Factor	Chapter 18	118 The Human Factor
20 Taking Stock	Chapter 19 pgs. 444–451; 22 pgs. 520–522	119 Taking Stock
21 "The Play's the Thing. . ."	Chapters 17, 18, 19 pgs. 444–451, & 22 pgs. 520–522	120 "The Play's the Thing. . ."
22 Keeping Track	Chapters 21 & 10 pgs. 209–219	121 Keeping Track
23 The Money Flow	Chapter 22	122 The Money Flow
24 Computers in the Small Business	Chapter 20	NO VIDEO
25 Risky Business	Chapter 23	123 Risky Business
26 Publish or Perish	Chapters 20–23 & 10 pgs. 209–219	124 Publish or Perish
27 For Everybody's Good	Chapter 16	125 For Everybody's Good
28 It's the Law	Appendix B of this book	126 It's the Law

Introduction

This is your telecourse guide. Treasure it; struggle with it; use it as your personal roadmap to the world of *Something Ventured*. Following the instructions in this guide will enable you to devote your time to absorbing course content rather than puzzling over what it is you are supposed to be learning.

Whether you are a newcomer to television courses, or an old hand, it is important that you become familiar with the components of *Something Ventured*, how they function with each other, and how they relate to you. Each of the elements in a telecourse contributes to the whole, effectively using the style of communication unique to that particular medium.

THE TELEVISION PROGRAM

The video component of *Something Ventured* calls your attention to key concepts and abstract ideas through a variety of formats. Using television for learning is not like watching a comedy series or sporting event. At first you may have to concentrate on *active* watching. It is very easy to slip into the passive, half-viewing stance used for entertainment television. In most instances, you will have a chance to review the lesson in an alternate time period, or watch video cassettes of the lesson at the learning center on campus.

If you have a video recorder, you can tape the program for viewing at a time convenient for you, or for review purposes. If you have an audio recorder available, tape the audio portion of the program as you are viewing it. After you have watched the program and can visualize it, the audio portion is an excellent source for review while you commute to and from work or take a morning jog, or at any time convenient for you. If you have any questions about content or wish additional information, contact the faculty advisor at the campus where you are enrolled. He or she is eager to help.

THE TEXT

The basic text for the course is *Small Business Management*, 11th edition, by Justin G. Longenecker, Carlos W. Moore, and J. William Petty, published by South-Western Publishing Company in 2000. The text is an essential part of the course, providing information most successfully adapted to the print media. It establishes a foundational background of knowledge and elaborates on concepts introduced in the television segment through charts, studies, and research. The assignment section of the study guide coordinates reading and review assignments with the television segment.

THE TELECOURSE GUIDE

The telecourse guide helps you to synthesize and integrate the materials presented in the text and television segments. With the exception of the business profile lessons (numbers 6, 12, 17, 21, and 26), each lesson contains the following sections:

- The objectives establish a structure for learning, suggesting what elements of the course require particular attention.

- The overview sets the stage and heightens interest in the material.

- The assignments section provides reading assignments in the text and shows the student how to proceed with learning activities.

- The key terms alert you to the important concepts covered in the lesson.

- The video viewing questions lay out some key questions that will be answered during the video program.

- The self-test shows what progress you have made in assimilating the material and beginning to apply it.

- The extend what you have learned section encourages you to apply concepts, integrate ideas, make choices, synthesize, and evaluate the material presented in the lesson.

As indicated earlier, each component in a telecourse contributes to the whole. The course is not any one of the elements by itself. It is a blending of all three: the television program, the text, and the telecourse guide.

Lesson 1

Small Business in a Big World

LEARNING OBJECTIVES

Upon completing your study of this lesson, you should be able to:

- Recognize the relative incidence of small businesses in today's society.

- Give examples of the contributions of small businesses to the economy.

- Describe the types of activities in which small businesses are engaged.

- Compare the advantages of a small firm to its problems and limitations.

- Specify reasons for the high rate of small business failure.

Going into business for yourself . . . it's always been considered one of the great American dreams. Today it's the dream of enterprising people all around the world. And it can be a smart thing to do, if you're prepared for the challenges that will confront you.

What constitutes a small business? In what industries are small businesses most successful? What sorts of contributions do small businesses make to the economy and to society? How great is the risk of failure, and what factors most strongly affect the success or failure of a new business? We'll be answering these questions, and more, in this lesson.

OVERVIEW

If you're the Bakersfield Dodgers, you seem like a small fry in comparison to the L.A. Dodgers. If, however, you're a semi-pro team in the piney woods of Georgia, chances are the boys in Bakersfield seem like pretty big stars indeed.

That's the way it is when we try to define "small" and "big" business. It all depends on your point of view. But to talk about small business, and its contributions to the economy and society, we have to try to define it. That way, we know we're all talking about the same thing.

Size Criteria Generally, when people define small business, they use a number of size criteria. Typical criteria across a variety of industries include the number of employees, the company's sales volume, its asset base, amount of insurance in force (in the insurance industry), and the volume of deposits (for financial service organizations).

Clearly, if we're talking about General Motors or IBM, we're talking big business—international in scope, vast in resources and asset value. But when we look at the incredible array of businesses in operation today, we've got to set different "big" and "small" criteria for every industry.

That, in fact, is just what the U.S. Small Business Administration has done in setting its standards for the definition of a small business. Some industries are measured in terms of sales volume, while others are ranked by the number of people they employ.

If, for example, you open an advertising agency and your billings grow to more than $3.5 million per year, you're considered "big business" by the SBA. But you may be considered a very big business with only one-fourth the billings if you're located in a small town or sparsely populated state.

Likewise, if you acquire land in Arkansas and set up a quartz mining operation, it will be considered "small business" if you have fewer than 500 employees. But, by local standards, you may be the big fish in a rural pond.

To create common ground on which to base our discussion, we'll define a small business as one in which:

■ there are limited capital resources; financing is provided by one or just a few individuals;

■ its operations (except perhaps its marketing) are generally local in nature;

■ it is small compared to other businesses in the same industry; and

■ it usually employs fewer than 100 people.

Where Does Small Business Operate? There are small businesses in virtually every industry in operation today. But they're more prominent in some industries than others. Take, for example, the auto industry. It's pretty obvious that you've got to be a big operation to compete in this industry.

But that doesn't mean you can't be important as a supplier to those big auto companies. What if your company manufactures door handles for the Big Three automakers? Your success is critical to their operations. So you may be a small business by measurable standards, but you're critical to your industry.

On the other side of that coin, a taxicab company in a small town may be an important business in a local sense, but it will play virtually no role in the success of the national transportation industry. That doesn't mean it's a worthless undertaking. It simply means it's not likely to have a significant impact on the transportation industry.

Small Business is Big Business! It may seem contradictory, but in the United States small business is actually big business. A few facts will help to explain what we mean. First, the SBA has classified about 98 percent of the 3.8 million businesses in its database—including corporations, partnerships and sole proprietorships—as "small." Those businesses employ one-half of the American workforce, excluding farm employment, and contribute about 40 percent of the gross national product. Two out of every three new jobs in the country are created by small businesses, so their impact on the economy is far from small!

Small business plays a significant role in the service and retailing industries. One-third of all service firms, and one-fourth of all retail operations, are classified as "small," and that trend is expected to accelerate, with the growth of a service-and-technology-oriented economy. But the presence of small business is felt in virtually all industries.

Contributions of Small Business Small business contributes to society and to the economy in a variety of ways. As we've already said, it is a strong provider of new jobs, since small firms are usually more growth-oriented than are larger business operations. In recent years, for example, firms with 20 or fewer employees added more jobs to the economy than did firms of 500 or more.

A second key contribution of small business comes in the area of innovation. It's not likely that a market analyst sitting in an office in some corporate enclave will identify the need for a pet-sitting or home construction referral service. Or see the market potential in paint-spattered sunglasses. Or devise a new filler for cat boxes and name it "Kitty Litter."

While large companies are more likely to improve or enhance existing products, it is the small business operation that is more likely to innovate and create. That doesn't mean employees of large organizations aren't creative. It's just more likely that their ideas don't fit into an ongoing operation, and the organization doesn't see a way to make them fit.

Some big businesses are entrepreneurially oriented. Take 3M, for example, where one research scientist's "mistake" in formulating a new adhesive turned into those little snips of paper known as Post-It Notes. The company encourages its employees to experiment, and to take the time to develop new ideas into marketable products. But that entrepreneurial focus is hard to maintain in a large organization, and that's why the major innovations often come from small firms.

Small business's third contribution is its stimulation of competition. When an industry is dominated by a few large organizations, it's hard to force those few to compete on price or service or anything else. But throw a few small companies into the marketplace and watch the price and service wars heat up!

Fourth, small business can be a powerful right arm to many big businesses, by providing services that the larger organizations couldn't do as efficiently. On the distribution side, for example, Procter & Gamble may be terrific at producing consumer products, but they're better off having their products sold by thousands of smaller firms than going into the grocery and drug store business, too. And on the supply side, General Electric may successfully manufacture an array of home appliances—but they rely on thousands of small businesses to supply them with the components for those appliances, rather than manufacturing each spring and latch and switch themselves.

Finally, small businesses are often more efficient at producing goods and service because they're not slowed down by a vast bureaucracy. Think about the difference: if you're a corporate employee and you come up with a new idea for product distribution, it could take months—or even longer—for the organization to consider the idea, analyze it, and finally give you the go-ahead. But if you own your own company—or if you're an employee in a ten-person shop, with direct access to the owner—that review and decision-making process is much more condensed. Have a good idea in a small business and you're much more likely to act on it in a matter of weeks, or even days.

The Down Side: Failure Rates It's no surprise to anyone that small businesses fare better in times of prosperity and struggle during economic recessions. What may be surprising is the finding by Dun & Bradstreet, Inc., that only about one percent of all businesses started in the United States end up in failure.

If there's just a one percent failure rate, you ask, why are news reports so glum on this subject? Many businesses don't fail in an economic sense, say

D&B's experts—they go out of business for other reasons. Perhaps the owner decides there just isn't enough profit to make the business worthwhile. Or maybe a business consolidated two locations into one. Or just relocated, leaving one community for another and creating the impression of failure. The discontinuation of a business isn't considered a failure by Dun & Bradstreet.

Even the SBA's studies show that failures are less common than we might believe. Their research shows us that 40 percent of all new firms survive six or more years, and that most that don't survive are closed voluntarily, with no economic loss to their creditors.

Why Businesses Fail To guard against failure in new business ventures, it's important to know why businesses do close. According to D&B, "economic factors" are most often cited as reasons for business closings. Included in this category are inadequate sales, insufficient profit and poor growth prospects. Running a close second are "finance causes"—such issues as heavy operating expenses and insufficient capital. Finally, there are "experience causes"—the lack of business knowledge, line experience, or managerial experience.

If we look at all of these causes, we can see that underlying each one is a management responsibility. It is the business owner's job to foster sales and growth, generate profit, control expenses, obtain capital, and run the business. So a firm grounding in management theory and practice is a key to success.

The failure of a business can be costly, even when there's no dollar loss involved. The entrepreneur and his or her creditors may lose the capital they've invested, which may create an economic crisis for them. But even if there is no financial loss, there can be losses to one's self-esteem.

In a larger sense, society loses, too, when a business shuts down. Jobs are lost to the local economy, unemployment increases, and government revenues are reduced because there's one less business taxpayer on the books. So when one business fails, many thousands of people can be affected, no matter how small that business may have been.

ASSIGNMENTS

■ Before you watch the video program, be sure you've read through the preceding overview, familiarized yourself with the learning objectives for this lesson, and looked at the key terms below. Then, read pages 14–18 in chapter 1 of Longenecker, Moore, and Petty, *Small Business Management*, "Entrepreneurship in the New Millennium."

- After completing these tasks, read the video viewing questions and watch the video program for Lesson 1, *Small Business in a Big World*.

- After watching the program, take time to answer the video viewing questions and evaluate your learning with the self-test.

- Extend your learning through the applications, exercises, or field experiences this lesson offers.

KEY TERMS

Size criteria   Measuring tools to determine whether a business is small or big. Typical criteria include number of employees, sales volume, asset size, insurance in force, and volume of deposits.

SBA standards   Criteria by which the Small Business Administration determines whether a business is small or big; SBA criteria include number of employees and sales volume.

Innovation   Creation of new products and services, often fostered by entrepreneurial firms.

Economic competition   Situation in which businesses vie for the greatest amount of sales.

Distribution function   Distribution of products and the establishment of intermediary relationships to guide and support the movement of products.

Supply function   Provision of the raw materials, parts, and other components needed in the production of goods and services, often provided by small business.

Failure rate   Measurement of the percentage of businesses that fail due to economic causes.

VIDEO VIEWING QUESTIONS

1. A variety of small business experts—Michael McGreevy, Oscar Wright, Jon Goodman, and others—describe the small business scene. Using their commentary, create a palette of words and phrases that, in combination, provide a comprehensive word picture of small businesses today.

2. Give examples of the contributions of small business that are illustrated in the video.

3. Although there is a vast difference in the size and complexity of the Los Angeles Dodgers and the Bakersfield Dodgers operations, you will notice that the two organizations perform many of the same functions. First list the functions you observed that are common to both. Then go back and indicate the similarities and differences in the way these business functions are carried out by the two organizations.

SELF-TEST

1. A typical small business in the construction industry is
   a. a roofing contractor.
   b. an appliance manufacturer.
   c. the corporation that acquires the land and builds all the homes.
   d. the bank that finances development projects.
   e. none of the above.

2. Small businesses employ approximately what percent of the U.S. labor force?
   a. 25 percent
   b. 40 percent
   c. 50 percent
   d. 98 percent

3. Small business is defined
   a. by the number of employees.
   b. by the volume of sales.
   c. by the value of assets.
   d. arbitrarily. There really is no universally agreed-upon definition.

4. Among small business's key contributions to society are
   a. increasing the number of available jobs.
   b. making it easier for big companies to conduct layoffs in economic downturns.
   c. encouraging the formation of monopolies by large companies.
   d. limiting the money supply available to large companies.

5. Business innovations occur most often
   a. in research and development (R&D) firms.
   b. in the research and marketing departments of major corporations.
   c. in small, entrepreneurial firms.
   d. in a home-based business.

6. Small businesses can help larger organizations with their
   a. management functions.
   b. supply and maintenance functions.
   c. research and development functions.
   d. supply functions.

7. Information technology
   a. is used by small businesses to overcome different obstacles than large companies.
   b. is used by small businesses to erase the advantages big businesses have.
   c. by companies of all sizes.
   d. All of the above.

8. The basic cause that underlies all business failures can be said to be
   a. a lack of good management skills.
   b. lack of trained employees in the area.
   c. poor bookkeeping practices.
   d. lack of commitment on the owner's part.

9. According to the television lesson, the growth of service industries as well as home-based businesses can be traced in large part to
   a. the emergence of a global economy.
   b. the impact of overcrowding and congestion.
   c. the personal computer.
   d. All of the above.

10. According to the Small Business Administration, what percent of new firms survive for six years or more?

    a. 10 percent.

    b. 25 percent.

    c. 40 percent.

    d. 65 percent.

EXTEND WHAT YOU HAVE LEARNED

1. Whether you live in a very large metropolitan area, or a small community, think of those businesses that are within reasonable distance of your home. Using the criteria established in this lesson, how many would be classified as small businesses?

    _____

    _____

    _____

2. Think of the businesses—large and small—that impact your life in a typical week. As a consumer, is there a difference in your relationship with these two categories of business? If there is, specify the differences.

    _____

    _____

    _____

3. Do you personally know someone who has owned or operated a small business that has failed? What are your observations regarding the reasons for the closure of the business? Do you think your perceptions would agree with the owner's? With the research regarding why most small businesses fail?

    _____

    _____

    _____

Lesson 2

On Your Own?

LEARNING OBJECTIVES

Upon completing your study of this lesson, you should be able to:

- Compare the rewards of entrepreneurship with its potential drawbacks.

- Recognize the characteristics of successful entrepreneurs.

- Analyze the personal needs, skills, and degree of commitment necessary to launch a new enterprise.

- Indicate personal considerations to contemplate before initiating a small business operation.

- Contrast the skills necessary for successful entrepreneurship with the skills necessary for successful small business management.

So, you want to go into business for yourself. You've got a great business idea, and you think you can make it fly. But how do you know whether or not you'd be a successful entrepreneur? How do you determine if you have the skills and characteristics that it takes to make it on your own? The best way to find out is to look at what others have found to be the most common characteristics of successful entrepreneurs, and to study entrepreneurial types. That's what we'll do in this lesson.

OVERVIEW

In studies conducted with entrepreneurs, and in discussions with business owners, management experts have drawn a number of conclusions about the traits that successful entrepreneurs have in common.

You won't necessarily find that your personality, or your reasons for going into business for yourself, are a perfect fit with those of the "typical" entrepreneur pictured by experts. But you should be able to identify many similarities between you and the people characterized as entrepreneurs in this lesson. If you can, and if your business idea is a good one, you're much more likely to find success in your own enterprise.

Here, according to the experts, is what the typical entrepreneur is like—and what he or she recognizes about striking out on one's own.

Incentives and Rewards There are three key reasons the typical entrepreneur decides to open up shop: profit, independence, and lifestyle.

The profit potential may be an end in itself, or it may simply be the benchmark by which the entrepreneur measures success. In either case, profit is a strong motivator for most people who head out on their own. They're confident that their business idea is strong enough to reap significant economic rewards. And they often believe, based on the strength of that business idea, that they can do better for themselves economically by taking the entrepreneurial route than by remaining in someone else's employ.

A desire for operating independence is the second common incentive. Entrepreneurs typically like to make their own decisions, take risks they've decided are worth taking, and reap the rewards of their actions. They're not satisfied with having to wait for approval from higher-ups to try out a new idea or to embark on a venture they're convinced is worth undertaking. Often they become frustrated in their efforts to get corporate bureaucracies moving—and moving quickly enough—on their recommendations. By going out on their own, entrepreneurs reason, they can make decisions quickly, and then act on them.

The third incentive revolves around lifestyle issues. Perhaps an employee's work involves too much travel, or prevents her from adapting her work hours to meet family needs. Or perhaps the employee doesn't mind the long hours, but would prefer to spend some of that work time in a home office, or work from home altogether. Maybe he wants to work outdoors, or has always dreamed of converting a hobby or avocation into a full time career.

Sometimes the motivation is simply the belief that it would be more fun to run your own business than to work for someone else. Whatever the motivation, lifestyle issues often play a big part in propelling the individual toward an independent work life.

Drawbacks and Costs Just as with any other speculative effort, there are risks involved in starting your own business. The first is obvious: it takes a great deal of time, effort, and money to launch a new venture on your own—

not to mention hard work and emotional energy—all of which take attention away from other activities, including family and friends. Business magazines are full of stories about the business that succeeded while the marriage failed. And those stories, unfortunately, often reflect the rule rather than the exception. You'll have a much easier time in the early months and years of a new venture if the people who mean a lot to you care as much about it as you do.

The second risk is obvious, too—and that's the risk of failure. By carefully constructing a business plan (which you'll learn more about in later lessons), and by conducting a detailed study of the marketplace in which you'll compete, you'll reduce the risk of failure.

Although you should recognize that failure is possible—even with the best idea and ample financing—careful preparation can reduce the possibility that you'll be conducting another job search in a year or two.

Entrepreneurial Characteristics So, just what is the "typical" entrepreneur like? How closely do your traits and attitudes match up with other entrepreneurs? Let's find out. Research has identified a cluster of traits that seem to clearly identify the entrepreneurial personality. They include a need for achievement, a willingness to take risks, a strong level of self-confidence, and the need to seek refuge from any of a number of "environmental" or external factors.

The need for achievement will vary from one entrepreneur to another, but it's there to some extent in virtually all those who seek to build their own businesses. If you were the kind of kid who set up the lemonade stand every day of every summer while your friends were inside watching television, you've got it. And if you've just come to the realization that being your own boss is something you want to do, you probably have it, too—your need just isn't as intense.

Your willingness to take risks can be measured in several ways: how willing you are to invest your own savings in the new venture; how willing you are to leave a secure job and set out on your own; how willing you are to risk failure, and the stressful feelings that failure would create.

If you're *self-confident*, you believe in your own ability to meet the challenges of a new situation. You believe that you can master problems you encounter. And, in all likelihood, you believe that your success depends on your own efforts, not on what someone else might do. In other words, you possess an internal, rather than an external, locus of control.

If you have a *passion for the business*, you will invest yourself in it. That is, you will be willing to work hard and will not be easily discouraged.

Finally, going into business often reflects the individual's need to seek renewal or refuge from something. Among the most common types are:

- *Foreign refugees*—Escaping the political, religious, or economic constraints of their homelands, immigrants often encounter discrimination in the workplace, or are handicapped by language and other barriers. Going into business for themselves is one solution.

- *Corporate refugees*—In an effort to reduce the impact of bureaucracy in their lives, some people go into business for themselves. Interestingly, they often do business with their former employers.

- *Paternal refugees*—People who are frustrated by a family business may begin a new venture just to prove they can make it on their own.

- *Feminist refugees*—Women who encounter sex discrimination in the workplace, may start a business of their own that will allow them to succeed on their own merits.

- *Housewife refugees*—Some women start their own businesses to free themselves from family responsibilities or to build new lives after their families are grown.

- *Society refugees*—Those who feel alienated from the dominant culture may seek an entrepreneurial way to support themselves apart from that culture.

- *Educational refugees*—Academicians who grow weary of life on campus and seek renewal may go into business for themselves, sometimes by providing consulting services in their areas of expertise or by striking out in entirely new directions.

Now, if you don't fit the entrepreneurial mold in every way and you still want to try to build your own business—take heart. Not every successful entrepreneur resembles the "ideal" model.

If, for example, yours is a sure-fire business idea—the market for your product is already guaranteed, or you know the need exists for your service and no one else is filling it—the fact that you're not much of a risk-taker may be irrelevant. If you knit elegant garments or create strikingly beautiful ceramic objects, you may not have to be the most self-confident, outgoing, energetic marketer for your product to sell. Your product will speak for itself.

Understanding that these characteristics do seem to influence entrepreneurial success will help in your endeavor. Incorporating them into your thought processes will help you identify the areas in which you may have to work a bit harder to finance your business and market your products or services.

Other Issues Among the other issues to consider when mulling over entrepreneurial possibilities are your age (admittedly an individual factor) and precipitating events that might push you toward a small business venture.

The age factor cuts both ways. If you're very young, you may not have enough experience, or the variety of experience necessary, to master the art of running your own business. Take, for example, a graphic artist who is working for an ad agency and decides to open a design studio. If he's only worked for a few years, he may not have enough experience in prospecting for new business or in managing client accounts. He may be the greatest artist in town, but if he can't run the business side of his operation, all his talent may go for naught.

On the other hand, your age might work against you—not in terms of your competency, your energy level or your abilities, but in terms of your economic flexibility. If you've been employed for some time, it may be economically impractical to give up the salary level you've reached, the pension plan and medical benefits, and "security" for a risky venture.

Many entrepreneurs can look back and point to a certain event or moment in time and say, "That's when I made up my mind to start a new business." An unexpected job termination or a business offer from a friend or relative may spark your interest in owning a small business. Or the push may be more gradual, as in the case of those who became disenchanted with corporate or academic life and slowly decide to seek their futures elsewhere.

Preparing for Entrepreneurship Some entrepreneurs prepare for their new business ventures by going to school. Others do so by working in their field of interest for a period of time. A balance between the two is often ideal. If you want to set up your own public accounting firm, clearly a college education is the first step. But if you plan to open a chain of floral shops, going to work at the neighborhood florist is probably the place to start.

Even if your business does not involve a professional service or require a college education, some formal education is likely to serve you well. Studies have shown that the owners of new businesses are, on average, better educated than the general public. And the recent advent of college-level entrepreneurship courses, such as the one you're taking, suggest that there's a lot to learn about running a business—any business.

Entrepreneurial People There are many kinds of entrepreneurs . . . a woman who, frustrated by her lack of opportunity in a traditionally male-dominated industry, sets up her own business to "beat the boys" at their own game . . . a duo who find themselves in agreement on how a travel agency ought to be run, and quit their jobs to open their own office . . . the inventor who establishes his company to market his new product . . . the fast-food restaurant manager who puts together the capital to buy her own franchise. All of these people have one thing in common: they are entrepreneurs.

In the life of a business organization there are generally two types of leaders. Founding entrepreneurs are those who start the business, who see the potential in an idea or a product and put together the capital and the facilities to market it. General managers are entrepreneurial types who continue to run the new business after start-up, moving from the innovative to the administrative phase of the operation. Often the skills required to be a successful entrepreneur and the skills required to be a successful manager once the business is up and running are quite different.

Business Styles Researchers point to two distinct styles of entrepreneurial operation—the craftsman entrepreneur and the opportunistic entrepreneur.

The craftsman entrepreneur brings technical job skills to the table, but lacks communications skills. He tries to make all decisions himself, hesitates to delegate, uses few capital sources for funding, defines market strategy in narrow terms (price, quality, and reputation), emphasizes personal sales efforts, and focuses on short-term rather than long-term objectives.

The opportunistic entrepreneur has supplemented her technical education with studies in economics, law, business, and communications. She tries to involve employees in decisions, delegates authority, shops for funding sources, uses a variety of marketing strategies and sales efforts, and plans carefully for long-term growth.

The closer your management style is to that of the opportunistic entrepreneur, the better your chances are for long-term success. It doesn't mean you must delegate everything, or that you should abandon a tried-and-true marketing strategy. But the more flexible you are, and the more willing you are to seek out other ideas and other sources of support, the more likely it is your business will prevail.

ASSIGNMENTS

- Before you watch the video program, be sure you've read through the preceding overview, familiarized yourself with the learning objectives for this lesson, and looked at the key terms below. Then, read chapter 1 of Longenecker, Moore, and Petty, *Small Business Management*, "Entrepreneurship in the New Millennium."

- After completing these tasks, read the video viewing questions and watch the video program for Lesson 2, *On Your Own?*

- After watching the program, take time to answer the video viewing questions and evaluate your learning with the self-test which follows the key terms.

- Extend your learning through the applications, exercises, or field experiences this lesson offers.

KEY TERMS

Refugee	In entrepreneurial terms, a person who seeks refuge from a negative factor in his or her work life by going to work for him or herself.
Locus of control	Whether a person is controlled primarily by internal or external forces; the entrepreneur typically has an internal locus of control.
Founding entrepreneur	The "pure" entrepreneur, who initiates a business on the basis of a new product or service, or on the basis of his/her skill as a craftsperson.
General manager	Administrator of the established, successful entrepreneurial organization.
Marginal firm	A small firm that has the potential only to return a small profit to its owners.
Opportunistic entrepreneur	Entrepreneur who has supplemented technical education with finance, managerial, and communications education.

VIDEO VIEWING QUESTIONS

1. The video features the comments of both experts and small business owners about the qualities and skills that seem common to successful entrepreneurs. Develop a list of these qualities and skills, and assess your own abilities in comparison to the inventory you create.

2. Carefully note the rewards, and the potential drawbacks, of owning your own business that are brought out in the video. Relate these comments to your own feelings as you contemplate starting a new business.

3. The video points out the difference between the entrepreneurial skills necessary to start a business and the savvy required to manage the small business long term. Match your skills to the attributes that are described.

SELF-TEST

1. Entrepreneurs are most often lured to independent business life by
    a. fear of failure, the potential for job security, and a preference for bureaucracy.
    b. potential for profit, freedom from supervision, and the excitement of being in business.
    c. the desire to work less while making more money.
    d. a successful corporate business career.

2. Starting and operating a business is risky because
    a. an individual needs extensive corporate experience to ensure success.
    b. it is necessary to hire so many specialists in the beginning.
    c. it could take more time than anticipated.
    d. there is no one to bail out the entrepreneur if the venture fails.

3. The typical entrepreneur has
    a. a low to moderate need for achievement.
    b. less education than the average corporate employee.
    c. a high need for achievement.
    d. a fear of failure.

4. Risks faced by the entrepreneur include
   a. career risk.
   b. financial risk.
   c. psychic risk.
   d. all of the above.

5. Typical precipitating events that lead one to entrepreneurship include all but
   a. being fired.
   b. graduating from business school.
   c. job dissatisfaction.
   d. unexpected opportunities.

6. An opportunistic entrepreneur would be characterized by which of the following?
   a. Guides the business in a paternalistic manner
   b. Tends to "fly by the seat of the pants"
   c. Is a well-educated, experienced manager
   d. Usually uses only one or two sources of capital to create his or her firm

7. The ideal time for entrepreneurship is generally
   a. before acquiring family responsibilities such as children and mortgages—generally from the late teens to the early 20s.
   b. later in life, when sufficient experience and financial resources have been acquired—generally after 50 years of age.
   c. when a balance between prepatory experience and family obligations has been reached—generally between the late 20s and early 40s.

8. Franchisees differ most from other entrepreneurs in
   a. the kinds of businesses they operate.
   b. the level of education they obtain.
   c. the amount of time they devote to their businesses.
   d. the degree of operating independence they possess.

9. The belief that one's success depends on one's own efforts is
   a. an internal locus of control.
   b. an external locus of control.
   c. the hallmark of a "pure" entrepreneur
   d. an identifying characteristic of the artisan entrepreneur

10. The three major rewards of entrepreneurship are profit, independence, and
    a. secure retirement.
    b. public influence.
    c. professional relationships.
    d. satisfying lifestyle.

EXTEND WHAT YOU HAVE LEARNED

THE ENTREPRENEUR'S QUIZ[1]

Who are these people called Entrepreneurs? Why do they seem more at home in a swivel chair than in an easy chair? What makes them lay their talent and skill on the line, not once, but over and over again? Why can't they just get a job? What's with them anyway?

Are they really smarter than the rest of us? Do they know something we don't? Or are they just crazy? Or maybe it's a combination of the three.

This entrepreneurial profile was developed from a series of questionnaire analyses performed by The Center for Entrepreneurial Management, Inc. Founded in 1978, the Center is the world's largest nonprofit association of entrepreneurial managers, with over 2,500 members. CEM is headquartered in New York City, with offices in Houston, and Santa Clara, California.

Check your own profile!

THE QUIZ

1. How were your parents employed?
   a. Both worked and were self-employed for most of their working lives.
   b. Both worked and were self-employed for some part of their working lives.
   c. One parent was self-employed for most of his or her working life.
   d. One parent was self-employed at some point in his or her working life.
   e. Neither parent was ever self-employed.

1. Copyright © 1983 Joe Mancuso. Reprinted with permission of Joseph R. Mancuso, The Center for Entrepreneurial Management Inc., 180 Varick Street—Penthouse, New York, NY 10014, (212) 633-0060.

2. Have you ever been fired from a job?
   a. Yes, more than once.
   b. Yes, once.
   c. No.

3. Are you an immigrant, or were your parents or grandparents immigrants?
   a. I was born outside of the United States.
   b. One or both of my parents were born outside of the United States.
   c. At least one of my grandparents was born outside of the United States.
   d. Does not apply.

4. Your work career has been:
   a. Primarily in small business (under 100 employees).
   b. Primarily in medium-sized business (100 to 500 employees).
   c. Primarily in big business (over 500 employees).

5. Did you operate any businesses before you were twenty?
   a. Many.
   b. A few.
   c. None.

6. What is your present age?
   a. 21-30.
   b. 31-40.
   c. 41-50.
   d. 51 or over.

7. You are the _____ child in the family.
   a. Oldest.
   b. Middle.
   c. Youngest.
   d. Other.

8. You are:
   a. Married.
   b. Divorced.
   c. Single.

9. Your highest level of formal education is:
   a. Some high school.
   b. High school diploma.
   c. Bachelor's degree.
   d. Master's degree.
   e. Doctor's degree.

10. What is your primary motivation in starting a business?
    a. To make money.
    b. I don't like working for someone else.
    c. To be famous.
    d. As an outlet for excess energy.

11. Your relationship to the parent who provided most of the family's income was:
    a. Strained.
    b. Comfortable.
    c. Competitive.
    d. Non-existent.

12. If you could choose between working hard and working smart, you would:
    a. Work hard.
    b. Work smart.
    c. Both.

13. On whom do you rely for critical management advice?
    a. Internal management teams.
    b. External management professionals.
    c. External financial professionals.
    d. No one except myself.

14. If you were at the racetrack, which of these would you bet on?
    a. The daily double—a chance to make a killing.
    b. A 10-to-one shot.
    c. A 3-to-1 shot.
    d. The 2-to-1 favorite.

15. The only ingredient that is both necessary and sufficient for starting a business is:
    a. Money.
    b. Customers.
    c. An idea or product.
    d. Motivation and hard work.

16. If you were an advanced tennis player and had a chance to play a top pro like Jimmy Connors, you would:
    a. Turn it down because he could easily beat you.
    b. Accept the challenge, but not bet any money on it.
    c. Bet a week's pay that you would win.
    d. Get odds, bet a fortune, and try for an upset.

17. You tend to "fall in love" too quickly with:
    a. New product ideas.
    b. New employees.
    c. New manufacturing ideas.
    d. New financial plans.
    e. All of the above.

18. Which of the following personality types is best suited to be your right-hand person?
    a. Bright and energetic.
    b. Bright and lazy.
    c. Dumb and energetic.

19. You accomplish tasks better because:
    a. You are always on time.
    b. You are super-organized.
    c. You keep good records.

20. You hate to discuss:
    a. Problems involving employees.
    b. Signing expense accounts.
    c. New management practices.
    d. The future of the business.

21. Given a choice, you would prefer:
    a. Rolling dice with a 1-in-3 chance of winning.
    b. Working on a problem with a 1-in-3 chance of solving it in the allocated time.

22. If you could choose between the following competitive professions, it would be:
    a. Professional golf.
    b. Sales.
    c. Personnel counseling.
    d. Teaching.

23. If you had to choose between working with a partner who is a close friend, and working with a stranger who is an expert in your field, you would choose:
    a. The close friend.
    b. The expert.

24. You enjoy being with people:
    a. When you have something meaningful to do.
    b. When you can do something new and different.
    c. When you have nothing planned.

25. In business situations that demand action, clarifying who is in charge will help produce results.
    a. Agree.
    b. Agree, with reservations.
    c. Disagree.

26. In playing a competitive game, you are concerned with:
    a. How well you play.
    b. Winning or losing.
    c. Both of the above.
    d. Neither of the above.

SCORING

This scoring is weighted to determine your Entrepreneurial Profile, the rating of which appears in Appendix A at the back of this book.

1.	a = 10	7.	a = 15	13.	a = 0	19.	a = 5	
	b = 5		b = 2		b = 10		b = 15	
	c = 5		c = 0		c = 0		c = 5	
	d = 2		d = 0		d = 5			
	e = 0					20.	a = 8	
		8.	a = 10	14.	a = 0		b = 10	
2.	a = 10		b = 2		b = 2		c = 0	
	b = 7		c = 2		c = 10		d = 0	
	c = 0				d = 3			
		9.	a = 2			21.	a = 0	
3.	a = 5		b = 3	15.	a = 0		b = 15	
	b = 4		c = 10		b = 10			
	c = 3		d = 8		c = 0	22.	a = 3	
	d = 0		e = 4		d = 0		b = 10	
							c = 0	
4.	a = 10	10.	a = 0	16.	a = 0		d = 0	
	b = 5		b = 15		b = 10			
	c = 0		c = 0		c = 3	23.	a = 0	
			d = 0		d = 0		b = 10	
5.	a = 10							
	b = 7	11.	a = 10	17.	a = 5	24.	a = 3	
	c = 0		b = 5		b = 5		b = 3	
			c = 10		c = 5		c = 10	
6.	a = 8		d = 5		d = 5			
	b = 10				e = 15	25.	a = 10	
	c = 5	12.	a = 0				b = 2	
	d = 2		b = 5	18.	a = 2		c = 0	
			c = 10		b = 10			
					c = 0	26.	a = 8	
							b = 10	
							c = 15	
							d = 0	

Lesson 3

Finding a Niche:
Investigating Entrepreneurial Opportunities

LEARNING OBJECTIVES

Upon completing your study of this lesson, you should be able to:

■ Suggest ways in which to assess the competitive merit of an idea for a potential product or service.

■ Determine which type of strategic advantage—cost or marketing—a new business idea may offer.

■ Understand the value of market segmentation strategies, and determine which type of strategy is most appropriate for an entrepreneurial venture.

■ Discuss the two primary types of segmentation variables—benefit and demographic—and apply them to a new business situation.

■ Describe the process involved in selecting a market niche and maintaining that niche potential over time.

It's been a lifelong dream—having a small business of your own . . . something you could create and nurture through the years . . . something that would become successful because of your skill, determination, and hard work.

But where does one begin? Is there some magic formula that makes one business idea good and another doomed to failure? And if you have an idea, how do you evaluate it realistically? Those are questions we'll be looking at in this lesson as we explore the topics of market segmentation, niche marketing, and customer service management.

OVERVIEW

One of the intriguing aspects of the small business scene is its diversity. If there is a common denominator, it's the fact that thriving businesses respond to a need that exists in the marketplace.

Once you've developed a new business idea, you'll want to test its viability by asking some tough questions. Does the business clearly appeal to an identifiable segment of the overall market? Can you design a marketing strategy that will appeal to the particular market niche (or niches) you identify as your initial target market? And can you design a business operating plan—and inspire your employees to internalize a management philosophy—that puts customer satisfaction first?

With any kind of new venture, you're likely to choose the business for one of several reasons. Maybe you've had business or personal experiences that convinced you this business is the right kind for you. Maybe you've enjoyed a particular hobby for many years and you've finally decided to make it your business as well.

Maybe it just happened—a serendipitous occurrence that caused you to dream up the latest incarnation of the legendary Pet Rock—and your entrepreneurial adventure is off and running. Or maybe you've conducted a deliberate search—consulting with friends, family, business associates, and community contacts to identify prospective business opportunities and decide which one is right for you.

A New-Venture Idea   You're a resident of an upscale suburban community in a prosperous metropolitan area, and you're thinking about opening a retail store. The business you're thinking about opening? "The Coffee Bean," a coffee and tea shop in which you'd sell gourmet coffees and teas, as well as coffee makers, coffee grinders, air pots, teapots, tea infusers, filters, gourmet cookies and breads—in short, all the supplies needed by the coffee or tea lovers in your town. But how do you find out if your idea is likely to be successful? How do you determine its market potential?

Clearly, you've got to do more than just guess at your prospective customer base. You'll want to test your idea by:

- identifying the likely market segments,

- determining whether you can best appeal to those segments on a cost or a marketing basis, and

- deciding whether you'll be most successful with an unsegmented, multisegmented or single-segmented marketing strategy.

The first step is probably the easiest. A list of prospective customers for The Coffee Bean might include local residents, the owners of area businesses and offices, and people who tend to give gifts to those with whom they do business. Area realtors, for example, may want to give a housewarming gift to a client who has just bought a home.

The second step—choosing between cost and marketing strategies—requires that you take a good, close look at your market. Since you're located in an upscale community, you probably won't need to compete on a cost basis. Your customers are more likely to be motivated by factors like product quality, uniqueness, convenience, and customer service, than by low-end pricing.

The third step—selecting the proper market segmentation strategy—will necessitate some careful consideration. Not only will you have to develop a preliminary sales forecast (which you'll learn more about in lesson 8), but you'll also have to decide whether there's a particular segment of your market that is most likely to offer your business the support it needs to succeed in the first critical weeks and months.

If, for example, yours will be the only coffee and tea shop in the community, you probably can pursue an *unsegmented strategy*. With no one else selling what you provide, you'll be able to offer an identical pricing, product and service mix to residents, local businesses and offices, and business gift-givers.

If, however, you will face competition, you'll have to decide if the potential is great enough to go after all three of those target segments from day one—employing a *multisegmentation strategy*. You may decide instead to target just the strongest segment for now, and hold off on going after the other markets until your hold on Market Number One is secure. If you choose that approach, you'll be following a *single-segmentation strategy*.

Your Market Niche—The Competitive Advantage   Assuming that you will have *some* competition—since utterly new business ideas are few and far between—let's talk about how you can carve out a market niche: the distinction that sets your business apart from all the rest.

Let's assume that the only other place in your community where people can buy fresh, gourmet coffees and teas is at a chain store located in the mall. Their prices are high because of their elevated rental costs. You plan to open in a smaller, community-oriented shopping center with lower rental rates, plenty of parking, and a friendly, informal ambience.

Your competitor's coffees are chemically decaffeinated, while you intend to market only water-decaffeinated products. They carry the same selection of coffees and teas at all times, while you plan to vary your product offerings and even create new concoctions on a seasonal basis.

To make your chances even better, your chain-store competitor can offer no special discounts or custom products to its customers. There's one price for everyone and the product selection is predetermined. You, on the other hand, could offer a free pound of coffee for every ten pounds purchased, and even create custom gift baskets for business customers.

Your market niche is already beginning to define itself in several ways. You'll be offering a pleasant, convenient location, lower-than-chain-store prices, product variety, healthier products, and discounts and specialized services for regular customers. Your business profile is beginning to take shape!

But you must remember that niche development is more than a one-time event. Carving out your niche is important initially, but it's also necessary to maintain that niche—or modify it—as time goes on. As the market grows and changes, as your competition increases or adapts, your niche strategy will have to adapt along with it. Otherwise, someone else may nab your great idea and carry it one step further.

But at the outset, your first step is research. When that research is complete—when you've analyzed your market, studied your competition, and developed a reasonably sound sales forecast—take a cold, hard look at what the data tell you. Is there a market for The Coffee Bean? Is that market substantial enough to support the investment that will be required? How sure are you that you can claim a solid share of the market segment or segments you'll be targeting? How long will it take for the business to turn a profit? The steps required to plan for and launch a new business are too demanding to begin with an idea that is doomed from the start.

Sustaining Your Competitive Advantage You've done it. You've done the research and have built a solid foundation based on available opportunities and organizational capabilities. You've planned your strategy and positioned yourself well, and now your business is a viable contender in its market or industry. Time to sit back and enjoy the fruits of your labor, right? Not if you want to maintain that competitive advantage you've worked so hard to gain! Staying competitive requires a forward-thinking attitude and a steady stream of strategies designed to generate increases in market share, customer satisfaction, and continued profitability.

The life cycle of a competitive advantage begins with the investment of the resources required to launch an endeavor, followed by the payoff for the initial investment in the form of sales or profits, and finally the erosion of the competitive advantage with the inevitable incorporation of similar strategies by the competition. In order to maintain performance over time, and to facilitate future competitive advantages, an organization must reinvest resources in its own maintenance and growth. Sustainable competitive advantage can be achieved only when an organization's external environment and internal capabilities are continuously evaluated and updated.

ASSIGNMENTS

■ Before you watch the video program, be sure you've read through the preceding overview, familiarized yourself with the learning objectives for this lesson, and looked at the key terms below. Then read chapter 5 of Longenecker, Moore, and Petty, *Small Business Management*, "Competitive Advantage in the Marketplace."

■ After completing these tasks, read the video viewing questions and watch the video program for Lesson 3, *Finding a Niche*.

■ After watching the program, take time to answer the video viewing questions and evaluate your learning with the self-test.

■ Extend your learning through the applications, exercises or field experiences this lesson offers.

KEY TERMS

Competitive advantage   Characteristic of a business that gives it an "edge" over the competition.

Cost advantage   Business advantage gained by pricing products or services at below- or bottom-of-market levels.

Marketing advantage   Business advantage gained by differentiating products or services on the basis of quality, convenience, customer service, visual appeal, or some other factor less tangible than price.

Market segmentation   Dividing a potential market into groups distinguished by demographics, buying behavior or product/service needs.

Unsegmented stragegy   Strategy useful in monopoly or near-monopoly markets, in which the business can appeal to all prospective segments on the same price, product and customer service bases.

Multisegmentation strategy   Strategy in which the business uses different price, product and customer service appeals for different market segments.

Single-segmentation strategy Strategy in which a new business owner targets just one segment of the market for its initial business push, choosing the one that offers the greatest potential competitive advantage.

Benefit variables Dividing a total potential market in terms of the benefits each market segment will derive from the product or service.

Demographic variables Dividing a total potential market in terms of the demographic factors that will make some prospective customers more likely to buy a product or service.

Niche marketing Creating a unique place for your product or service in the marketplace; distinguishing it in some way from the competition.

VIDEO VIEWING QUESTIONS

1. Oscar Wright, Kathleen Gurney, and Alan Tratner suggest a number of different sources of startup ideas for someone interested in starting a new business. Make a note of their recommendations, and the fields they feel offer growth potential. For each category that is suggested, begin a list of service or product needs that are not being met in the area in which you live. Keep this list around for several months, adding to or modifying it as you come up with new ideas. Check the business section of your local newspaper, watching for the emergence of new businesses to fill the needs you've identified.

2. What are the crucial elements to consider in conducting a feasibility study? Why not start with family and friends? Aren't they the very people who would most like you to succeed?

3. According to Oscar Wright, how does the Small Business Administration support innovation research?

4. Analyze the ways in which the three businesses profiled in this lesson—CBI Labs, Sundance Expeditions, and Mascoll Beauty Supply—investigated entrepreneurial opportunities and found their niche. In each case, how did Cain, Patterson, and Mascoll differentiate themselves from others in the field?

SELF-TEST

1. Systematic investigation of a new business opportunity should involve *all but*
   a. examining opportunities, risks, and resources.
   b. deciding on alternatives and adopting a basic strategy.
   c. keeping the strategy informal and unwritten, to allow for modification.
   d. periodic reevaluation of the strategy chosen.

2. The only time a business owner doesn't need to identify market segments is when
   a. the competition has already identified them.
   b. the business is still in the planning stages.
   c. the marketplace is heterogeneous.
   d. the business has monopoly control of the market for its products or services.

3. Among the five forces that determine the nature and degree of competition in an industry are *all but*
   a. product quality.
   b. the threat of substitutes.
   c. buyers' bargaining power.
   d. rivalry among existing competitors.

4. Competitive advantage is
   a. the difference between the list price and the selling price of an existing business.
   b. the difference between a company's cost and the price it sets for its products or services.
   c. the advantage gained by commencing a startup business rather than buying out an existing business.
   d. the element of a new business' products or services that gives it a competitive edge.

5. The value of initial and ongoing market research was most pointedly demonstrated in the television lesson by
   a. Dr. Paul Cain and his natural cosmetics business.
   b. Beverly Mascoll and her Mascoll Beauty Supplies.
   c. Judo Patterson and his Sundance Kayaking School.
   d. Oscar Wright and the Small Business Administration.

6. The strategy which requires the entrepreneur to become the lowest-cost producer within a market is called the
   a. market penetration strategy.
   b. marketing advantage strategy.
   c. cost advantage strategy.
   d. production ratio strategy.

7. The three major components of the competitive advantage model include *all but*
   a. building a foundation through environmental and organizational assets.
   b. selecting a marketing strategy.
   c. determining an acceptable profit margin.
   d. sustaining the competitive advantage.

8. Differentiating your product or service from that of competitors is called the
   a. differentiation advantage strategy.
   b. marketing advantage strategy.
   c. cost advantage strategy.
   d. competitive advantage strategy.

9. The text considers this the market segmentation strategy that is likely to be most beneficial for new businesses:
   a. multisegmentation strategy.
   b. competitive advantage strategy.
   c. unsegmented strategy.
   d. single-segmentation strategy.

10. Developing a niche strategy could involve all of the following *except*
    a. concentrating on a single product and emphasizing its superiority.
    b. focusing on several market segments rather than risking a more concentrated effort.
    c. emphasis on a single product or service.
    d. sticking to one geographic region.

EXTEND WHAT YOU HAVE LEARNED

1. There are very few of us who have not considered, or dreamed about, starting a small business. Think back—at least a few years—and list those businesses that you have considered starting. What stopped you? Or what

now prompts you to go forward with one of the ideas you have considered?

_____

_____

_____

2. Conduct a preliminary, but diligent, investigation of your business idea. Find the answers to such basic questions as:

    — Who are my potential customers?

    _____

    — Where are they located?

    _____

    — What are their major needs?

    _____

    — What kinds of service do they want?

    _____

    — What's the best way to reach them?

    _____

3. A number of secondary research sources are suggested in the video program and the background material you read for this lesson (such sources as local Chambers of Commerce, industrial development commissions, trade associations, and the Bureau of Labor Statistics). What research resources do you find most valuable? Does your enthusiasm for the product or service you are considering impair your ability to analyze data objectively?

    _____

    _____

    _____

Lesson 4

New or Used?
Buying a Firm or Starting Your Own

LEARNING OBJECTIVES

Upon completing your study of this lesson, you should be able to:

- Recognize the various options that are available to a person interested in acquiring or starting a small business operation.

- Distinguish between Type A, Type B, and Type C business startup ideas.

- Indicate the advantages and disadvantages of buying an ongoing business versus starting your own.

- Suggest ways in which a person interested in purchasing a small business can find one to buy.

- Discuss approaches to use in investigating and evaluating an existing business.

- Indicate factors to consider in establishing the value of a company, negotiating price and terms, and closing the deal.

Imagine, as you did in Lesson 3, that you've decided to open a gourmet coffee and tea store in your community. But imagine that, instead of having just one option—starting your business "from scratch"—you could also buy out an existing retailer. How would you decide which option is preferable?

In this lesson, we'll talk about the process that can be used to determine the pros and cons of each option and come to the best decision.

OVERVIEW

When you talk about starting a new business, people generally assume you mean starting from the ground up; and indeed, many new businesses begin this way. But if you know how to analyze the value and the potential of an existing business, it might be possible to buy out an existing company and "jump-start" your entrepreneurial venture.

The Startup Option You'll learn about three types of startup ideas in this lesson: Type A ideas, for marketing a product or service that exists elsewhere but not in the target market; Type B ideas, for brand new processes or products; and Type C ideas, performing old services or offering existing products in new or better ways.

Sometimes, you have no choice but to go the startup route. If you've created a completely new product, or if yours is the first such business in your community or region, clearly you're not going to find a similar business to buy.

There are certain advantages to the startup option. You can choose the best possible location, and buy or lease exactly the equipment you prefer. You can select the range of products or services you'll offer, without feeling compelled to offer something just because the former owner did.

You'll have free rein when it comes to deciding policies and practices for your business; there will be no negative precedents to tie your hands. Nor will you be saddled with any legal obligations that make it harder for you to run your business and make a profit.

Contemplating a Buyout If your entrepreneurial idea allows you to consider a buyout—instead of opening The Coffee Bean, for example, you're considering buying the neighborhood Gourmet Caffe, which you've just learned is on the market—you've got to do a great deal of research.

Choosing to buy out the owner of Gourmet Caffe offers a number of potential advantages. You're buying an existing business, which means it's already got a track record, its location has been tested, it has a customer base, and it provides you with an instant inventory and equipment base from which to begin operating.

In addition, the owner of Gourmet Caffe already has established working relationships with employees, suppliers, landlord, utilities companies, lenders and so on. You'll want to find out, of course, if those relationships are positive, but if they are, you'll be off and running more quickly.

And finally, you may be able to go into business for a price that is a "bargain," compared to the cost of starting up your own business and slowing building your own goodwill with customers, employees, and other publics.

But—and "but" is the operative word when looking at a buyout—you must be cautious. It's easy to be persuaded that an ongoing business is a great opportunity, and it's *very* hard to uncover the problems that may be hiding below the surface.

You must do a great deal of research when considering a buyout, and that research should take a number of forms. First, visit the business and observe its operations. If you were visiting Gourmet Caffe, you'd want to ask yourself a variety of questions: Are the employees courteous with customers? Is the location busy? Do customers seem to know the staff, or are employee-customer interactions perfunctory? Is the store inviting? Do you feel comfortable being there?

Talk with the owner and find out why she is selling. Will she be leaving the community—or is there a chance she is just leaving this location . . . and secretly planning to open up a bigger shop in the newer, even more attractive shopping center a few miles away? (And, of course, taking many of Gourmet Caffe's customers along with her!)

To unearth that kind of information, you'll want to talk with other people who work with the owner of Gourmet Caffe—suppliers, bankers, customers, accountants, lawyers and so on. Work hard to learn the owner's *true* reasons for selling—they may be quite different from the reasons she gives you.

The Financial Investigation Then you'll need to do your financial investigation—examining the company's financial records, commissioning an independent audit, and having your financial advisers prepare an adjusted, audited statement. (This will tell you what the true income potential of the business is, by adjusting for the possibility that the owner has understated income for tax reasons, put several relatives on the payroll, or recorded personal expenses on the business' books.)

Your audit should also determine whether the value of assets you'd be buying is stated realistically. If Gourmet Caffe has been in business for 15 years and declares the value of its aging cappuccino machine at $1,000—when you know you can buy a brand new one for half the price—you know you've got to adjust the stated asset value accordingly before setting a price you're willing to pay for the business.

Your financial advisors should also look at the business' federal tax returns, state sales tax statements, invoices, receipts, bank statements—anything that will help you determine the true financial valuation of the business.

Several different approaches are used to establish the value of a business: *asset-based valuation* (which includes the modified book value, replacement value and liquidation value approaches), *market-based valuation*, *earnings-based valuation*, and *cash-flow-based valuation*.

Asset-based valuation determines the value of a business by examining the value of its assets in one of three ways. Using *modified book value*, you will determine asset value by comparing the historical cost and the current value of all business assets. *Replacement-value* analysis determines how much it would cost in current dollars to replace business assets. And *liquidation-value* analysis asks what payment you would receive if you were to sell off the business' assets. None of these approaches, however, recognizes the business' value as a going concern, so they should be used only as a highly conservative measure of value.

Market-based valuation relies on the marketplace to set the business' value. It is useful only if other similar businesses have sold recently. But if Gourmet Caffe is the only game in town, market-based valuation won't work, since you'll find no appropriate businesses for comparison.

Earnings-based valuation—which is most often used by people considering a buyout—calculates the business' income potential in the coming year, applies a desired rate of return to that amount, and determines the amount of investment you'd need to achieve that rate of return. You'll learn a great deal more about this method—also called *capitalization of profit*—in the textbook.

Finally, *cash-flow-based valuation* compares your expected rate of return on your investment with the rate of return you must realize to make the investment economically feasible. It requires that you ask whether putting your funds in another similar investment would be more likely to give you the required rate of return than would the investment in question.

Other Considerations   So, you've looked at Gourmet Caffe from all sides and you're convinced it's a good buy. You're ready to make an offer. Well . . . not just yet. You still need to look more closely at a number of issues.

One is competition. Not just what competition exists today, and whether Gourmet Caffe's owner is planning to open up again on the other side of town—but also whether Gourmet Caffe is currently gaining ground, remaining static, or losing market share to existing competitors. What does its business trend look like?

And how big is the market? Is it big enough to keep you in business, along with all those other competitors? Or is there likely to be a shakeout in the coming months or years? And if so, is Gourmet Caffe likely to survive?

Another issue—community growth and political plans. Is a massive rezoning underway that will enhance—or impair—your operations? Is the city planning major road construction, or changes in traffic patterns? If so, how will they affect traffic flow at your location? Is the local transit company planning to reroute local bus traffic? What if it's rerouted away from your shopping center? You get the idea.

Fourth, has the owner of Gourmet Caffe entered into any legal commitments, union agreements (unlikely in a small retail business, but watch for the question if you're contemplating buying a larger industrial concern), or other obligations which you will be required to uphold?

These may seem like insignificant concerns, but "little things" can be real budget-busters. Just ask the two nationally-recognized classical ballet dancers who discovered only after buying an existing ballet school in a suburban L.A. community that the former owner had committed to "Yellow Page" ads in dozens of southern California telephone directories. That commitment cost the new owners more than *$400 a month* for their entire first year of operation but brought few students from the remote locations in which many of the ads had been placed.

Look, too, for the possible impact of a national or regional emergency. If you're in a drought-susceptible area and you're buying a water-slide park, one or two dry winters could put you out of business. So could a hurricane or other natural disaster.

Take a careful look at the property on which your new business will be located. Make sure it's in good condition and that there are no restrictions to access (either physical or legal) that aren't apparent to the casual observer.

Do some comparison shopping. Check prices at Gourmet Caffe against those of its competitors. Will you be firmly rooted as the "high end" retailer—and if so, will the market allow you to stay there? Or is Gourmet Caffe's owner "lowballing" her prices to maintain volume—and if so, what will that do to your ability to earn sufficient profit when you take over?

If you have reasonably good answers to all of these questions, you'll probably want to give your legal or financial representative the go-ahead to open negotiations. And if those negotiations succeed, you'll soon be the proud owner of Gourmet Caffe—and on your way to entrepreneurial success.

ASSIGNMENTS

■ Before you watch the video program, be sure you've read through the preceding overview, familiarized yourself with the learning objectives for this lesson, and looked at the key terms below. Then read chapter 4 of Longenecker, Moore, and Petty, *Small Business Management*, "Startup and Buyout Opportunities."

■ After completing these tasks, read the video viewing questions and watch the video program for Lesson 4, *New or Used?*

■ After watching the program, take time to answer the video viewing questions and evaluate your learning with the self-test which follows the key terms.

■ Extend your learning through the applications, exercises or field experiences this lesson offers.

KEY TERMS

Startup	Starting a new business "from scratch." Most appropriate for businesses offering a completely new product or service, or a product or service new to the area.
Buyout	Acquiring an existing business.
Type A ideas	Startup ideas for businesses that will offer a product or service new to the geographical region.
Type B ideas	Startup ideas for totally new products or processes.
Type C ideas	Startup ideas for providing goods or services in a new and improved way.
Business valuation	Establishing an accurate value for a business that is up for sale.
Asset-based valuation	Establishing the value of a business by measuring the value of its assets, using either modified book value, replacement value or liquidation value.
Modified book value	Comparing the historical cost of a business' assets with their current value.
Replacement value	What it would cost to replace business assets at current-market rates.
Liquidation value	How much money could be obtained if business assets were sold off.
Market-based valuation	Establishing the value of a business by comparing the business with other similar businesses that have sold recently.
Earnings-based valuation	Establishing the value of a business by estimating future returns expected on the investment.
Cash-flow-based valuation	Establishing the value of a business by comparing the expected rate of return for the business with the expected rate of return that could be obtained through a similar but safer investment.

Capitalization of profit Process used to valuate a business by the earnings method.

VIDEO VIEWING QUESTIONS

1. Murray Garrett makes it very clear how he feels about the choice between starting a new business or buying an existing one. What reasons does he give for his preference?

2. Outline the suggestions provided in the video program for evaluating what a business is worth prior to entering into a purchase contract.

3. Placing a value on "good will" is admittedly difficult. Does that mean that it has little worth? What precautions should a potential owner take in dealing with this aspect of the purchase negotiation?

4. Compare the ways in which Murray Garrett and Betty Robertson gained information about the two companies they ultimately purchased: Diener Industries and XIT Grounding. Do you feel they had sufficient information to proceed with the transactions?

5. Provide examples of how "good will" entered into the business packages they were buying. Did this "good will" allow them to get started more efficiently than would have been possible if they had invested in a startup operation, or did it prove problematic?

6. Illustrate how Garrett and Robertson expanded on the basic product lines of Diener Industries and XIT Grounding. Were their new ventures compatible with the original focus of the two businesses?

7. Why did Cec Taylor choose a different route in establishing Varey House?

SELF-TEST

1. A study conducted by the National Federation of Independent Business Foundation found the largest percentage of startup ideas were the result of
   a. chance happenings.
   b. personal interests and hobbies.
   c. business classes.
   d. prior job experience.

2. Typical routes to entrepreneurship include
   a. startups, family businesses, franchises, and ownership transfers.
   b. franchises, selloffs, family businesses and startups.
   c. family businesses, startups, franchises and buyouts.
   d. buyouts, selloffs, startups and franchises.

3. People usually choose the startup option for *all but one* of the following reasons. Which answer does not belong?
   a. They've invented a brand new product or service.
   b. They can't secure the financing to buy out an existing business.
   c. They want the freedom to set up the business as they see fit.
   d. They don't want to be saddled with an existing business' procedures and legal obligations.

4. An advantage to buying an existing business is
   a. the avoidance of undesirable policies.
   b. precedents have been set by the previous owners.
   c. the freedom to select an ideal location.
   d. the existence of established customers or clientele.

5. The most common reasons for offering businesses for sale are *all but one* of the following. Identify the item that does not belong.
   a. The need for modernization.
   b. A desire to relocate.
   c. Old age or illness.
   d. The unprofitability of the business.

6. A potential disadvantage of purchasing an existing business is
   a. its customer base.
   b. loyalty of employees to former owner.
   c. proven location.
   d. acceptance of the product or service.

7. Evaluating the financial health of a firm involves
   a. reviewing 5 years of financial statements and tax returns and conducing an appraisal or valuation.
   b. measuring the amount of profit that is likely to be realized by the business under consideration in the coming year.
   c. learning whether asset book values are realistic.
   d. determining the accounting methods used in preparing the financial statements.

8. The market-based valuation approach to business valuation is based on
   a. the amount of potential income that may be produced by the business in the next year.
   b. the replacement value of the property being purchased.
   c. previous sales of similar businesses.
   d. the salvage value of the business if operations cease.

9. The valuation approach based on future returns from investment is
   a. the market value approach.
   b. the earnings approach.
   c. the liquidation value approach.
   d. the replacement cost approach.

10. Three non-financial factors to evaluate when considering the purchase of a business are
    a. union contracts, employee longevity, future community development.
    b. legal commitments, buildings, stock on hand.
    c. competition, buildings, goodwill.
    d. adequacy of the market, future community development, competition.

EXTEND WHAT YOU HAVE LEARNED

1. If you are considering the purchase of an existing business, there are certain documents that you will want to examine in association with your accountant and attorney:

   — Financial statements (Balance Sheets, Profit & Loss Statements, etc.) for three years—the current year and two years prior.

   — Sales Tax and Federal Income Tax reports for the past three years.

   — Copies of the building lease or purchase contract, and any applicable addenda.

   — Value of the inventory of goods for resale.

   — Replacement value (used) of the furniture, fixtures and equipment.

   — Disclosure of any lawsuits, contracts payable or receivable, and bad debts.

   — Non-competition contract.

Why are each of these elements important in establishing a value for the business, and in determining whether or not it is a good buy?

_____

_____

_____

2. In analyzing a business that is for sale, ask yourself if there are any intangible assets such as trademarks, copyrights, patents, trade secrets that are of value. What about good will—the continued public patronage you might expect to enjoy if you purchase a business that has an established clientele? How does this assist you with cash flow?

_____

_____

_____

3. If you purchased the business, and decided a year or two later to sell it, how easy or difficult would it be for you to sell out quickly, easily and profitably?

_____

_____

_____

Lesson 5

The Ties that Bind:
Franchising Opportunities

LEARNING OBJECTIVES

Upon completing your study of this lesson, you should be able to:

- List and give examples of various types of franchises and franchise arrangements.

- Compare the advantages and disadvantages of franchising.

- Summarize factors to consider in evaluating and financing a franchise opportunity.

- Recognize the legal aspects of franchise arrangements, in particular the contractual obligations that permeate the relationship.

- Describe the process involved in selling a franchise.

A drive-through coffee-aspirin-and-morning paper concession. A local quick-print establishment. Your community's business magazine. An area-wide maid service. The neighborhood brake repair outlet. What do all of these businesses have in common with one another—and with the corner Shell station, Century 21, and even the mammoth McDonald's restaurant chain? They're all franchises—a business form whose growth has actually outstripped the American economy in recent years.

Franchises have enjoyed this tremendous growth because they offer what can be an easier, safer approach to business ownership. In this lesson, we'll find out why they're so popular and learn how to determine whether or not a franchise opportunity might be worth pursuing.

OVERVIEW

You don't need to come up with a brand new product or service to go into business. In fact, many of the world's most successful entrepreneurs do extremely well by taking someone else's good idea and running with it. That's what franchising is all about.

In franchising, as you'll learn in this lesson, you simply recognize a market need for a particular product or service, and work to meet that need by using proven marketing strategies. Those strategies—if you're working with a reputable, successful franchisor—have already been tested and proven effective. That's one of the chief advantages of becoming a franchisee.

In this lesson we'll look at franchising from two points of view—that of the franchisor, or seller of the business opportunity, and the franchisee, or buyer of that opportunity. So whether you're looking to sell a great business idea to others or seeking a business that you can buy into, franchising may be the answer to your needs.

How Franchising Works Franchising is based on a legal agreement between two parties—the franchisor and the franchisee. If you're Joan Kroc, the wife of the founder of McDonald's, you're a franchisor. If you own the local McDonald's restaurant, you're a franchisee.

By signing a franchise agreement, the franchisee is given the right to conduct business as an individual owner of a franchise outlet. The franchisee may use the franchisor's company name, logo and other identifying symbols, and may benefit from the company's advertising and overall reputation—assuming, of course, that the franchise is respected by potential customers!

To receive the advantages of association with the franchisor company, the franchisee agrees to run his or her business according to the methods and terms set by the franchisor. You probably won't be able to serve stir-fried rice at your McDonald's franchise, or cut back on the amount of ketchup on a double cheeseburger, or change the uniforms your employees wear. But that's a key reason to buy into a franchise opportunity. Its market appeal is based on the uniformity it offers to customers who frequent the business. They're comfortable with the fact that they know exactly what they're buying.

Types of Franchises A McDonald's franchise represents one of the four main types of franchises in operation today—the *business format franchise*. Entrepreneurs who become franchisees in this kind of operation are buying full-fledged marketing systems, as well as ongoing business assistance and guidance, from their franchisors.

If you buy the right to a product or its trade name, you're the owner of a *product and trade name franchise*. About two-thirds of all franchises fall within this category; including Coca Cola bottlers, gas station owners, and Xerox copier retailers, to name just a few.

The third type of franchising is *piggyback franchising*, in which the owner of a store—called the "host store"—operates a smaller franchise business within the store. Maybe it's a Kinko's copy outlet inside a stationery supply store, or a fast-food restaurant on the grounds of a local university, owned and operated by the university itself.

And then there's *master licensee*. In this situation, the master licensee is a person who serves as a sales agent for the company offering franchise opportunities. It's the job of the master licensee to find new franchisees in a given territory. These are the people whose "business opportunity" ads you're likely to see in the local news or business press. In addition to attracting franchisees to the business, the master licensee also may provide support services on behalf of the franchisor company.

We can look at franchises one other way—in terms of the system under which they function. You'll learn there are three types of franchise systems:

- One in which the producer/creator of a product (the franchisor) grants a franchise to a wholesaler (the franchisee). This is a common choice in the soft drink industry.

- A second in which the wholesaler (franchisor) grants a franchise to a retailer (franchisee). Typical users of this system are hardware stores.

- The third type of franchising is the most widely-used system, in which the producer/creator (franchisor) grants a franchise to a retailer (franchisee). You'll find these types of franchises in all areas of business, from the auto industry (GM is the franchisor, the local Pontiac dealer the franchisee), to fast food chains, gas stations, and quick-print shops.

Why be a Franchisee? If you're ready to go into business for yourself, why might you choose the franchise route? If you have not had the opportunity to go to college, or didn't study business when you did attend, you might choose a franchise opportunity because of the formal training it may offer. (Not every franchisor operates a training program as comprehensive as McDonald's Hamburger U, so you've got to do some careful research to find out if a franchisor offers the kind and extent of training you need.)

A good franchisee training program will include course work at a central training school, followed by on-site training at a franchise outlet. And it will provide you with ongoing guidance, whether it's in the form of refresher courses, meetings with your franchisor representative, or updated training manuals. The goal of training is to help you overcome any managerial weaknesses you may have and to help you run your business successfully—from employee training, scheduling, and supervision to product or service delivery.

Another reason to opt for a franchise business is the financial assistance you may receive from the franchisor. Even if a franchisor won't lend you money directly, the fact that you're associated with a larger enterprise may help you obtain funding from other sources. Sometimes franchisors will even intercede on behalf of prospective franchisees, helping them to obtain the loans they need. And franchisors often provide favorable payment terms for the goods and operating supplies a franchisee needs.

The third key advantage to franchisee status lies in the realm of marketing and management. When you buy a franchise, you're usually buying a company with name recognition and proven products or services. That's why you pay a franchise fee. And you benefit from any recognition that the company's name, trademark, logo, or mascot might offer, as well as from the company's tested and proven marketing and management practices.

The significance of these advantages? You're likely to be up and running more quickly, since your franchisor has been through the experience many times and can help you negotiate the tough spots. And you run a lower chance of failure, if statistics on business failure among franchisee and independent businesses are any indication.

On the Other Hand But becoming a franchisee isn't *all* roses. As with other big decisions in life, there are down side impacts as well. First and foremost is cost. It may be more expensive to buy a franchise than go into business for yourself. You'll have to pay a franchise fee (the amount will reflect how well-known and successful other franchises in the chain have been), royalty payments, promotion costs, predetermined inventory and supplies costs, and building and equipment costs. You may save money by avoiding these franchisor-imposed charges, but the trade-off lies in the benefits a franchise offers. If the cost of being a franchisee can be offset by the marketing, management, and training benefits a good franchise should offer, it may be money well spent. Only you can decide, after looking at a particular franchise opportunity.

The second negative is the potential for restrictions on growth that may be imposed by the franchisor. To keep all of its franchises operating successfully, the franchisor may have to limit the number and size of franchises in a given geographic area. That means you may not be able to grow as much as you'd like.

Third, you won't have absolute operating independence. You will have to live by certain policies and practices set by the franchisor, and you will be restricted in terms of the products or services you may offer.

You'll have to decide for yourself whether the tradeoff is worth it—whether you absolutely must have total control, or whether you will be happy running a franchise, knowing that you've exchanged a degree of control and freedom for the support the franchisor can offer you.

Investigating Franchises To decide if a franchise is right for you, there are several sources of information. First, of course, is the franchisor company. Although you'll have to take what they tell you with a grain of salt—their goal, after all, is to sell franchises—they can provide you with a great deal of information. And you'll get a feel for the kind of working relationship you're likely to encounter if you buy one of their franchises.

The franchisor is also required by the Federal Trade Commission to provide you with a complete disclosure document, which is designed to give you information on everything from the business experience of the franchisor's directors and officers to how the franchisor goes about the process of site selection. Look at it carefully, and have a franchise attorney and a CPA review it, too.

Then, you should visit existing franchises and talk to their owners. Find out what it's *really* like to work with the franchisor company, and what it's like to run the franchise itself. Better yet, find someone who's sold one of the franchises you're thinking about buying, and find out why.

Finally, there are third-party sources—the government (which produces a number of handbooks and other publications on franchising), trade associations, business magazines, bankers, and franchise specialists, including consultants, attorneys, and CPAs. Not surprisingly, business magazines often provide some of the best information, since they're most likely to investigate a particular franchise operation from all sides, good and bad

Why Sell Franchises? If you're looking at franchising from the franchisor's point of view, you've got a different set of questions to ask. It might be hard to justify selling part of your operation—relinquishing some of your potential profit and some control over business opportunities to other people—unless you understand why franchising can be advantageous.

If obtaining sufficient capital for expansion is a problem, franchisees are a potential solution. They help you grow your business by paying some of the costs of expansion into new locations. That, in turn, speeds up the pace of your expansion program.

Besides, franchisees are much more highly motivated to succeed than the average employee. They've invested their own money, or they've committed themselves to paying back borrowed funds. And their egos are invested in the idea of being in business for themselves. So they *want* to succeed. Franchising isn't just another job.

Experts tell us the best way to sell a new franchise idea is to set up a model store or business operation and use it to demonstrate your business concept to prospective franchisees. As the saying goes, sometimes you have to see it to believe it. So let them see how your idea will be brought to life.

ASSIGNMENTS

■ Before you watch the video program, be sure you've read through the preceding overview, familiarized yourself with the learning objectives for this lesson, and looked at the key terms below. Then, read chapter 3 of Longenecker, Moore, and Petty, *Small Business Management*, "Franchising Opportunities."

■ After completing these tasks, read the video viewing questions and watch the video program for Lesson 5, *The Ties that Bind*.

■ After watching the program, take time to answer the video viewing questions and evaluate your learning with the self-test.

■ Extend your learning through the applications, exercises, or field experiences this lesson offers.

KEY TERMS

Franchising	Two-party legal agreement in which the buyer (franchisee) gains the right to run a business but must do so according to methods and terms dictated by the seller (franchisor).
Franchise contract	Legal agreement that establishes a franchisor/franchisee arrangement.
Franchise	The business privileges purchased by the franchisee in a franchise arrangement.

Franchise fee	Fee charged a franchisee for the right to operate a business under the franchisor's business name/logo; the better-known the franchise, the higher the franchise fee.
Disclosure document	Document prepared by a franchisor which is expected to disclose all relevant information about a franchise opportunity to a prospective franchisee; its provision is required by the FTC.

VIDEO VIEWING QUESTIONS

1. In aggregate, the comments of Gerold Morita, Douglas Kinney, Robert Kahan, and Oscar Wright depict the advantages and disadvantages of franchise ownership. Make a list of the points they make and assess the degree to which the factors that are mentioned would encourage or discourage your involvement in a franchise operation.

2. What is the best approach to use in evaluating a franchise opportunity?

3. Compare the three franchise operations featured in the video: Bellini Juvenile Designer Furniture, Johnny Rockets, and Sir Speedy. From the information provided in the video, answer the following questions:
   a. Which of the three franchisors seems to provide the most support for the franchisee? What is the basis for your answer?
   b. What common reasons did the franchisees give for selecting this form of business ownership?
   c. Did you sense or see any evidence of excessive control on the part of the franchisor?
   d. Given a choice, which of the three franchises would you want to own? Why?

SELF-TEST

1. A franchisee who buys the right to use a widely recognized product or name has bought a
   a. piggyback franchise.
   b. product and trade name franchise.
   c. business format franchise.
   d. master franchise.

2. A McDonald's restaurant is an example of a
   a. business format franchise.
   b. master franchise.
   c. piggyback franchise.
   d. product and trade name franchise.

3. Which of the following does *not* represent one of the three types of franchising systems? One in which the
   a. producer/creator of a product franchises to a wholesaler.
   b. wholesaler of a product franchises to a retailer.
   c. producer/creator of a product franchises to a retailer.
   d. manufacturer of a product franchises to the consumer.

4. A franchise opportunity can offer the prospective franchisee
   a. a way to get into business for less money.
   b. a proven store location.
   c. business training needed to run the franchise.
   d. the opportunity to take an idea and diversify it.

5. Which of the following types of financial support is a franchisor *least likely* to offer a franchisee?
   a. A direct loan for the purchase of the franchise
   b. A flexible payment schedule for franchise costs
   c. Delayed payment options for supplies and merchandise
   d. Assistance in obtaining bank loans

6. Typical costs for franchisees include *all but* the
   a. franchise fee and royalty payments.
   b. promotion costs and inventory and supplies costs.
   c. insurance premiums and employee training charges.
   d. building and equipment costs.

7. The three most important reasons to sell franchise opportunities are
   a. reduced capital requirements, lower business taxes, and ease of expansion.
   b. reduced capital requirements, increased management motivation, and ease of expansion.
   c. ease of expansion, increased management motivation, and reduced public visibility for products or services.

8. Important sources of information for evaluating a franchise opportunity include
   a. the disclosure statement.
   b. existing and previous franchisees.
   c. *The Wall Street Journal.*
   d. All of these are sources of information.

9. The disadvantages of owning a franchise include
   a. unlimited opportunities for growth.
   b. absolute operating independence.
   c. costs associated with owning and operating a franchise.
   d. the lack of marketing and managerial support.

10. Which of the following is the least objective, and perhaps reliable, source of information about a franchisor?
   a. An informative booklet prepared by the franchise company
   b. Disclosure document required by the Federal Trade Commission
   c. Visits to existing franchises and discussions with their owners
   d. Third party sources: government, trade associations, business magazines, bankers, and franchise specialists

EXTEND WHAT YOU HAVE LEARNED

1. Get as much information as you can about one or two franchises that are offered in an area that is of interest to you. (It would be particularly valuable for you to secure information about franchises whose products or services are closely aligned with startup or buyout opportunities you've considered.) Thoroughly read the prospectus and the contract, and record answers to the following:

   a. What is the length of the franchise agreement? _____

   b. What is the initial franchise fee? _____

   c. What is the estimated cost to build a store? _____

      To buy the equipment?_____To buy inventory? _____

   d. Are you required to buy supplies from the franchisor? _____

   e. Is there a continuing royalty based on sales, and if so what percentage of gross revenues must you pay? _____

f. What kind of training is provided?

_____

_____

g. What controls does the franchisor have over your operation?

_____

_____

h. Under what conditions can the agreement be cancelled?

_____

_____

2. Review the franchisor's projected income statements and the company's financial data. If the franchise was a business you were considering, would you buy it based on the financial information that is provided?

3. Stop by and observe the operations of several franchise holders. What similarities and differences do you notice among the various locations? Make an appointment to talk to at least two franchise holders at length. Ask them about their profitability, and in particular, their relationships with the franchisor.

4. Finally, ask yourself these questions:

    — Does this franchise have a strong chance of competing in my community?

    — Does it have a potential for future growth, or does its success depend on the longevity of a fad?

    — Will franchise ownership be an advantage in this line of business, or could I do as well on my own?

Lesson 6

A Different Look:
The Nicole Miller Story

If you're interested in taking the entrepreneurial route to success, one of the best ways to test the water for an entrepreneurial idea is to do so while swimming in someone else's pool. Namely, spend a year or two working for someone else in the same industry, to learn all you can about the business and to make sure it's right for you. And if you've completed coursework or other training to help prepare you, all the better. That's the route followed by Nicole Miller, who today is one of America's best-selling young fashion designers.

Nicole Miller Her clothes are worn by a veritable Who's Who of the entertainment and communications industries, as well as fashion-conscious businesswomen in New York City and across the U.S. Her novelty ties—created as a prank—are a hit with young urban men who want their attire to make a visual statement. And her shop on New York's Madison Avenue is one of the biggest success stories in the boulevard's hotly competitive history.

Nicole Miller set out to be a leading U.S. fashion designer—and by all accounts, she's done just what she intended to do.

"I knew by the time I was in high school—maybe even earlier," Miller recalled, "that I wanted to be a designer. We lived in Massachusetts, and I'd take the bus all the way to New York City whenever I could, just to see Betsey Johnson's clothes at Paraphernalia."

Education Came First Her first step toward entrepreneurship was an education at the vaunted Rhode Island School of Design. While at RISD, Miller spent a year in Paris, studying design at the same school which gave Yves St. Laurent his start. "Being in Europe was an incredible experience. It gave me a sense of discipline and a sense of aesthetics that I simply would not have picked up in an American school."

For a short time after graduation from RISD, Miller ran a Massachusetts boutique, but her heart kept pulling her toward the Big Apple. So, in the mid-

1970s, Miller headed to New York—sans apartment, sans job, but on the way toward her dream.

A miserable first job—"the kind you hear about in school and vow never to take"—lasted just five days. Fortunately for Miller, and for the world of fashion design, she soon landed another job, designing raincoats for P.J. Walsh, a company owned by Bud Konheim, a fourth-generation design industry professional with 35 years of experience.

There, Miller clicked. By 1982, her line of dresses, dubbed "Nicole Miller for P.J. Walsh," was so popular that she and Konheim decided to create a new company, called simply "Nicole Miller."

In less than a decade in the business, Miller had proven herself to the design community, made the key connection that would get her business off the ground, and convinced herself—not to mention the rest of the fashion world—that she and fashion design were meant for each other. She knew the business from the inside out, she was aware of its advantages and its pitfalls, and she'd tested her ideas in the marketplace and found them sound. Not a bad start for an entrepreneur.

Getting Started But it wasn't all as easy as that. In an industry where multi-million-dollar startups are common, Miller and Konheim established their company with just $215,000 in startup capital. That didn't bother Miller: "I've seen a lot of companies spend millions on promotion and advertising and fashion shows, and flop miserably. There were plenty of low-capitalization success stories to learn from—Liz Claiborne among them. And I'm still convinced that the money doesn't make the difference—the clothes do. If it doesn't sell, it doesn't matter how much funding you had going in."

Her confidence—and her distinctively stylish, yet never faddish designs—helped make Nicole Miller an instant success. Sales reached $4 million the first year, and they've climbed steadily since, reaching $35 million in 1990.

Even one of her not-so-successful designs—dresses made from fun, novelty silks—turned into gold in 1990, when Konheim took some of the unsold merchandise and used the fabric to make 36 ties. Made of fabric printed with theatre ticket stubs, the ties were an instant hit at the Nicole Miller shop on Madison Avenue, and at the Metropolitan Opera House, which sold over 4,500 "ticket stub" ties and 3,000 scarves in 1990 alone.

Today, the company's tie line includes kicky cravats featuring everything from football motifs to Italian pasta or popcorn and candy—whatever tickles the fancy of Miller's fabric designers. And it was worth some $8 million of the company's $28 million in wholesale volume for 1990.

And Miller is venturing farther afield from her original day-into-evening one-piece dress, on which she focused in the early years, adding to her line with softly styled suits, evening wear, sportswear, fun-print camp shirts, ties, scarves, belts, handbags and accessories, and even—harking back to her early days with P.J. Walsh—raincoats.

Finding her Niche Miller can afford to experiment today, with her design niche so carefully carved out. Her focus, she says, always was on "things I'd be happy wearing every day. I wanted to be known for stylish clothes, but stylish clothes that are *wearable*. They have to work for people—and they have to look good on *real* bodies, not just on models." Her silhouettes, never form-fitting, are nonetheless feminine and flattering.

In terms of pricing, Miller's designs come in somewhat above the price of good quality off-the-rack merchandise, but they're not so out-of-sight that only the wealthiest women need inquire. Her dresses typically range from $200 to $300, evening wear from $350 to $450, and her sportswear in the $100 to $200 range.

"The fact that I try to keep my designs stylish but timeless helps too," Miller said. "My clothes are known for working this year—and next year, and the year after that. They're not the kind of things you'll wear for one season and then stuff in the back of your closet for a decade. That makes them a better value."

Distribution and Marketing The sophistication of the Nicole Miller distribution and marketing effort has grown right along with the company. Miller and Konheim targeted specialty stores right from the outset since, as Konheim put it, "we're not a high-volume, mass-merchandise company. We're offering a more exclusive product, and that type of product is more effectively marketed in a specialty store, where the people who select the merchandise deal directly with the customers who will buy it."

That philosophy has taken the Nicole Miller line into some 3,800 specialty shops in the U.S. and 18 foreign countries, as well as to some major department stores where purchasing decisions are given the kind of attention a high-fashion line require. One chain—Marshall Field's in Chicago—has even moved her designs from its "better-priced" department to the designer area, signifying the increasing seriousness with which fashion retailers now treat Nicole Miller designs.

The company's move into direct retailing—taken in 1986, when the Madison Avenue store was opened—was the happy result of a contest of wills between Miller and Konheim. "Nicole wanted to do a fashion show," Konheim recalled, "and I didn't want her to. I thought doing that would cause her to design for the critics and not for the customers. So instead of doing the fashion show, we gave ourselves a stage by opening the store."

"And I still won," laughed Miller. "Last year, we had our first fashion show! With my line composed of a variety of pieces—not just dresses, but suits, sportswear, evening wear, and so on—I can mount an effective show today."

"But the store works well as a testing ground, too. Often, if I've got a new design I want to try out, I'll take it to the shop to see how it does. That's far less expensive—and probably less risky—than putting on a show every time I want to present something new."

Always testing, ever searching, constantly on the lookout for a new idea and a new market—that's business as usual at Nicole Miller. And, in all likelihood, at every other highly successful entrepreneurial venture.

Because entrepreneurs are, it seems, never satisfied to run in place. There's always a new horizon to explore. And that's what makes entrepreneurship so much fun.

APPLYING THE CONCEPTS FROM LESSONS 1–5

Before you watch the video program for Lesson 6, *A Different Look*, review chapters 1 and 3–5 in the text. Then answer the following questions:

1. Was Nicole Miller well-prepared for her move into the entrepreneurial ranks? Why or why not?

2. Does Nicole Miller have what you would call an entrepreneurial personality? What characteristics can you point to that cause you to draw the conclusion that you do?

3. How do you measure market potential for a product whose appeal changes with each season?

4. Where can you acquire the knowledge you need to go into an entrepreneurial enterprise in your industry?

5. Why might a bad job be a good experience for a prospective entrepreneur?

6. Is creation of a niche a necessity for businesses like Nicole Miller? Why or why not?

7. What do you think is the greatest risk for entrepreneurial businesses in the fashion industry? What has Nicole Miller done to lessen that risk?

8. What kinds of distribution methods can the small company use to get products out to the right retailers?

9. Should Nicole Miller open stores in a number of U.S. cities? Why or why not?

Lesson 7

The Business Plan

LEARNING OBJECTIVES

Upon completing your study of this lesson, you should be able to:

- Recognize the purpose of a business plan and how it is used.

- Give examples of techniques that can be used in preparing a business plan.

- Describe the elements of a business plan and what is emphasized in each section.

Imagine that you've decided to take the big step. You're going to open that store we discussed earlier—Gourmet Caffe. Your initial research suggests there's a market for such a shop, and you're determined to make your idea fly. There's just one problem—and it's the problem shared by virtually all fledgling entrepreneurs: how to convince those who need convincing that yours is a good idea, and one they should support.

The tool you'll use is the business plan. In this lesson, we'll find out what goes into a business plan, and how you should go about developing one.

OVERVIEW

There's no one right or wrong way to prepare a business plan, but there are certain similarities among business plans that do the job they're intended to do. That job is two-fold. First, you'll want your business plan to fully describe your idea—what kind of business you plan to open, where it will operate, who are its likely customers or clients, how it will be financed, how much money it should make. Whatever *you* know about your business, what you expect of it, and how you will define its operational and geographic boundaries should be in the plan. Second, the business plan should provide a full description of how you'll run your business for the first three to five years—your marketing, operational, financial, and managerial game plan.

It'll take you time—and, if you have it professionally written and pre-pared, it'll cost you money—but a proper business plan can *save* you money, and grief, down the road. Think of it as the football coach's game plan for the fall season, and imagine what that season would be like if the coach failed to prepare one. Does he build on his team's offensive strength, or depend on its defensive capabilities? Can he call on a star running back, who's ready to break through the line and head for the end zone? Or must he rely on his quar-terback to throw the long bomb because the running game is suspect? How will he prepare for the big cross-state rivalry? Will he offer up any trick plays? And what if someone's injured or is declared ineligible when he flunks his chem exam—what's the coach's contingency plan?

By thinking everything through, and by carefully studying all factors that will affect your business, you'll be more sure of your ability to run the busi-ness, more confident in your decision to open it, more aware of the actual costs that will be involved, and better prepared for any surprises that occur along the way. And—most importantly—you'll be more likely to gain the financial support that you'll need.

Other Uses for the Plan If you recognize that the business plan can be used long after your business is up and running, the justification for taking the time to prepare it properly will be stronger still. Smart business owners realize that their business plans can serve them throughout the years. In fact, they re-vise and update them as their businesses grow and change.

Not only will the business plan convince prospective investors that yours is a venture they should support, but it also will give bankers the information necessary to secure a line of credit or other banking services you will need.

A business plan also serves as an internal motivational tool. It can explain your vision of the business to employees in a manner that is clear, rational, and factual. You'll even want to show it to key recruits—the people you will need on staff to make the business succeed.

Even suppliers and key customers will be interested in your business plan. For suppliers, the information it contains may be all they need to decide you're a good risk, convincing them to extend trade credit—a critical com-modity for a young, growing business. And customers will be interested to know that you've thought things through, and that you're likely to be there next year when they may need additional service or replacement goods.

Once your business is underway, the business plan can—and should—serve as a management tool. The business goals you have established become your targets for operational control. If, for example, your business plan for

Gourmet Caffe predicted monthly gross sales of $10,000, and you're only reaching the $7,500 mark, you'll know that other projections which rely on that $10,000 target must be adjusted as well.

Preparing a business plan isn't easy—in fact, it's hard work. But by forcing yourself to deal with the tough questions now, it will be easier for you to get through the difficult times that may lie ahead as you open for business.

Writing the Plan   The style and format of a business plan are almost as important as what it says. It's important to prepare a plan that is not too long (40 to 50 pages at the most), visually attractive, easy to read, well-organized, logical, and persuasively written. The pages must be numbered, and you should provide readers with a table of contents and section tabs to help them find the sections in which they have the greatest interest.

Beyond that, you're wise to position the information in your plan from a market perspective. What does that mean? Don't tell prospective investors or lenders why you love your great new business idea—they assume that! Tell them why the marketplace will embrace it, and to what extent. Among the message points to highlight: information that points to cust-omer acceptance of your product or service; financial projections for three to five years; recognition of the investor's need for a satisfactory return on investment; a business focus that is manageable in scope; and, if you have it, information on proprietary rights (copyright, patent, or trademark) to the product or service.

Conversely, certain messages will cause potential investors to cringe, such as: an inability to clearly identify market needs because of an infatuation with your idea, unrealistically rosy financial or growth projections, and the need for custom or applications engineering which may limit business growth.

Besides using a computer for its word processing abilities in writing the business plan, you'll want to run your financial and growth projections on a good spreadsheet program to simulate the impact of different levels of market activity on your bottom line. You'll also want to liven your presentation with top-quality photos of your product (if appropriate), as well as any graphs, charts, tables, or other graphic elements that can help get your information across. If you can't write well—and be brutally honest with yourself—hire someone to write the plan for you. But be sure you know the finished product inside and out, because *you're* the one to whom any questions will be directed!

Elements of the Plan   Let's walk through the preparation of the business plan for Gourmet Caffe and identify some of the topics it will cover. You'll write the first section last. Why? Because the first section is the *executive sum-*

mary, which offers readers a quick look at the plan's highlights. Most investors read only the Executive Summary before deciding thumbs-up or thumbs-down on an investment—so it *has* to be good.

Following the executive summary comes the mission statement, which is a concise description of a firm's strategy and business philosophy. While mission statements vary considerably in length and content, they should always be simple, believable, and achievable, and should set your firm apart from all others. You may not be able to generate this summary of your business philosophy on your first try. Try jotting down a list of ideas, then going back through them, narrowing down the choices, and fleshing out the better option or options until you are happy with your work. You might begin jotting down ideas when you start the plan and continue to weed and refine over the entire project or until you think you have summed up your philosophy.

The first section you'll write, then, is the *general company description*. You'll say that Gourmet Caffe is a startup business which hasn't opened yet but is targeted to open six months from now in your community. You'll describe the community and discuss the attributes that make it hospitable to a gourmet coffee and tea shop. You'll tell about the range of products and services you plan to offer. You'll discuss the fact that there's just one competitor in the area, saddled with more restrictive corporate policies and higher operating costs than the Gourmet Caffe will have. You'll also discuss your short- and long-range growth objectives, and talk about the special characteristics that will set Gourmet Caffe apart from other similar businesses.

Second, you'll prepare the *products and services plan*. You'll go into additional detail about the products and services to be offered by Gourmet Caffe, including your business gift packages, free-pound-of-coffee for repeat customers policy, health-conscious water-decaffeinated products, and the full range of complementary products you'll sell to accompany the coffees and teas. You'll compare your products with those of your key competitor to demonstrate the qualitative differences between the two.

Third is the *marketing plan*. You'll identify your target market, discuss its size, and break it into segments—area residents, businesses in the area, and special business-gift customers. Then you'll provide a demographic description of those customers—age, income level, lifestyle characteristics, buying characteristics (in terms of coffee and tea purchases), and so on.

In this section, you'll also talk about market growth trends that are anticipated for the community, about the reactions of prospective customers with whom you've talked, about the share of market you expect to snare and how you'll go about competing with the mall-based coffee store. You'll discuss whether you plan to offer catalog or mail-order sales to customers, how and where you'll advertise or promote your store, how you'll set prices, and what kind of credit and collection practices you'll institute. You'll also talk about employees—how many people you'll hire, the qualifications you'll look for, and how much you'll pay them. And much more!

Then you'll present your *management plan*. Will you be the sole owner, or will you have a partner? If ownership is shared, how is it divided? What are your qualifications for business—and what are the qualifications of others who will play a significant role? If you're setting up a corporation, who are the directors and why are they qualified to serve?

Will you retain any consultants—attorney, CPA, advertising or PR person—and if so, what skills do they bring to the table? How will you select employees, and how will you motivate and reward them? What is your management style? How will you foster a sense of commitment and loyalty among your employees?

Once you've answered those questions, you'll move to the *operating plan*. Where will you locate Gourmet Caffe, and how large a store will it be? How will you handle inventory, and what kinds of supplies and equipment will you need? Who are your sources of supply, and what kind of arrangements have you made with them? What will your operating costs be?

Then, you'll discuss your *financial plan*, telling how you developed your financial projections, and what those projections are. You'll look at projected expenses, revenues, and cash flow for the first 12 months, quarterly for the next two years, and annually for at least the two years beyond that. You'll tell when you expect to reach the break-even point, and how you arrived at that conclusion. And you'll talk about where you expect to get the money to *get* to that break-even point—who your sources of funding are, what proportion of your funding will be debt or equity, and what kind of stake in the company you're offering in exchange for funding support.

Supply an appendix of supporting documents that will help readers to better understand the plan. Items such as resumes of key players, photographs of products and/or facilities, research studies, and professional references are appropriate materials for the appendix.

If You Need Help Many accounting firms and financial organizations offer publications to prospective entrepreneurs, to help them produce thorough, effective business plans. Guides to business plans are also included in many business textbooks, including your textbook for this course. But to really talk yourself through the process, you'll probably want to show your draft plan to someone—an attorney, a CPA, a business consultant, a colleague—anyone who's been down this road before and knows what should be included in a business plan. And once you know its content, you'd be wise to turn it over to a skilled writer, to turn your important information into compelling, persuasive prose.

ASSIGNMENTS

- Be sure you've read through the preceding overview, familiarized yourself with the learning objectives for this lesson, and looked at the key terms below. Then, read chapter 6 of Longenecker, Moore, and Petty, *Small Business Management*, "The Role of a Business Plan."

- This lesson does not include a video program. Your instructor will provide you with information regarding individual, small group, or class meetings to discuss the development of a business plan as a part of course requirements.

- After completing these tasks, take time to review what you've learned. Be sure to evaluate your learning with the self-test.

- Extend your learning through the applications, exercises, or field experiences this lesson offers.

KEY TERMS

Business plan   A description of a new business idea that gives a 3-to-5-year projection of its marketing, operational, managerial, and financial components.

Executive summary   Opening section of the business plan; it summarizes overall plan contents and gives prospective investors or lenders a quick look at the proposed business.

Products and services plan Section of the business plan that describes the product or service to be offered by the new business; highlights any unique product/service features.

Marketing plan   Section that identifies the business's customer base and describes the marketing strategy that will be used to reach it; analyzes competition the business will face.

Mission Statement   A concise written statement of a firm's strategy and philosophy.

Management plan   Section that provides biographical and skills information on the new venture's management, direc-
tors, and investors.

Operating plan   Section that tells how products or services will be
produced, and what facilities, raw materials, and
equipment will be needed.

Financial plan   Section that lists financial needs and identifies prospective sources of funds; also offers cost, revenue,
and profit projections.

SELF-TEST

1. Which of the following statements is *not* true concerning utilization of the business plan?
   a. The business plan may present a proposal for launching an entirely new business.
   b. The business plan may be a response to a change in the external environment that may lead to new opportunities.
   c. The business plan may be used internally to more efficiently handle the business.
   d. The business plan may not be useful for planning major expansion of a firm that has already started operation.

2. The business plan is used most often to
   a. recruit key personnel.
   b. help the entrepreneur avoid costly mistakes.
   c. help the entrepreneur obtain investor support.
   d. communicate the company's mission to employees.

3. The section of the business plan that receives the greatest scrutiny from potential investors is the
   a. financial plan.
   b. general company description.
   c. marketing plan.
   d. executive summary.

4. "Turn-ons" for prospective investors include *all but*
    a. evidence of customer acceptance of the product or service.
    b. products produced through custom or applications engineering.
    c. a proprietary position for the product or service.
    d. focus on a limited number of products or services.

5. The business plan section that identifies likely customers and tells how your business will reach them is the
    a. marketing plan.
    b. operating plan.
    c. general company description.
    d. management plan.

6. A key question to answer in the operating plan section of a business plan is
    a. what the basic nature and activity of the business will be.
    b. what unique characteristics the product or service offers.
    c. how and where the product or service will be produced.
    d. how customers will be attracted to the new company.

7. This part of the business plan explains why people will buy the product or service.
    a. The marketing plan
    b. The financial plan
    c. The products and/or services plan
    d. The executive summary

8. The financial plan should provide quarterly projections of revenues and profits for at least the first
    a. five years.
    b. two years.
    c. one year.
    d. three years.

9. In developing a business plan, the entrepreneur should
    a. critically evaluate his or her ability to write.
    b. limit its length to 15 pages.
    c. avoid any discussion of employees since they have not been hired.
    d. turn the project over to an attorney, since the attorney will be the one to answer questions and defend it.

EXTEND WHAT YOU HAVE LEARNED

The process of putting a business plan together forces you to take an objective, systematic, critical, and unemotional look at your entire business proposal. In its finished form, the document becomes an operational tool that, when properly used, will help you manage your business and work toward its success. It provides the basic information necessary to secure financial support for your business, and serves as a means for communicating your ideas to others.

As you begin to establish the game plan for your prospective business, answer the following questions. Some of your answers may change in the weeks and months to come as your information base broadens and your plan becomes more defined. But consider this a place to start.

1. How would you describe the basic nature and activity of your business?

    _____

    _____

2. What is its primary product or service?

    _____

    _____

3. Who will be served by your business?

    _____

    _____

4. Is your company involved in manufacturing, retail sales, service, or another type of industry?

    _____

    _____

5. Is it a new startup, the expansion of an existing business, the purchase of an ongoing business, or a franchise operation?

    _____

    _____

6. What is your actual or projected startup date?

    _____

    _____

7. What achievements have you made to date?

   _____

   _____

8. How and why will your business be successful?

   _____

   _____

9. What makes your company's product or service unique?

   _____

   _____

10. What are the dangers of the product or service becoming obsolete?

    _____

    _____

11. What kinds of licenses or approvals will be necessary for you to begin operation?

    _____

    _____

12. What liabilities are involved?

    _____

    _____

13. What is your experience in this business?

    _____

    _____

14. What are the skills, education, and experience of those who will assist you?

    _____

    _____

Lesson 8

Taking Aim:
The Marketing Plan

LEARNING OBJECTIVES

Upon completing your study of this lesson, you should be able to:

■ Describe the relationship between the marketing philosophy a new firm establishes and its marketing activities and consumer orientation.

■ Identify the components of the marketing mix and understand how they interrelate.

■ Distinguish between the three most distinct marketing philosophies and determine which is most appropriate for a particular new business.

■ Recognize the role of the sales forecast and its relationship to cash flow.

■ Summarize the steps involved in the forecasting process.

■ Understand the process involved in conducting the market research and analysis necessary to develop a formal marketing plan.

■ Develop the marketing strategy and determine the marketing mix for a given company.

■ Specify the elements that are included in a formal marketing plan.

Think back to lesson 3, where we first began discussing how to determine the feasibility of a business plan. Remember learning that a customer satisfaction strategy is the key element in developing your marketing philosophy? And remember how we began to explore the process of market segmentation for that hypothetical new business, Gourmet Caffe?

In this lesson, we'll take a closer look at the marketing plan—how it is developed, how it reflects your marketing philosophy, and how it affects the success of a new business.

OVERVIEW

A marketing plan does more than assure potential investors and lenders that you know what you're doing. It also guides you through the decision-making process, to help you determine the upside and downside extremes of your proposed venture. And, perhaps most important, it helps you define the marketing philosophy of your new business—which, if it's to be truly effective, will adapt big-business marketing ideas to the smaller venture, while focusing on the consumer.

Small Business Marketing Many entrepreneurs assume, when they establish their new businesses, that they can't do the kind of marketing research and planning that's done by large firms. Some may even think it's not necessary—their idea is so terrific, they reason, that it will simply sell itself.

That kind of thinking isn't just unrealistic—it's also counterproductive. Not only may the entrepreneur without a plan head off down the wrong road, he may also find himself without adequate funding, since a well-developed marketing plan is a prerequisite to lending approval.

So the entrepreneur must adapt full-scale market research techniques to his small-business situation. He must *identify his target markets*; *determine the market potential* of each one; and prepare, communicate and deliver a *"bundle of satisfaction"* to each market.

For the new owner of Gourmet Caffe, that means identifying the three key markets—area residents, local businesses and offices, and businesspeople with gift-giving needs. It means measuring, through quantitative market research, the market potential of each of those three groups. And it means developing a plan that responds to the distinct wants, needs and preferences of each market.

Finally, Gourmet Caffe's owner must be sure that his operating procedures and sales practices are designed to maximize customer satisfaction. Because if the customer's satisfaction isn't the end goal of his efforts, he might as well forget going into business at all.

Marketing Research Intuition will tell you a lot about your prospective market and its customers—and that's a good thing, since intuition is inexpensive and research funds are likely to be in short supply when you first go into business. But you can use many of the market research tools that are used by larger enterprises—and use them you must.

If you define marketing research as gathering, processing, reporting and interpreting marketing information, you can see that there is no mandate in that definition for costly computerized analyses or high-priced market research firms. There's just the simple expectation that you will study your market and analyze the facts that you uncover.

The steps you'll want to take in conducting your marketing research are simple, too.

First, you'll need to *identify the problem*. Just what is it you need to know? For Gourmet Caffe, a representative set of questions might be, "How many businesses and offices are located within a five-mile radius of the store? How many of them have coffee and tea supplies on hand for their customers or employees? Of those who do, how many actually enjoy the products they're using, and how many wish they had a higher quality, tastier product? Of those who don't, how many might be interested in providing coffee and tea to their customers or employees?" (Notice that these questions apply to just one of Gourmet Caffe's market segments; similar questions would need to be asked for each market segment.)

With those questions identified, you can begin searching for answers. *Secondary sources* might be in short supply for Gourmet Caffe—unless the local newspaper has just written an article on the growing popularity of gourmet coffees—but for many businesses, they're quite useful, and often free. Among the most common secondary information sources are your own internal business information; magazines and other publications; trade associations; and government agencies. Secondary information may not be completely relevant to your situation, and statistics can often be out of date, but these sources should be considered.

Primary sources are easier to research, because they're your prospective customers. You can observe them. You can communicate with them informally, simply by talking with them (in person or by telephone), or more formally, by asking them to respond to a written questionnaire.

In each case, you should develop a list of questions you'd like to have answered, and pretest those questions to be sure they don't confuse people or elicit inappropriate or irrelevant responses.

Then, after you've asked your questions—whether formally or informally—you'll have data which you can study and analyze. If you've asked the right questions, of the right people, you'll have a far better reading on the potential success of your new business idea. And that's what you'll need to attract investors and develop your marketing plan.

The Sales Forecast To develop a sales forecast—which will tell you how much of your product or service is likely to be bought by your target market over a set period of time—you would need to conduct separate research activities for each of your market segments.

For Gourmet Caffe, for example, you'd conduct interviews or do phone research with a representative sampling of area residents. Another sampling, of area business owners or office managers, would provide gift purchase projections and data regarding in-office or in-store coffee and tea use.

Assume that your residential research told you the following: the people most likely to buy your products are women between the ages of 30 and 55 who live in the town's most affluent neighborhoods. Residents in "starter home" areas, who tend to be younger, are interested in your products but tend to buy coffees and teas on the basis of price and convenience of purchase rather than for their health advantages or status value. They're much more likely to pick up a jar of instant coffee when they run to the market.

Of the residents in those more affluent neighborhoods, which include some 50,000 households, 65 percent told you they'd be very likely to buy products from you. That's 32,500 households. Of those households, 60 percent said they'd be likely to visit your store once a month or more, buying one to two pounds of product on each visit.

So now you know that 19,500 households might visit your store once a month, buying an average of 1-1/2 pounds of product per visit. At an average price of $7 per pound, that's more than $200,000 worth of product in a year from your personal-use customers—not counting any filters, brewing equipment, mugs, cookies or any of the other products you'll be offering.

Do the same sort of analysis for your business-use and gift buyers, and you'll quickly arrive at a realistic assessment of your likely sales volume for the first year. But remember that the quality of that assessment depends on the quality of your research. Smart entrepreneurs spend enough time, effort and money to conduct thorough, reliable research studies.

The sales forecast is important because it will tell you a great deal: how much product you're likely to need and how often you'll need it. Which products are most likely to sell, at which times of the year, and to whom. How many people you'll need to hire to handle the sales volume you anticipate, and so on.

The only way you can adequately plan for your business needs is to know what those business needs will be, and the only way you can do that is through a carefully-conducted sales forecast.

To do a good forecasting job, you'll want to decide which of the two forecasting processes—*breakdown* or *buildup*—is more appropriate for your business. The breakdown process begins with a "macro-level" analysis—for example, the total population of the community in which Gourmet Caffe is located—and systematically works its way down to the sales forecast. It's usually the choice for consumer goods forecasting.

The buildup process works the other way. It identifies all potential buyers in each submarket and then adds up the estimated demand for all submarkets. It is used more often in industrial goods forecasting.

The Formal Marketing Plan Only when you've gone through the entire process—determined your marketing philosophy, conducted your market research, analyzed market potential, selected your market niche, segmented your market, and developed your sales forecast—can you sit down to write your formal marketing plan. It will detail what you've learned about all of these subjects and provide specific, quantifiable evidence of the potential worth of your business idea. That's what you'll need to convince investors and lenders that yours is an idea worth supporting.

Among the key components of your marketing plan are the market analysis and customer profile, the sales forecast, a description of the likely competition, and an explanation of the marketing strategy you intend to employ.

Your customer profile will describe the benefits customers will enjoy by purchasing products from Gourmet Caffe, and it will identify and describe each of your key target markets.

The sales forecast will offer a range of sales assumptions—optimistic, likely, and pessimistic—drawn from the sales forecasting research you undertook.

Your discussion of competition will talk not only about existing competition and how your venture compares with their market positioning, but also about the possibility of other competitors entering the same market once they see that your venture is a success. You'll need to talk about how you'd handle such a challenge and the marketing strategies you'd employ to prevent it from succeeding. (Maybe you'd offer additional incentives to repeat customers, or change your pricing strategy. Whatever your approach, you'll want to discuss it in this section of the plan, to convince investors that you're aware of the risks.)

And finally, you'll want to provide a detailed description of your tactical plan for marketing. What product qualities will you promote the most, and how will you promote them? If you'll be buying advertising, how much and in what media? How much will it cost, and how much business do you expect it to bring in?

What distribution methods will you offer? Will all customers have to visit the store, or will you provide a small catalog and mail- or phone-order service? Will that service be available to all customers, or just to large volume buyers?

Will large-volume buyers get any kind of price break? And how will you price your products overall? Will you be known as the low-price leader, or as a retailer with competitive prices (but not the *lowest* prices) who offers special services as part of that price?

Answer all of those questions effectively, and your marketing plan will do more than get you the financial backing you need to start up your business. It also will give you a road map for your first months in business—usually the most critical time for any fledgling enterprise.

ASSIGNMENTS

■ Before you watch the video program, be sure you've read through the pre-ceding overview, familiarized yourself with the learning objectives for this lesson, and looked at the key terms below. Then read chapter 7 of Longe-necker, Moore, and Petty, *Small Business Management*, "Developing the Marketing Plan."

■ After completing these tasks, read the video viewing questions and watch the video program for Lesson 8, *Taking Aim.*

■ After watching the program, take time to answer the video viewing ques-tions and evaluate your learning with the self-test which follows the key terms.

■ Extend your learning through the applications, exercises or field experi-ences this lesson offers.

KEY TERMS

Small-business marketing Business activities that relate directly to identi-fying target markets; determining their market po-tential; and preparing, communicating and deliver-ing a "bundle of satisfaction" to those markets.

Marketing research Gathering, processing, reporting, and interpreting marketing information.

Primary data Data obtained from primary sources; in the case of marketing research, primary sources are your cus-tomers and prospects.

Secondary data	Data obtained from secondary sources, which may include internal business information or external information, obtained from such sources as publications, trade associations, private information services, and government agencies.
Market	A group of customers or prospects who have purchasing power and unsatisfied needs.
Market analysis	Process in which target markets are identified and market potential is measured.
Sales forecast	Prediction of how much of a product or service will be bought by a market or market segment over a specific period of time.
Breakdown process	Sales forecasting process which begins with a macro-level variable and systematically works down to the sales forecast.
Buildup process	Sales forecasting process which identifies all potential buyers in each market segment and adds up their estimated total demand.
Direct forecasting	Forecasting method which uses sales as the predicting variable.
Indirect forecasting	Forecasting method which uses other information to predict sales.
Customer profile	Section of the marketing plan that identifies likely customers and describes the benefits they'll obtain from the product or service being offered.

VIDEO VIEWING QUESTIONS

1. Why is a marketing plan based on research critical to the success of a new business?

2. Summarize Luke Strockis' analysis of the comparative advantages and disadvantages of acquiring professional help versus doing your own market research.

3. Several different approaches to primary market research are discussed in the program. Cathy Walters talks about personal observation and questionnaires; Luke Strockis describes focus group research. Ideally, you'll be able to implement several different types of primary research as you start your business. But if you could use only one approach, which method would you choose based on their commentary?

4. In researching the market potential for Skullduggery prior to purchasing the business, the Koehl family discovered a market potential beyond that which the existing business served. What was this market segment, and how did it affect their business plan? What part has market research continued to play in their business?

5. Describe the focus of the market research Pablo Preisser conducted with Janice Ellis, a professional marketing consultant, prior to the launching of Videostay.

6. Because Kidsmetics is a manufacturing firm, its research took a different path. Sketch the approach the Merlos took to market research, including the advice they sought in pricing the product.

SELF-TEST

1. Entrepreneurs need formal marketing plans to
   a. convince investors to fund the new venture and decide on their product mix.
   b. guide them through the early months of operation and convince investors of the worth of the venture.
   c. decide on a business location and determine pricing strategy.

2. Business activities that seek to identify target markets, determine market potential, and provide satisfaction to those markets are examples of
   a. customer-satisfaction strategy.
   b. strategic decisionmaking.
   c. small-business marketing.
   d. marketing research.

3. The most commonly-observed marketing philosophies include *all but*
   a. retail orientation.
   b. consumer orientation.
   c. production orientation.
   d. sales orientation.

4. Gathering, processing, reporting and interpreting information for a new business venture is termed
    a. secondary source research.
    b. marketing research.
    c. preliminary investigation.
    d. market analysis.

5. According to the text, an excellent source of free market research data is
    a. gut instinct.
    b. trade journals.
    c. networking with colleagues and others.
    d. the Internet.

6. Marketing research includes all of the following steps *except*
    a. searching for secondary data.
    b. identifying the informational need.
    c. writing the marketing plan.
    d. searching for primary data.

7. Information collected by an organization and later used in its own research is called
    a. internal secondary data.
    b. primary data.
    c. external secondary data.
    d. tertiary data.

8. Among the most common questioning methods of market research are *all but*
    a. telephone surveys.
    b. personal interviews.
    c. mailed questionnaires.
    d. observation.

9. The three elements that define a market are
    a. demographics, product preferences, and perceived benefits.
    b. customers, purchasing power, and unsatisfied needs.
    c. market segments, marketing niche, and product selection.

10. The best method of sales forecasting is
    a. qualitative.
    b. interpretive.
    c. quantitative.
    d. intuitive.

EXTEND WHAT YOU HAVE LEARNED

A critical element of any business plan is its formal marketing strategy. Who are the potential customers? What devices will you use to attract them to your business? And how will you lure clients from competitors who are in a similar line of business?

Customer Analysis

Describe your market in terms of its customer profile—age, education, annual income, buying patterns—and other significant data regarding potential customers. Where are these customers located in relation to your business? (If you envision several target markets, each segment must have its corresponding customer profile.)

_____

_____

_____

_____

_____

Sales Forecast

Projecting sales is a difficult, but necessary, task for the aspiring entrepreneur. Trade associations will be one of your most helpful sources of information.

Sales Activity Year		PRODUCT OR SERVICE SALES		
		Most likely	Optimistic	Pessimistic
Year 1	1st quarter	$	$	$
	2nd quarter	$	$	$
	3rd quarter	$	$	$
	4th quarter	$	$	$
Year 2		$	$	$
Year 3		$	$	$
Year 4		$	$$	$
Year 5		$	$	$

Competition

An objective analysis of the competition is an aspect of your marketing plan that potential funders will expect to see. The chart below will assist you in developing a profile of existing competitive firms.

Company Name and Addresses	Key Management Personnel	Related Products/ Services	Share of Market (%)	Competitor's Strrengths	Competitor's Weaknesses

Product/Service Strategies

What is the name of your product or service and why was it selected?

_____

_____

_____

If packaging is a consideration, describe how you developed the packaging and provide a sample drawing.

_____

_____

_____

What warranties, repair, or replacement policies will your business offer?

_____

_____

_____

Promotional Plans

If you plan to use sales personnel in creating customer awareness of your product or service, how many people will be employed, how will they be trained, and how will they be compensated?

_____

_____

_____

What advertising will you use to sell your product or service to potential customers?

Form of Advertising	Size of Audience	Frequency of Use	Cost of Single Ad	Estimated Total

Distribution Plans

Describe below what channels of distribution you will use in getting your product or service to the end user. Be sure to indicate whether or not you will take advantage of intermediary support, licensed subdistributors, export opportunities . . . and, if so, how. If you are opening a retail store, describe its layout and configuration.

_____

_____

_____

_____

Pricing Plans

The prices that you set must reflect the costs of bringing a product or service to the customer. However, setting a break-even price ignores other aspects of pricing. If you have a unique niche, you may be able to charge a premium price, at least in the early days of your business when you are the only game in town.

Study your closest competitors to find out what they are charging, and then indicate in your plan what you intend to charge, and why.

Product or Service	Per-unit Cost to Produce Product/Service	Price Range of Competitive Products	Projected Price of Product or Service

Lesson 9

Where to Hang the Sign

LEARNING OBJECTIVES

Upon completing your study of this lesson, you should be able to:

- Understand the process involved in conducting a trade area analysis.

- Indicate factors to consider in selecting a region in which to establish a business; in selecting a city or town within the region.

- Given a specific product or service, establish and rank criteria that should be considered in choosing the site for a new business; in evaluating the site of an existing business.

- Compare the advantages and disadvantages of building, buying, and leasing business facilities.

- Recognize the benefits that can accrue from planning and implementing a functional layout of facilities.

- Given a specific product or service, project the basic equipment, supplies, and inventory required to establish the business and to maintain the ongoing business operation.

Coming up with the idea for a new business may be the hardest part of entrepreneurship—but it's not the only challenge you'll have to face. There's another crucial component of a successful startup or buyout: locating your business in the right place. That's the purpose of this lesson: to help you determine the best possible location for your new business.

OVERVIEW

Consider yourself lucky if you're in the market for a business location, because you've got the perfect opportunity to do it right. But consider yourself forewarned, too—the process isn't simple!

Whether yours is a brand new business or one looking to relocate or expand, the process of deciding on a new location is essentially the same. And the decision is crucial. It could, quite literally, mean the difference between success and failure—or, at least, between a smashing success and mere survival. If you choose the wrong location, your customers may never find you, or they may find it too inconvenient to visit you very often. If the atmosphere isn't appropriate for your kind of business, it may discourage the kind of customer you want to attract to your business.

Since you won't want to move again for a while, and since you may not be able to *afford* to, your selection must be very well-thought-out.

Overall Considerations Beginning with general considerations, and moving toward more specific issues, you'll want to decide first whether locating in your hometown is a good idea. Clearly, you know the community well, and people in town know you—and those facts may be a factor in helping you build your business.

But if Hometown, U.S.A., is off the beaten track and your business will require airplane, rail, or highway access, you'd better broaden your search. And if business trends in general are weak, with no upturn in sight, it might not be wise to stake your future on a community in crisis. Look closely and critically at your community before committing your business's future to it.

Other general factors you'll need to consider are such "environmental" issues as weather, competition, local laws, and even public attitudes. (You'd be taking a big risk by opening a swim-suit shop in northern Minnesota—or a snowblower rental store in Tucson, for instance.) Also take into account where your suppliers and others significant to your business are located.

Competition is a pretty clear-cut question, too. If you live in a sunny climate, and people in your town are avid exercisers, chances are your town is well fortified with nonfat frozen yogurt shops. But if you're located in an industrial city in the Northeast, you may not have too many challengers on the yogurt-shop front. If market research tells you the product would be popular, you've got a "go."

A good source of information on competition is area wholesalers. They'll know how well businesses in your industry can handle demand for their products or services, and they may even be able to offer advice on a particular market niche that isn't being well-served. Another way to evaluate the need for added competition is to look at population data for the region and compare it with figures on the average population required to support your type of business. You should also look at the income level of the population, and its proximity to your proposed location.

Take a look, too, at the local laws, governing everything from zoning and taxation to business licenses and employee benefits. Make sure you can live with the laws and regulations that will be imposed on your business if you locate in a particular community.

The fourth environmental factor—public attitudes—is a bit harder to gauge. Your market research must tell you what prospective customers in your target market think; about your product or service and its impact on their lives. A family counseling center that specializes in pregnancy counseling and birth control would be welcomed in a community where public attitudes support the notion of choice; it would be greeted with great hostility in an area where public sentiment is strongly against abortion and family planning.

Resources and Customers Consider the resources you'll need to run your business. If you're opening a plant nursery, you'll need land that is zoned for agricultural use. You'll also need access to water and a steady supply of unskilled labor. If you're engaged in heavy manufacturing, you'll need to check on access to waste disposal facilities and on the availability of raw materials used in the manufacturing process. You'll need to make sure that state laws and environmental controls allow such businesses to operate. And you'll need semi- skilled or skilled workers.

Whatever your business, certain resources will be critical to its success. Identify those resources and then make sure they're amply available in the area you're considering for your business location.

Then you'll need customers. If you're opening a clothing store, you'd better choose an area where the population is large enough—and preferably growing—to sustain the level of business you need to move into the black. If, on the other hand, you're establishing a scientific research consultancy and you can communicate with clients via fax or phone, you can set up shop in the wilds of Idaho, far from any population center, and still work with people around the world.

Regional Choices Some businesses, as we've already said, can set up shop just about anywhere. Others must choose an area based on transportation, communication, climate, or other factors. If your business must be in a particular region, you'll want to study these factors in selecting a location within that region:

■ *Nearness to market*—try to locate your business in the center of your market, to cut shipping and transportation costs.

■ *Availability of raw materials*—if the raw materials you use are heavy, or hard to transport, locate your business as close to the source of those raw materials as possible, again to cut costs.

■ *Adequacy of labor supply*—choose a town or city where a good supply of employees with the level of skill you need is available. Don't count on training unskilled workers if you need skilled employees—you can't afford to do that at first.

Choosing a City   Once you've identified the region in which you will locate your business, you'll need to select a city. Again, the questions are pretty straightforward. Is the city in growth—or in decline? Are income levels advancing? Is the city keeping up with technological change? Don't plan on being the white knight who rides in to save the town. You may go down with it.

Are major shifts in local markets taking place? That can be good *or* bad. If it's a one-industry town, and that industry is drying up, opening up in that town might seem like a smart thing to do. You'd be giving jobs to people who need them, you reason. But the city's troubles may send your business into bankruptcy, too. On the other hand, if the city is coping with change by aggressively pursuing new business, you could get in on the ground floor of a new era of growth and prosperity.

Take a look, too, at transportation patterns. Is the city on major rail or air routes? Is it served by major state or interstate highways? Does it have a good rapid transit system? Can city streets and highways handle the traffic they receive, or is the city heading toward gridlock?

Finally, take lifestyle considerations into account, if you'll use them to lure employees to join your staff. Can they zip off for a weekend in the country, or the mountains? Can they enjoy opera or theater, or the tri-county rodeo? Are there plenty of public parks, and good schools, and a variety of religious institutions? If *you'd* care about the availability of a particular amenity, chances are your employees would, too.

Choosing the Site   Once you've narrowed your choice to a particular city or town, it's time to consider the facilities for your business. Choosing the site and deciding whether to buy or lease often comes down to weighing the costs and benefits of each option.

If you buy—or build—your own facility, you've got complete control over it and you can build or remodel it to your specifications. But if your business grows more quickly than your business plan anticipates, you may need more space—and that could mean selling your existing facility to buy another. All of that costs money.

By leasing, a new business usually gains advantages that outweigh the benefits of ownership. You'll spend less up front, and have the flexibility to lease additional space if growth occurs more quickly than you expect.

You can even rent space in one of the new facilities called "business incubators," if it's appropriate for the type of business you're starting. There, you not only lease space but also administrative services and management advice. You won't need to buy or lease office equipment, hire office help, or even acquire phones—the incubator provides them all for you.

Or, if yours is a business that could be started from your home, you might want to consider that option. Home-based businesses offer a level of convenience and definite cost savings, but they also require a great deal of patience on the part of family members—and a great deal of discipline on the part of the business owner. Consider this option if working from home won't impair the image of your business, if it's a business that can be confined to one area of your home, and if the nature of your work won't cause disruptions in normal family activities and vice versa. And do some reading on home-based businesses to be sure you fully understand all of the advantages and disadvantages they present.

Site Selection Factors   Key factors to consider when choosing a business site include the following:

- *Cost*—What is the cost to rent, or to buy, in different areas of the city? In which areas would it be most appropriate to locate your type of business? Your business neighbors should complement the nature of your business. Housing your new accounting firm located next to a fried-chicken take-out restaurant won't do much for your credibility.

- *Customer accessibility*—If your business is one that needs to attract customers as they drive by, make sure your location is visible from the road—and make sure it's a well-traveled road. If you need heavy foot-traffic to succeed, don't locate in a business park where few retail customers will venture. Instead, head to a shopping center or mini-mall, and choose a visible, easy-to-reach space within that facility.

  To check the vehicle- or foot-traffic patterns, do a count. That means standing at the site and counting cars or people, at different times of day, and on different days. (Check to see if your community has such data available. It is routinely gathered to assist in the placement of traffic lights.) Get a good sense for the amount of traffic a location is likely to enjoy *before* you lease or buy.

■ *Parking*—Is there enough parking for employees and customers? If you will be shipping or receiving sizeable deliveries, is a ramp or loading area available?

■ *Utilities/comfort factors*—Seemingly detailed questions may make a great deal of difference once your business is underway. Is there sufficient electrical power? sufficient water? sufficient air conditioning or heat? Don't hesitate to call in an expert if your engineering capabilities are questionable.

■ *Neighborhood conditions*—Is the area growing? thriving? Or are nearby stores slipping into disrepair? Be sure you'll want to stay in your location for several years to come.

■ *Suburban shift*—Are businesses leaving the central city and heading to outlying areas? If they are, you may be left behind if you don't head to the suburbs, too.

The Property   Now that you've chosen an area of the city, it's time to zero in on a particular property. The building—if you're not building one yourself— must be suitable to the kind of business you'll be opening, and it mustn't be too large or too small. If it offers some space flexibility in the coming months and years, so much the better.

The quality of the property should match the image you're trying to project, while not breaking your budget. You can find perfectly presentable office space—clean, modern, and comfortable—without springing for mahogany paneling and ultra-thick carpets. Save those luxuries for a few years down the road when your business is booming.

Look for space in a general-purpose building if you don't need specialized facilities. It will be easier to sublease if you need to move before your lease is up. And be sure the space layout will permit your work to proceed smoothly, particularly if you'll be using the space for manufacturing or distribution processes. The more efficient the layout, the more profitable the firm.

If yours is a retail establishment, you'll want a layout that maximizes sales, customer convenience, customer service, and store security. Your choice of a layout—grid, free-flow, or self-service—will be determined in part by the kind of merchandise you offer and the level of service you'll want your employees to offer your customers.

Once you've made decisions concerning your business layout, you can acquire the equipment and furnishings you'll need to do business.

ASSIGNMENTS

- Before you watch the video program, be sure you've read through the preceding overview, familiarized yourself with the learning objectives for this lesson, and looked at the key terms below. Then, read chapter 9 of Longenecker, Moore, and Petty, *Small Business Management*, "Selecting a Location and Planning the Facilities."

- After completing these tasks, read the video viewing questions and watch the video program for Lesson 9, *Where to Hang the Sign.*

- After watching the program, take time to answer the video viewing questions and evaluate your learning with the self-test.

- Extend your learning through the applications, exercises, or field experiences this lesson offers.

KEY TERMS

Business incubator — Facility that provides space, as well as administrative services, some office equipment, and management advice, to startup businesses.

Process layout — Manufacturing facility layout in which similar machines are grouped together.

Product layout — Manufacturing facility layout in which equipment is laid out to facilitate continuous-flow mass production of products, with similar machines at the same points on each conveyor line.

Grid pattern — Block-like layout used in retail stores to enhance merchandise display and simplify restocking, security, and cleaning; used most often in supermarkets, drugstores, etc.

Free-flow pattern — A less space-efficient, more attractive retail store layout than a grid, this layout is visually appealing and encourages customers to wander through store.

Self-service layout — Store layout that enables customers to reach all merchandise; keeps employee costs down by minimizing need for customer service, while encouraging customers to inspect merchandise.

General-purpose equipment Equipment that can be used for more than one purpose; less expensive to acquire, but can be less precise than special-purpose equipment.

Special-purpose equipment Equipment designed for a specific use; its higher cost is justified when it will be used for high-volume production of standardized products.

VIDEO VIEWING QUESTIONS

1. How do the general location needs of manufacturing/distribution, retail, and office operations differ?

2. In choosing a city in which to locate what should the business owner look for? Are "no growth" initiatives that some cities have adopted a negative factor for all types of businesses?

3. Summarize the comments of Nadler and Torgeson regarding what is important to consider in the selection of a business site.

4. Beverly Feldman and Oscar Wright talk about establishing a business at home or within a small business incubator. How would either of these options fit your business plan?

5. Why do Nadler and Torgenson recommend a team approach in the negotiation of a lease?

6. Compare the experiences of Audree MacClelland, Maxine Weinman, and Mike Holman in their selection or "inheritance" of a place of business. If you were a consultant to each of their businesses, what advice would you have given them when they were considering a place to locate or trying to figure out what to do with a current location ?

SELF-TEST

1. Actual site-related factors taken into consideration when selecting a retail location include
   a. future advertising costs.
   b. the labor supply.
   c. raw material availability.
   d. customer accessibility.

2. Locating a business in your home community
   a. should always be the entrepreneur's first choice.
   b. enables the entrepreneur to call on familiar sources for business and financial support.
   c. isn't a good idea unless you've been in the community for more than five years.
   d. is generally unwise, especially during a growth period in which a lot of new businesses are being established.

3. The four general factors to consider in choosing a business location are
   a. personal preference, cost, convenience, and traffic patterns.
   b. cost, traffic patterns, environmental conditions, and regional demographics.
   c. equipment needs, space needs, personal preference, and resource availability.
   d. personal preference, environmental conditions, resource availability, and customer accessibility.

4. Among the key issues to consider in making a regional site selection for a manufacturing plant are
   a. personal preferences, cost, and environmental conditions.
   b. availability of raw materials and transportation, and adequacy of labor supply.
   c. adequacy of labor supply, cost, and personal preferences.
   d. customer accessibility, advertising costs, and neighborhood conditions.

5. One of the most important reasons to lease, rather than buy, space for a new business is
   a. the risk of new-business failure.
   b. the avoidance of real estate closing costs and brokers' fees.
   c. the ability to change locations or add space as business demands.
   d. favorable lease options offered by the landlord.

6. All home-based business owners should
   a. establish boundaries between the home office and the home.
   b. expect to move their businesses to conventional business space within one to three years.
   c. assume that their businesses will be less successful in the early months, due to their unconventional location.
   d. obtain a comprehensive homeowner's insurance policy.

7. A business incubator
   a. expects all businesses located there to remain for at least five years.
   b. provides only space and will not offer management advice to tenants.
   c. provides financial support to fledgling companies.
   d. encourages businesses located there to grow and eventually move to other locations.

8. The functional character of a business is used to determine
   a. geographic location of a business.
   b. suitability of a building.
   c. labor requirements.
   d. spatial requirements.

EXTEND WHAT YOU HAVE LEARNED

"Where to hang the sign" is an important consideration for most people who start new businesses. Answer the following questions in relation to the business you have been researching and planning:

General Considerations

Indicate where, in general, you plan to locate your business, and your reasons for choosing that particular location. Some options you may have considered:

— a downtown business location

— an area adjacent to the downtown business area

— a residential section of town

— a major highway outside of town

— a suburban shopping center

— an undeveloped area away from centers of population

_____

_____

_____

_____

Economic Factors

Is the area in which you plan to locate supported by a strong economic base? As you write your analysis, consider these questions and resources:

— Are new industries and businesses scheduled to open in the near future? Have any gone out of business?

— What is the occupancy rate of office buildings and retail locations in the area?

— Is the population of the area growing, declining, or maintaining? What do you know about the income levels of people who live in the area?

— Does the community support or offer incentives for new business activity?

— How restrictive are local ordinances, zoning regulations, and environmental requirements?

_____

_____

_____

_____

_____

Resource Availability

Rate the importance of each of the following resource factors in locating R = your retail, service, manufacturing, or warehousing facility:

Is the area you are considering close to the markets you will be serving?

_____

_____

_____

If your business requires raw materials, are you close enough to the sources of these materials to operate economically?

_____

_____

_____

If your business is labor intensive, does the area you are considering have an adequate pool of highly skilled, semi-skilled, or unskilled labor that your operation will require?

Skill Classification			Number of Persons Needed	Pay Rate	Availability
Highly Skilled	Semi-skilled	Unskilled			

Site Considerations

To assist you in developing a list of specifications that will be important in selecting the site for your business, answer the following questions:

Will customers come to your place of business, and if so, how frequently? Is parking available? Is public transportation nearby?

_____

_____

_____

How much space will you need initially? A year or two down the road?

_____

_____

_____

Must the building meet certain standards in terms of electricity, heating, ventilation, air conditioning?

_____

_____

_____

What is the competition in the area you have picked? (Does it matter?) Do surrounding buildings looked cared for and prosperous? Is the neighborhood becoming run down, or is it new or on its way up?

_____

_____

_____

What is the occupancy history of the site you have selected? Is it in good physical condition? What improvements is the landlord or seller willing to make?

_____

_____

_____

What are the terms of the lease or the sales contract? Can you justify the cost? What services does the landlord provide?

_____

_____

_____

When you think you have selected an appropriate site for your business, or have narrowed the selection to several possible locations, enlist the assistance of your attorney and accountant before making the final judgment and signing a long-term lease.

_____

_____

_____

Lesson 10

The Buck Starts Here:
Startup Capital

LEARNING OBJECTIVES

Upon completing your study of this lesson, you should be able to:

■ Describe the process involved in determining the financial requirements for a new business, including profit forecasting, current-asset capital, fixed-asset capital, startup expenses, and funds for personal expenses.

■ Given a specific product or service, calculate the assets needed to start a business. Verify your calculations with both breakeven and empirical analyses.

■ Develop pro-forma financial statements (balance sheets, income statements, cash flow projections) that will communicate funding needs to a prospective lender.

■ Differentiate between debt capital and equity capital.

■ Compare and contrast sources of startup capital for a new business.

Having a good idea for a new business is the first step in establishing a successful enterprise. And it can be fun. But it's only the first step. And, all too often, entrepreneurs find themselves so caught up in the idea, so eager to produce the exciting new product, so hungry to begin providing the essential new service, that they give little attention to the financial underpinnings of their new enterprise.

Attend any seminar on developing a new business, and you're likely to hear the leader declare, "Most new businesses that fail do so because their owners didn't plan adequately for capital requirements." To avoid this unhappy outcome, the savvy entrepreneur learns how to calculate the financial requirements for a new business, and how to obtain the capital needed to keep the business afloat in the early months and years.

OVERVIEW

A contractor wouldn't begin to build a home without first consulting a floor plan. And a chemist wouldn't conduct an experiment without first developing a formula. So it stands to reason that an entrepreneur shouldn't begin a new business venture without the business world's equivalent of that floor plan or formula—the business plan.

Without a comprehensive business plan, you're not likely to obtain the financial support you need to get your business off the ground. And you're certainly not likely to have a clear picture of the road ahead of you—a fact that's just as critical in the long run as financial support.

Doing a good job of initial financial planning is a rather straightforward task that involves several steps: calculating financial requirements and conducting both break-even and empirical analyses of that calculation; conducting a cash-flow analysis; preparing the financial plan; and identifying and approaching the most promising funding sources. Let's take a look at each step of the process.

Calculating Financial Requirements   To determine how much money you'll need to get your business going—and how much you'll need to keep it going in the early months and years—careful planning is the key. A profitability forecast, which will tell you how much profit your new venture is likely to bring in (profit that can be used to help finance the business once it's underway) is the first step.

Profitability depends on four factors: the amount of sales you expect to have, your operating expenses, your interest expenses (on the funds you borrow to open up shop), and your tax obligations.

To determine the *likely profit level* for your new venture, you must:

- compute the *cost of goods* you will sell, and your likely *operating expenses*;

- subtract these amounts from your anticipated sales, to determine your likely *operating profit* (also known as earnings before interest and taxes);

- calculate your anticipated *interest expenses*;

- estimate the *income taxes* you will pay; and

- subtract those two amounts from your operating profit, to determine your estimated *net profit*.

Then, by conducting both a breakeven and an empirical analysis of that estimate, you'll have a reasonably good idea about the validity of your estimate.

Next, you'll need to do a cash flow analysis, to project the amount of money you will need and when you will need it. This analysis will measure financial need in four areas: current-asset capital, fixed-asset capital, other asset capital, and personal expense funds.

Current assets appear on the plus side of your working capital needs equation. They include such assets as cash, inventories, and accounts receivable. You'll need cash on hand to cover expenses—to pay for merchandise or supplies, to cover employee salaries, to pay for other types of overhead, and to deal with emergencies. The amount of cash you're likely to require is determined by your anticipated sales volume, and the regularity of cash receipts and cash payments.

Inventory needs will vary from one business to another, but they often constitute the bulk of a business' working capital requirement. The worst mistake you can make when business is booming is to run out of products to sell—so having enough cash or credit to obtain inventory is crucial.

Accounts receivable play into the current assets equation because of their impact on cash flow. If your company sells on a credit basis, or if your customers are slow in paying for merchandise or services received, you'll need an extra cash cushion to keep the business rolling until those payments are received. It is not uncommon for a new business to wait 90 days before seeing a single credit on their accounts payable ledger. Most companies recognize the need to have six months of working capital to offset startup costs.

Fixed assets include all of the relatively permanent assets you'll need to run your business—the things you won't sell but will use in the operation of your new enterprise. Those fixed assets can be tangible, intangible, and security investments. Tangible fixed assets include buildings, machinery, equipment, and land assets. Not every new business has intangible fixed assets, which include everything from patents and copyrights to goodwill. And most new businesses don't have fixed security investments, which include stock of subsidiary companies, pension, and contingency funds. Normally, you'll begin a new business without intangible fixed assets.

If you're opening a service business—a bookkeeping and accounting practice or a personal shopper service, for example—your fixed asset requirements may easily be limited to a few pieces of office equipment and furniture. But if you're establishing a manufacturing plant, your fixed asset requirements will be much greater.

The important rule to remember when calculating fixed asset needs is that your operating flexibility will be inversely related to your investment in fixed assets. Stated simply: the less you spend on fixed assets at the outset, the more flexibility you'll have in responding to economic demands.

You may need a professional to assist you in determining cash require-ments—the amount of cash needed to operate your business for a specific period of time, usually one year. This means that you will need to estimate the amount of cash required to carry accounts receivable, pay bills (accounts pay-able), buy or lease equipment, purchase inventory, make payments on loans, and pay taxes. Prior to actually starting your business, it is important to project your cash flow from collections of accounts receivable and what you will need to secure from other sources, such as loans.

Be sure that you also consider *spontaneous short-term debt*—the debt that arises out of your success! For, as your sales grow, your need to replenish inventory will grow, too. And that will mean increased accounts payable—or spontaneous short-term debt. Be sure you have sufficient credit lines to carry that added debt, or your business could be destroyed by its own success.

An important step in this entire process is the development of a profit and loss statement. This statement and its indication of net profit or net loss will provide you with the data necessary to determine if the net profit warrants the time and effort that you, the owner-manager, have to put into the business.

Other asset capital requirements will include covering the cost of such items as printed materials about your business, insurance premiums, utility deposits, and any promotional activities you'll undertake to tell the world about your new business.

First-time entrepreneurs are often surprised when they add up the cost of printing letterhead and business cards, paying for startup telephone service, making deposits to gas, water, and electric utilities, and securing insurance for the new venture. These costs are a necessary part of any new business, so your expense calculations must include them.

Whether you plan to promote your business yourself or retain an advertis-ing or public relations consultant, you should allocate sufficient funds for marketing and promotion activities. After all, if no one hears about your new business, customers or clients will be hard to come by.

Funds for personal expenses are just that—a set-aside fund that enables you to keep paying your personal living expenses while you build your new business. While these funds aren't usually included in your business capitali-zation plan, *you* need to be certain they're available. There's no guarantee your business will realize enough profit in the early months to pay you a sal-ary. Most financial experts advise setting aside between six and 18 months' worth of personal funds before opening a new business.

Developing the Financial Plan Developing a financial plan is more than a number-crunching exercise. It's the key to convincing potential funding sources that your business idea makes economic sense. The plan is presented in the form of pro-forma financial statements.

Pro-forma financial statements provide the same kinds of information about a proposed business as actual financial statements offer about an ongoing enterprise, only the figures are projected rather than real. By using pro-forma financial statements—which include an income statement, balance sheet, and cash flow budget—you offer prospective investors and lenders information about your business in a form they're used to seeing.

These statements will tell prospective lenders and investors when you expect to begin showing a profit, when additional infusion of funds might be needed, and when you expect to begin drawing income from the business. You'll need to prepare pro-forma financial statements for the first three to five years of operation, to give potential funding sources the long-range view they need to determine whether or not to support your new venture.

Obtaining Funding Determining how much money you'll need to launch your new business is a relatively straightforward process—particularly when that effort is contrasted with the search for funds. That adventure requires a combination of business acumen, professional presentation, and sheer salesmanship.

Most small businesses are funded largely with personal funds—the savings of the business owner, and loans from his or her family and close friends. Some manager-owners take on "bridge-jobs" to finance the startup of their business. But when your financial requirements are greater than the amount you can earn, or when your personal funding sources are insufficient, you'll need to look to more formal sources of capital, which include banks and venture capitalists.

If you've done a good job of preparing your pro-forma financial statements and business plan, prospective lenders and investors will be much more likely to take you and your business seriously. And, if you observe the owner capital/creditor capital rule-of-thumb ratio—between half to two-thirds of the initial capital from you, and the balance from lenders—you'll be perceived as an entrepreneur with a serious stake in your new business and a strong motivation to see it succeed.

There are two fundamental categories of financing available to the entrepreneur: debt financing and equity financing. Debt financing is money that is borrowed and that must be repaid at some predetermined date in the future. Equity financing represents capital that is raised when the entrepreneur invests personal funds, or convinces others to do so in exchange for ownership in the business.

Among the primary sources of *equity financing* are personal savings, venture capitalists, business "angels," who use their considerable resources to help fund new enterprises, and the securities market. Included on the list of *debt financing* sources are individuals, commercial banks, government-assisted programs, and asset-based lenders. Let's look briefly at each funding source.

Equity Financing   You already know what it means to use *personal savings* to help finance your venture, so we won't belabor the point.

Included in the *venture capitalist* category are both individuals outside your immediate social circle (lawyers, physicians, and others looking for investment opportunities), and professional venture capitalist organizations. Both groups will risk funds in a new venture *only* if they think it will offer a rate of return significantly higher than what they can receive elsewhere. So you've got to have a great idea with a strong likelihood of substantial profit to convince these people to invest.

Although this may be a tough group to sell on your new business, it's a smart approach to take. More funds are obtained by small firms from venture capitalist sources each year than from the public funding market. So, you'll want to tap into your community grapevine to see if there are any venture capitalist "clubs" in your area.

Business angels are much like venture capitalists. They're wealthy individuals who like to invest in fledgling enterprises and see them succeed. Again, hooking up with your local grapevine will help you identify any prospective angels in your midst.

Both venture capitalists and "angels" may also be able to give you management and operating advice, depending on the background and experience of the particular individuals you work with. And that advice can be very valuable to the new business owner.

If your business is of significant size, you may prefer to offer stock in the company, either through a private placement or a public sale. *Private placement* is difficult because your company isn't yet a known entity. On the upside, it avoids many of the securities requirements placed on public offerings.

A *public sale* is more costly and involves a great deal of public regulation, but it does get word of your organization to a much wider investing audience. You can expect to pay between 10 and 30 percent of your profit as your fee to securities underwriters, and you'll also pay for options and other fees. You need to be careful about the timing of any public offering. In a tight market, where venture capital is scarce, your quest for public funding may very well fail.

Unless yours is a very impressive business undertaking, any initial public offering isn't likely to succeed. Your firm simply has no operating history on which prospective investors can base a purchase decision.

Debt Financing   On the debt financing side, you may wish to seek out *individuals* who know you well and who know a lot about your business idea. They may be interested in supporting the new venture, given a good prospective rate of return and a relatively short projected payback period. Be sure to carefully delineate their rights as investors, however, or you may find yourself forced to seek their approval for every business decision you make.

A less personally taxing debt financing source is the commercial bank. Although they often limit their lending to the working-capital needs of established businesses, you may obtain some funding if your business is adequately financed and you have a strong reputation in your field. Collateral or personal guarantees may be required before commercial banks will issue a new-business loan.

You should look to commercial banks primarily for two types of assistance: a line of credit and long-term loans for permanent working capital and the acquisition of fixed assets.

You might also investigate *federal, state* and *local government agencies* that lend money to small businesses. Though funding may be significantly limited, the management insights gained from the process are often well worth the effort. The federal government makes loans available through the Small Business Administration and the Small Business Investment Company program. The latter, created in 1958 to help new businesses get over their initial capital crunch, established a group of privately organized and managed investment firms licensed by the SBA. These firms provide investment capital to new and ongoing small businesses.

In recent years, state and local governments have stepped up their involvement in small business financing. But their efforts are usually directed at augmenting other funding sources, so don't count on them to assist in the establishment of your business.

You might also turn to potential *business suppliers* who recognize that assistance in starting your business will benefit them. They can help by extending trade credit—giving you time to pay for the merchandise they deliver to you—or by selling you equipment on an installment basis.

Asset-based lending Finally, there's *asset-based lending*, or financing secured by your working-capital assets. Loans are most often secured by your accounts receivable or inventory, but they may also be secured by equipment or real estate owned by the new business. Asset-based lending is a good source of funds for young companies that are growing and find themselves in a cash-flow bind.

At the core of any financing commitment, however, one thing stands firm: the strength of your business idea and the professionalism with which you present your plans, along with your financial calculations, are the keys to success. Do those jobs right, and the funds you need are likely to be found.

ASSIGNMENTS

- Before you watch the video program, be sure you've read through the preceding overview, familiarized yourself with the learning objectives for this lesson, and looked at the key terms below. Then read chapters 10 and 11 of Longenecker, Moore, and Petty, *Small Business Management*, "Accounting Statements and Financial Requirements" and "Finding Sources of Financing."

- After completing these tasks, read the video viewing questions and watch the video program for Lesson 10, *The Buck Starts Here*.

- After watching the program, take time to answer the video viewing questions and evaluate your learning with the self-test which follows the key terms.

- Extend your learning through the applications, exercises or field experiences this lesson offers.

KEY TERMS

Current assets   Cash, inventory and accounts receivable—the "plus" side of your ledger.

Fixed assets   Permanent assets used in the business and not sold, such as furnishings and equipment.

Average collection period	Average length of time a business in a given industry must wait to receive payment on a credit sale.
Current ratio	Ratio of current assets to current liabilities; guide to proper degree of liquidity.
Break-even analysis	Determines relationship between sales revenue and cost of producing that revenue to identify a business' break-even point.
Owner equity capital	Capital invested in a business by its owner—usually half to two-thirds of initial capital required is owner capital.
Creditor capital	Initial capital obtained from investors in a business (also known as *debt capital*).
Asset-based lending	Financing secured by working-capital assets (also known as current assets: cash, accounts receivable, and inventory).
Factoring	Providing cash to a business before accounts receivable payments come in, by selling accounts receivable to a firm known as a "factor."
Pro-forma financial statements	Projected financial statements for a new business; usually cover the first 12 months of operation and follow the same form as financial statements for an ongoing business.

VIDEO VIEWING QUESTIONS

1. One of the first questions any potential entrepreneur needs to ask is "How much money is this venture really going to take?" What guidelines do Jon Goodman and Robert Gipson suggest?

2. In initiating a search for new business capital, what are the most fruitful leads to follow, according to Gerold Morita, Robert Gipson, and Oscar Wright?

3. Robert Gipson divides potential sources for financial backing into two camps: debt and equity financing. How does he differentiate between the two?

4. When a new, untested company seeks capital from a bank, what can the new owners do to increase their chances for a successful response? (Gerold Morita addresses this point.)

5. Oscar Wright, Regional Director of the Small Business Administration, talks about the support the SBA provides small businesses to secure loans. What incentives does the SBA provide to bankers?

6. What are the advantages and disadvantages of securing financial support from a venture capitalist?

7. In securing the financing necessary to create Didee Snugs and his company, Vencor International, did Culley Davis choose the debt or equity route? How does he feel about this choice now that the business is six years old? In a similar situation, what would your approach have been?

8. Analyze the multiple financial sources Mike Smith drew upon to purchase Aero Haven, the charter airline and flight instruction school.

9. When Pauline Parry's catering service moved from a home operation to a business location, what new costs did she face? When it became obvious that she was in financial difficulty, what was her recourse? What steps could she have taken to avoid the problems she experienced?

SELF-TEST

1. In analyzing capital requirements for a business, you should consider the need for
    a. current-asset capital.
    b. fixed-asset capital.
    c. personal expenses.
    d. all of the above.

2. An example of a current asset is
    a. buildings.
    b. inventories.
    c. equipment.
    d. patents and copyrights.

3. The amount of cash needed by a new business is determined in part by
   a. volume of sales.
   b. regularity of cash receipts.
   c. regularity of cash payments.
   d. all of the above.

4. An example of a fixed asset is
   a. cash.
   b. accounts receivable.
   c. the company's delivery truck.
   d. inventories.

5. Startup expenses include everything *but*
   a. equipment maintenance costs.
   b. promotional fees.
   c. insurance premiums.
   d. utility deposits.

6. Current assets divided by current liabilities is the formula for
   a. financing needs calculations.
   b. determining the necessary amount of equity capital.
   c. calculating the necessary degree of liquidity.
   d. projected sales ratios.

7. Renting, rather than buying, property for a new business makes sense because
   a. it costs less over the long term and offers operating flexibility.
   b. it reduces the initial cash requirement and offers operating flexibility.
   c. it allows for easier dissolution of a sole proprietorship.
   d. it is a tax incentive for the small business.

8. Which of the following is not among the "Five Cs of Credit" that a banker looks at in making a loan decision?
   a. The borrower's character
   b. The conditions of the industry and economy
   c. The borrower's clarity of purpose
   d. The collateral available to secure the loan

9. Commercial banks are likely to offer a line of credit to a young business
   a. if the owner demonstrates that the business' financial condition will make it possible to repay the loan.
   b. if the business owner waits until there's a critical need for the cash.
   c. if the line of credit will be used for business expansion.
   d. if the line of credit will be used to pay debts.

10. The primary providers of debt capital to small businesses are
    a. federal assistance programs though agencies like the Small Business Administration.
    b. venture capitalists.
    c. commercial banks.
    d. friends and relatives.

EXTEND WHAT YOU HAVE LEARNED

At this point, take some time to think about what your business plan requires in terms of dollars. First, list anticipated startup costs for your company. Because each new business is somewhat unique, the list that follows may not include all of the startup costs you will incur. Add categories that should be included for your particular operation.

Startup Costs

Fixtures and equipment . . . . $_____

Starting inventory . . . . $_____

Office supplies . . . . $_____

Decorating and remodeling. . . . . $_____

Installation of equipment . . . . $_____

Deposits for utilities . . . . $_____

Legal and professional fees. . . . . $_____

Advertising for the opening . . . . $_____

Owner's living expenses during startup period . . . . $_____

TOTAL. . . . . $_____

Like most businesses, your new firm will probably require financial support during startup and over its first months—even years—of operation. Realize that many businesses do not show a profit until the second or third year. If this is the case with your business, you will need to secure the financial reserves necessary to carry you through this period of time.

Before approaching a bank or venture capitalist, it is important to determine whether or not your plan is economically feasible. This will require sets of projections. The forms that follow are designed to help you with this task.

ESTIMATED CASH FORECAST

	Jan	Feb	Mar	Apr	May	June	July	Aug	Sept	Oct	Nov	Dec
(1) Cash in bank (start of month)												
(2) Petty cash (start of month)												
(3) Total cash (add 1 & 2)												
(4) Expected accounts receivable												
(5) Other money expected												
(6) Total receipts (add 4 & 5)												
(7) Total cash & receipts (add 3 & 6)												
(8) All disbursements (from Sales and Expense Statement)												
(9) Cash balance at end of month in bank & petty cash (subtract 8 from 7)												

*This balance is your starting cash balance for the next month

SUMMARY STATEMENT OF SALES AND EXPENSES

	Jan	Feb	Mar	Apr	May	June	July	Aug	Sept	Oct	Nov	Dec	Annual Total
SALES (a)													
Cost of goods sold (b)													
Gross profit (subtract a from b)													
EXPENSES													
Variable expenses													
Gross wages													
Repairs & maintenance													
Operating supplies													
Advertising expenses													
Shipping & postage													
Telephone													
Travel													
Misc. expenses													
Fixed expenses													
Rent													
Utilities													
Insurance													
Taxes & licenses													
Interest													
Depreciation													
Total expenses													
NET PROFIT													

If you are having difficulty projecting sales and expenses, start first with the sales volume you expect to do in the first twelve months. Base your answers on the market research you have conducted.

After looking at the cost figures and comparing them to how much you could potentially earn by investing dollars in a money market account, or stocks and bonds, you may decide that you'd be better off investing your money than trying to establish a small business.

Lesson 11

Making it Legal

LEARNING OBJECTIVES

Upon completing your study of this lesson, you should be able to:

- Recognize the characteristics of a proprietorship.
- Describe the following aspects of the form of business ownership known as a partnership:
    - a. qualifications of partners
    - b. rights and duties of partners
    - c. the tax and liability consequences of partnership
    - d. termination of a partnership
    - e. the articles of partnership
    - f. the limited partnership.
- Discuss the legal aspects of a corporation, including:
    - a. the rights and status of stockholders
    - b. tax considerations
    - c. the liability of stockholders
    - d. the death or withdrawal of stockholders
    - e. the corporate charter.
- Recognize the difference between regular, or C, corporations, and sub-chapter S, or S, corporations.
- Identify the criteria for choosing the proprietorship, partnership, or corporate form of ownership.
- Discuss the relationship between federal income taxes and the form of ownership chosen.
- Analyze the role of the Board of Directors in a small company, and discuss the potential advantages of its alternative, an advisory council.

From an economic perspective, selecting the form of legal ownership of a new business is one of the most important decisions an entrepreneur will make. That decision will affect everything from the provision of tax-free employee health benefits and liability to the rate at which business income will be taxed.

Identifying the major characteristics of each of the three forms of legal ownership most often used by small businesses is the purpose of this lesson.

OVERVIEW

A variety of business forms exist, but the three most often chosen by the founders of small businesses are the proprietorship, the partnership, and the corporation.

Proprietorships have only one common form of ownership, but within the partnership, two options exist: the general partnership and the limited partnership. And there are two types of corporations, regular, or C, and Subchapter S. Deciding which form of legal ownership is best will depend on the type of business you're establishing and whether you're going into business for yourself or with partners. Here are a few quick examples of the kinds of decisions you may need to make.

If yours is a home-based office, solo-practitioner psychological counseling service, you won't need to consider the partnership option. But you may face substantial legal risk, since the nature of your business is such a personally sensitive one. Given that potential, you might want to look at a Subchapter S corporation, which (as you'll soon learn) will protect your personal property from legal claims against the business while offering you certain corporate tax advantages.

Open up a two-person psychological counseling service, however, and a partnership also becomes an option. That form of ownership will increase the capital and assets available, and, if you subscribe to the belief that better decision-making will occur when two intelligent people are involved, it will decrease the risk for each partner. A Subchapter S corporation *could* be another option if you and your partner are interested in the employee benefits offered by that business form.

On the other hand, establish a freelance writing business from home—one in which you go to clients' offices for meetings and use your home office only for writing and telephone work—and the legal liability issue declines significantly. For your business, a proprietorship is probably a good option.

And, if you're establishing a computer peripherals development and manufacturing firm, you'll need the skills and oversight of a wide variety of business experts. You'll probably also need the economic resources that only the sale of stock can provide. In your case, a corporation is the likely answer.

As you can see, we need to take a closer look at each of the legal forms of ownership.

The Proprietorship Simply put, a proprietorship is a business owned and operated by one person. That person owns all the business' assets, and only creditors' claims may impinge on that ownership. The proprietor receives all profits from the business, assumes all losses, is responsible for all debts, and bears all the business' risks. When you're the proprietor, the buck stops with you.

The proprietorship is the easiest, least expensive form of business to establish. And since there are no partners, directors, stockholders, or officers, it's the easiest form of business to operate, and the easiest form to dissolve. Maybe you're asking yourself right now: "If it's so easy to establish, run, and dissolve, why doesn't everyone begin this way?" You've already heard some of the reasons in the examples above, but here's the complete rundown.

First, there are no limits on the owner's personal liability. So if your proprietorship fails, and you owe creditors a great deal of money, they can target your personal assets—your home, your car, anything you own—to satisfy your debts.

Second, the proprietorship doesn't offer some of the tax-free employee benefits—such as insurance and hospitalization—offered by corporations. If you want them, you must pay for them yourself with after-tax dollars.

Third, the death of the proprietor means the end of the proprietorship. The business assets belong to the heirs, not to any employees or creditors of the business. The business can continue only if the proprietor's will gives the power to run the business to an executor—and even then, only until the heirs take over or sell the business.

Fourth, if the proprietor is incapacitated, the business may simply cease to operate, unless the proprietor has given someone power of attorney to continue business operations.

And fifth, if the nature of your business exposes you to significant legal risk, the proprietorship won't protect your personal assets if you're sued. So to be sure you won't jeopardize your personal security, you must look carefully at the legal risks involved in operating a proprietorship.

The Partnership The partnership is just what the name suggests: an agreement between two or more people to establish a business together and run it for mutual profit. Unless the partnership terms state otherwise, partners are to share an equal risk and receive an equal reward for their efforts.

Because establishing a partnership is a voluntary act, there aren't as many procedural requirements as there are for incorporation. So, a partnership can be set up relatively quickly and painlessly. But if it's not set up correctly, there could be a great deal of personal pain or problems down the road.

For starters, anyone who is legally capable of signing a contract may enter into a partnership agreement. That doesn't mean the person is capable, honest, or physically able to do the job, or even compatible with the other partners. It just means the partnership agreement is binding.

If you're considering a partnership, approach it just as carefully and deliberately as you would a marriage (or as carefully and deliberately as you *should* approach a marriage!). After all, the relationship between partners is much like a marriage. Personality clashes and individual idiosyncracies can ruin a partnership as easily as they can break up the hottest romance.

If you're reasonably convinced that the personalities, tastes, viewpoints, values and—not least important—skills of all the partners will mesh, the partnership can offer a number of advantages. It puts each partner at less risk, since they're going into the venture together. It enables individuals to share decisionmaking responsibilities and to benefit from each other's strengths. And it often serves as a great motivator to be part of a team, rather than a lone crusader. The old saying about two heads being better than one is often true.

On the down side, it's not easy to dissolve a partnership, unless you've taken care to write your articles of partnership to cover every eventuality— death, disagreement, financial failure, incapacity of a partner, and so on. Most importantly, you must have full trust and faith in your partners, since each partner has what is known as agency power—the right to bind all other partners to an agreement into which the individual partner enters.

So partnership can work, but it relies heavily on two factors: the partners' ability to trust one another completely, and the preparation of thorough, precise articles of partnership. Once you've refined your thoughts on how you want your partnership to operate, and how you'll take care of problems if they occur, you should have those articles of partnership reviewed and revised as necessary by an attorney. No matter how much you trust each other, it's always better to spell out the ground rules in advance.

The Limited Partnership The limited partnership is a special breed of partnership. It includes one general partner, who runs the organization and is liable for its debts, and one or more limited partners, who contribute capital to the organization but have no role in running it, and whose liability is limited.

Often used as tax shelters (in which the limited partners invest as a way to reduce their personal tax obligations), limited partnerships are less common since the Tax Reform Act of 1986 reduced the tax advantages they offer.

The Corporation   The corporation may be big or small, it may manufacture goods or distribute them, it may provide a service or operate retail stores. Virtually any type of business can be incorporated.

The ordinary corporation, often called a C corporation to distinguish it from more specialized forms of corporations is, in effect, a legal entity. It can sue and be sued; it can own, buy or sell property; and it can engage in the type of business activities that are described in its charter. The corporation exists independently of any person—its officers, managers, stockholders, or directors. They may operate it, and make decisions about what it will do, but the corporate entity "lives" independently of all individuals. They may die, but the corporation lives on!

As a result, the corporation—not its owners or directors—is liable for its debts. So, clearly, the corporate form of ownership protects individuals from personal liability for corporate obligations. In addition, the corporation can offer a wide variety of tax-advantaged benefits to its employees, another incentive for incorporation.

Individuals who choose not to incorporate usually make that choice because of the expense and complexity involved in the process, not because incorporation isn't a good idea. Sometimes it's just too costly and time-consuming a process for the kind and size of business being established.

Corporations are owned by stockholders who purchase shares of stock. That ownership gives stockholders the right to receive dividends on their investment (if dividends are declared by the corporation's directors), the right to buy new shares before they're offered to the general public, and the right to vote at annual meetings (receiving one vote for each share of stock they hold).

Stockholders have only limited liability for the obligations of the corporation unless, as individuals, they have agreed to assume financial liability by endorsing notes to the company. Their shares in the company are easily transferred either by sale or by bequest to their heirs.

The death of a majority shareholder could, however, pose problems for the corporation. An heir, executor or buyer of the stock could easily insist on direct control of the company, and that could spell disaster if his or her intentions conflict with those of the other shareholders. So it's important to determine before incorporating just how management continuity will be assured to the surviving shareholders, as well as how the rights of the majority shareholder's heirs can be protected.

If a corporation is small, it might be wise to determine up front how major blocks of stock may be transferred or sold, and to whom. This may help prevent one stockholder from tearing apart the company by deciding to sell—or refusing to sell—at a critical time.

One tool often used by new corporations to reassure prospective investors is "section 1244" stock. This type of stock protects the stockholder, in case the business fails, by allowing up to $100,000 in investments to be treated as an ordinary tax-deductible loss.

The Board of Directors is the corporation's governing body. It elects corporate officers to manage the firm. It sets or approves management policies. It receives and evaluates reports on the company's operations. And it declares whether stockholders will receive quarterly dividends on their investments.

It may appear that the corporate form of ownership protects the business from overwhelming control by one individual, and in large corporations, that's usually the case. But in smaller corporations, a majority owner can be just as dictatorial as the sole proprietor, by insisting that minority stockholders elect him or her the president and general manager of the organization.

It even happens on occasion in major corporations. Armand Hammer's long-lived rule at Occidental Petroleum is just one example of how an individual can *be* the organization. So even the corporate form of ownership isn't an absolute guarantee of management by consensus and operation by teamwork. It just increases the odds.

Establishing the corporation requires the preparation of a corporate charter, a job for a corporate attorney. In essence, the charter represents a request to the state government for permission to incorporate. When the charter is approved and articles of incorporation (or, in some states, a certificate of incorporation) prepared, the charter usually declares:

- the name of the company;

- a formal statement of corporate formation;

- an explanation of the corporation's purposes and powers—its reasons for being;

- its planned life-span;

- the classes and preferences of stock to be offered;

- the number and value of shares of each class of stock to be authorized;

- voting privileges for each class of stock;

- names and addresses of incorporators and first-year directors;

- names and addresses of, and amounts subscribed by, all subscribers to capital stock;

- a statement concerning stockholders' limited liability; and

- a statement concerning any alterations in directors' powers from those generally granted by state law.

Obviously, the more thoroughly the charter is prepared, the greater the odds that the corporation will successfully weather any unexpected events.

The Subchapter S Corporation Finally, there's the Subchapter S corporation, a structure that allows the corporation to retain the limited liability provisions of a general corporation while enabling it to be taxed as a partnership. This form offers significant tax advantages to its owners. To qualify for Subchapter S status:

- the corporation must be owned by 35 or fewer stockholders (with husband-and-wife owners counting as one);

- all owners must be individuals or certain types of qualifying estates and trusts;

- the corporation must offer just one class of stock to all stockholders;

- the corporation must be within the state, as opposed to outside the state in which it was organized;

- there may be no nonresident alien stockholders; and

- the corporation may not own more than 79 percent of the stock of another corporation.

Among the chief advantages of this structure: the corporation pays no corporate income tax. Instead, taxable income is passed through to stockholders who receive these dividends without the double-taxation that would otherwise occur (corporate taxes and then personal taxes on the dividends).

Setting up a Subchapter S corporation has become more complicated since the Tax Reform Act of 1986, so an attorney should be consulted if this option seems viable.

Choosing the Ownership Form So just how can you decide which form of ownership will be best for your new company? There are a number of criteria to use in making the decision, but in the end, you'll be left with a list of advantages and disadvantages for each option. And it'll be up to you to decide which approach offers the greatest advantage and the least downside risk.

Among the criteria you should use to help you come to a decision are:

- organizational costs,

- limited versus unlimited liability,

- continuity (What happens if an owner, partner, or majority shareholder dies?),

- transferability of ownership,

- control (Who has it?),

- ability to raise new equity capital,

- income tax implications.

The final criterion, income tax implications, is crucial. If yours is a sole proprietorship, you will report income from the business on your individual tax return, and you will be taxed at the rates set by Congress for people in your income bracket.

A partnership reports its income to the IRS, but it doesn't pay taxes. That income is allocated to the partners according to their partnership agreement, and they each report their share of income on their individual tax returns. Again, your individual income bracket will determine your taxes for partnership income.

As a distinct legal entity, the corporation reports its income and pays taxes on that income. The owners (or stockholders) do not report corporate earnings on their individual tax returns, except for any dividends they receive during the year from the corporation.

Only you can determine which of these forms of ownership makes the most sense from a tax standpoint.

The Board of Directors in the Small Company The last topic we'll cover in this chapter concerns the role that can be played by the Board of Directors of a small company.

Often, the majority owner of a small company will appoint board members simply to meet his or her legal obligation, appointing friends, neighbors or relatives to what amount to figurehead posts. Doing that is foolhardy, for the owner misses out on the opportunity to bring people into the corporate inner circle who can offer the benefit of their skills and experience to the operation. An effective board of directors can help by:

- reviewing major policy decisions,

- offering advice on external business conditions that will affect the corporation,

- providing the insights and counsel on specific problems for which their expertise makes them valuable sources of information,

■ offering an objective evaluation of corporate actions and plans, and

■ monitoring the ethical performance of the corporation.

Obviously, then, directors should be chosen carefully. Talk with your attorney, banker, accountant, other business executives, and management consultants to identify strong candidates. Choose people in part on the basis of their qualifications and the specialized expertise you need to help you lead your organization, and in part on the basis of chemistry—how well you think their personalities and outlooks mesh with yours and with the character of your organization.

Compensation of board members varies greatly, but usually ranges from $200 to $300 monthly (for participating in a once-a-month, half-day board meeting of a smaller firm).

If prospective board members seem hesitant to join your board, for fear of becoming responsible for illegal company actions about which they may have no knowledge and over which they may have no control, you may want to consider another alternative. That option: the advisory council.

Instead of being officially elected as board members, individuals become informal advisers to the organization. The group functions much as a board of directors would, but its actions are strictly advisory and present little or no risk of legal liability to its members.

ASSIGNMENTS

■ Before you watch the video program, be sure you've read through the preceding overview, familiarized yourself with the learning objectives for this lesson, and looked at the key terms below. Then read chapter 8 of Longenecker, Moore, and Petty, *Small Business Management*, "Selecting the Management Team and Form of Organization."

■ After completing these tasks, read the video viewing questions and watch the video program for Lesson 11, *Making it Legal*.

■ After watching the program, take time to answer the video viewing questions and evaluate your learning with the self-test which follows the key terms.

■ Extend your learning through the applications, exercises or field experiences this lesson offers.

KEY TERMS

Proprietorship	A business owned and operated by one person, who assumes all risk and reaps all rewards or consequences.
Partnership	An agreement between two or more people to operate a business, share in the risk as well as rewards or consequences.
Articles of partnershi	Papers that set the terms of operation for a partnership and establish all partners' rights and obligations.
Agency power	The right of any partner in a partnership to sign an agreement or contract that is binding on all partners.
Limited partnership	Partnership involving a general partner, who runs the business and assumes liability for its debts, and one or more limited partners, who risk capital but do not run the business and have only limited personal liability.
Corporation	A legal entity that can own and sell property, sue and be sued, and engage in the business activities specified in its charter; its owners, directors and officers have limited personal liability.
Board of Directors	Governing body of a corporation, it elects officers to manage the firm, sets or approves management policies, receives and reviews operating reports, and declares dividends.
Corporation charter	Papers that authorize the incorporation of a company, detail the business activities it will undertake, and explain the rights and obligations of its directors, officers, and stockholders.
Subchapter S corporation	Corporation that offers the same limited liability benefits to its owners while offering them the tax benefits of a partnership.
Advisory council	A group of qualified outsiders asked to serve in an advisory capacity; substitutes for a board of directors when individuals are concerned about the significant risk of legal liability that comes with board membership.

VIDEO VIEWING QUESTIONS

1. Is the choice of a legal form of ownership a fairly straightforward question that leaves little to doubt? What do Robert Gipson and Oscar Wright have to say about this?

2. As you listen to the comments of Michael McGreevy, Denise Lamaute, Robert Gipson, and Oscar Wright, construct your own "good news-bad news" analysis of sole proprietorships, partnerships, and corporations.

3. What is the difference between general or limited partnerships? Between regular, or C, corporations, and Subchapter S corporations?

4. Compare Mildred Hughes' experience in a partnership with that of Larry Longobardi and Doug Lovosin. From your observation, what factors led to the success of one operation and the demise of the other?

5. Why did Randy Olsen choose to incorporate the Celebrity Valet operation? Did similar considerations influence Signs and Glassworks?

SELF-TEST

1. If you wanted to operate a business on your own, with no board of directors and no stockholders, and your business presented minimal legal risk, you'd probably establish a

   a. Subchapter S corporation.

   b. proprietorship.

   c. limited partnership.

   d. C corporation.

2. If you needed investors for a business venture but wanted to maintain full operating control, the best form of ownership might be the

   a. partnership.

   b. proprietorship.

   c. limited partnership.

   d. Subchapter S corporation.

3. The most costly, complex form of business to set up is the
    a. corporation.
    b. limited partnership.
    c. partnership.
    d. proprietorship.

4. A business in which two or more owners pool their managerial talent and capital is a
    a. Subchapter S corporation.
    b. corporation.
    c. limited partnership.
    d. partnership.

5. To become a partner in a partnership, an individual
    a. must contribute to capital resources.
    b. may be any age.
    c. must be capable of contracting for the partnership.
    d. must always have the right to a share of the assets.

6. The right of any partner to sign a contract that is binding on other partners is called
    a. the articles of partnership.
    b. agency power.
    c. limitations of partnership.
    d. partnership risk.

7. A corporation is
    a. a state-chartered organization that continues to function independently of the lives of its owners.
    b. a body that cannot be sued for the actions of its officers and directors.
    c. an association of two or more owners.
    d. an association that is dissolved on the death of a member of the Board of Directors.

8. Owning shares of stock in a corporation gives one the right to
    a. elect officers, manage operations, and declare dividends.
    b. set and approve management policies, and receive and approve reports on operating results of the company.
    c. receive dividends, buy new shares, and elect the corporation's directors.
    d. manage the company with the right of agency.

9. Key criteria for choosing the best form of ownership include all of the following *except*
   a. transferability of ownership.
   b. ability to raise new equity capital.
   c. limited versus unlimited liability.
   d. paperwork requirements.

10. If the individuals establishing a new venture do not want to personally pay income tax on its profits, they must establish
    a. a general partnership.
    b. a corporation.
    c. a limited partnership.
    d. a sole proprietorship.

EXTEND WHAT YOU HAVE LEARNED

1. Interview a tax attorney or an attorney specializing in business organizations concerning the factors involved in establishing the different legal forms commonly used by small business.

   _____

   _____

   _____

2. Identify three fictitious businesses that you feel, given the information provided in this lesson, would be suitable for each type of legal structure.

   _____

   _____

   _____

3. Secure information from local and state agencies concerning documents, licensing, registrations, and state laws that govern small businesses in your area.

   _____

   _____

   _____

4. Given your specific business idea and emerging business plan, indicate the advantages and disadvantages of organizing the business yourself.

_____

_____

_____

From the Ground Up:
RAW Architectvre

Entrepreneurial organizations are often the brainchild of those who are disillusioned with the corporate or cultural circumstances in which they find themselves. Young, bright, ambitious individuals attend college, earn the degrees, and acquire the licenses which enable them to practice a particular profession, and go to work for the industry leaders, expecting a swift climb up the corporate ladder. After all, they were at the top of their class in college—why should the work world be any different?

But it is—and for those who cannot or will not wait years, even decades, for recognition and control, entrepreneurship often is the best alternative.

That is how it was for Roland A. Wiley, Steven Lott, and R. Steven Lewis, who encountered both corporate complacency and lingering discrimination in the predominantly white architecture industry, and who chose to establish the young, inventive and already successful Los Angeles-based RAW Architectvre.

RAW Architectvre By the time that Roland Wiley, Steven Lott, and A.Steven Lewis hung out a shingle together, one of them already had become so disillusioned with the "corporate" practice of architecture that he'd given up on the profession altogether.

When Roland Wiley decided in 1984 to leave Gruen Associates, one of America's largest architectural firms, to start his own practice, he set up a drafting office in space owned by Steven Lott. He and Lott had met at Gruen, where both had begun their architectural careers.

But, although Lott became Wiley's financial partner, he refused at first to become involved again in architecture. Lott already had walked away from the profession and was busy running an ice cream parlor, operating a children's day care center, providing licensed products to the Olympics, and operating a magazine mail-order business. Anything, it seemed, but the practice of architecture.

But then R. Steven Lewis returned to Los Angeles from New York, where he'd been working at his father's architectural firm, and joined the young partnership. Together, he and Wiley began building the business.

Watching their success, and observing their satisfaction at working for themselves and practicing architecture the way they thought it *should* be practiced, Lott felt the old pull. A year later, he was working once more as an architect, helping to build RAW Architectvre into what is today; one of L.A.'s fastest-growing, most highly-respected architectural firms. They established a partnership because, as Wiley put it, "the simplicity of structure was appealing. And we trust each other."

Education and Experience   The most important assets the three men brought to their young business were their education and their experience.

Wiley, a graduate of the Ball State University College of Architecture and Planning, and a registered architect in the state of California, worked first for Gruen Associates. There, he handled architectural assignments and served as construction coordinator on several major high-rise office and luxury condominium projects in the L.A. area. He is active in the industry as a member of the L.A. chapter of the American Institute of Architects and a member and former L.A. Chapter President of the National Organization of Minority Architects.

Lewis grew up in the business. He came to the partnership from his father's New York architectural firm, Roger C. Lewis and Associates, where he worked on a number of urban redevelopment projects as well as more conventional architectural assignments. Earlier, he'd worked in L.A. as a planning associate with the city's Community Redevelopment Agency, helping to formulate plans for the redevelopment of North Hollywood, Chinatown and Little Tokyo. He earned his architecture degree at Syracuse University, and he is a registered architect in New York, California, and Nevada.

A graduate of California State Polytechnic University, Pomona, Lott earned a dual degree in architecture and behavioral science. He worked first on the technical staffs of Gruen Associates and Skidmore, Owings and Merrill—as a job captain and design coordinator at Gruen, and a specialist in curtainwall development and mid- and high-rise construction at SOM. He is a member of the L.A. chapter of the National Association of Minority Architects, the American Society of Planning Officials, and the National Trust for Historic Preservation.

Building a Client Base But the threesome also brought a great deal of commitment to their new business—as well as a sense of mission. "We tried first to focus our efforts on providing architectural services to Black clients in southern California," Lott said, "but we began to realize a certain irony. Many blacks have the resources and the authority to retain our firm, but they often choose to hire white architects instead of looking to black-owned firms. Affluent blacks are so well assimilated into the southern California mainstream that they often didn't think of sending business our way."

So RAW Architectvre decided to fight fire with fire. They'd go after mainstream clients—major businesses, big-time developers, government agencies doling out assignments for large-scale architectural projects—everyone they'd targeted when they'd worked for mainstream firms.

The strategy seems to have worked. "We were hired to design the L.A. and Chicago showrooms for Waterford/Wedgwood Crystal," Lott said. "We've worked for Baskin Robbins and Dun and Bradstreet, Kaiser Permanente and a leading Beverly Hills physician, Pacific Bell and Southern California Edison, the Los Angeles Wholesale Produce Mart and the L.A. Unified School District—just to name a few."

They got the mainstream assignments, Wiley said, by "being highly efficient and highly creative. We try to demonstrate to prospective clients that they'll get the most value for the dollar, both in terms of project management and architectural creativity, by working with us."

And they have also acquired an identity in recent years as a firm to which black-owned businesses ought to look for architectural services. When the mall in L.A.'s Baldwin Hills—a prosperous black community—was renovated, RAW Architectvre served both of the mall's black business owners, Golden Bird Fried Chicken and Armando's Clothing.

Creating a Niche Knowing that, because of their size, they couldn't do everything a major architectural firm can do, RAW Architectvre's partners honed in on a range of services that created a special niche in the marketplace.

That niche, Lewis said, includes "a mixture of interior design, project coordination, and 'shell' exterior architectural services. We fit into the spaces left by major architectural firms when they take on big projects—or when they decline to take on smaller and mid-size projects."

Whatever the project type, the firm takes advantage of Lewis's special skill—his ability to use computer assisted design systems on RAW Architectvre assignments. Using CAD technology not only makes the job easier for the firm's architects and draftspeople; it also convinces clients that the firm can play the game just as professionally as much larger firms.

Another business target—one that has developed as a result of Lewis's experience in redevelopment and low-cost housing development in New York—is the area of urban re-development. "We hope to be a major player in rebuilding the crumbling infrastructure of major U.S. cities," he said, "and of creating new, more livable urban environments for everyone—not just those with plenty of cash."

Getting Started Choosing their niche was just one part of the planning process for RAW Architectvre's partners. The three architects put together a full-blown business plan long before they put pencil to paper on their first commission. "When we established the partnership," recalled Wiley, "we put together a five-year business plan, based on financial goals. We determined that our goal was to gross $1 million by the fifth year. And we did it by the end of the fourth year."

Proud of their success, and busy meeting the myriad demands of a growing clientele, the partners forgot just one thing: to update that business plan to ensure that it reflected current reality. "When we reached our goal, and reached it a year early," Wiley said, "we kind of lost focus—we forgot to sit back and think, 'what next?' "

"So . . . we started the planning process again. The three of us went on a retreat, and we started to formulate our personal goals for the firm. We decided that the focus shouldn't be just on financial growth anymore—that we needed to establish some goals in terms of project type. We started asking what kind of work each of us wanted to do for our own personal growth and development. And that got us thinking ahead again."

A second retreat kept the long-term planning process in full gear. And now the three partners plan to make the exercise an annual event.

One change they expect to make is to shift their form of business ownership from a partnership to a corporation. "We've always had a sense of complete trust in one another, and nothing has ever happened to make us feel otherwise," said Wiley. "But because of the size and the complexity of the firm we're running today, and the fact that we plan to acquire property that the firm will own, we need to be incorporated. It's time."

Startup Economics The financial aspects of startup were easy to handle, Wiley said, because of the "rather unique nature of the architectural practice. All you really need to get started are a drawing board and drawing materials, and a little startup capital for letterhead and supplies. And," he added, "because I simply moved into an empty office in Steve Lott's suite, the initial expense of opening an office was reduced."

Wiley estimates that opening his first office cost about $700—for equipment, phones, business cards, stationery, and the like. As projects came in, he plowed as much as possible back into the business—buying additional phones, drafting stations, and a typewriter (and later computers).

"And for project expenses—blueprinting, xeroxing, and so on—I just put them on my credit card, and when a payment came in from a client, I paid off the card. I was my own lender at first."

After Lott and Lewis joined the firm, revenues increased, enabling the partnership to acquire additional space and equipment. "In the beginning," said Wiley, "we really sacrificed in terms of our personal income. We all agreed to put whatever money we could back into the business. It wasn't until about two years ago that we began to pay ourselves a little more. It's still our goal to make a significantly better income—to reap the rewards of our efforts. But in architecture, it takes a long time to reach the level where you can make a really good living."

The only time the partners took out a loan was when the firm moved to new offices. "We borrowed $25,000 to cover the anticipated cost of new furniture and to give us an emergency cushion. But when the move was done and we compared what we'd spent with what we'd taken in, we still had the $25,000. So we've just used those funds as an emergency account. It's given us a level of comfort that is really important."

Choosing the Location   At first, RAW Architectvre's location was dictated by the location of Steven Lott's existing business office. When the architectural firm outgrew that space, the partners leased space in Baldwin Hills, in keeping with their plan to target L.A.'s affluent black business community.

Today, their primary office, housing the company's 14-person staff, is in downtown Los Angeles, close to the heart of the city's business and governmental operations and convenient to many of their clients. But they've kept the Baldwin Hills office space to handle anticipated growth, and they expect to move soon to a larger site.

But wherever the new office may be located, its appearance is certain to reflect the upbeat, trend-setting, contemporary flavor of the people who own it and the work that they do. Because that, too, will help propel RAW Architectvre into the forefront of the southern California design community.

And that's where Roland Wiley, Steven Lott, and R. Steven Lewis plan to be—now and for many years to come.

APPLYING THE CONCEPTS FROM LESSONS 7–11

Before you watch the video program for Lesson 12, *From the Ground Up*, review chapters 6–11 in the text. Then answer the following questions:

1. As you analyze the decision RAW Architectvre's owners made in establishing their firm, what particular steps made good business sense when they set up their firm? What mistakes do you think they made in the early years?

2. Is it possible to start a firm with little or no capital? What kinds of firms might succeed more readily with a limited funding base?

3. What can a business owner do to overcome a lack of capital in the early years of operation?

4. RAW Architectvre had a business plan from day one. What could the firm's partners have done to avoid the "drift" that occurred around the fifth year of operation?

5. How did RAW Architectvre seek to distinguish itself from other Los Angeles-based architectural firms?

6. How much do you think the location of RAW Architectvre's offices has affected its success? Where do you think its office, or offices, should be?

7. How important is the appearance of RAW Architectvre's offices to its clients? Why?

Lesson 13

The Right Mix:
Product/Service Strategies

LEARNING OBJECTIVES

Upon completing your study of this lesson, you should be able to:

■ Recognize the psychological factors that influence consumer behavior and the decision to purchase a product or service.

■ Summarize concepts related to market segmentation.

■ Compare and contrast product/service strategy alternatives for a one product/service, a modified product/service, multiple products/services and unrelated products and services.

■ Describe the product development curve.

■ Discuss the introduction of a new product or service in terms of:
   a. its relationship to existing product lines or service strategies
   b. the costs of development and introduction
   c. its impact on personnel and facilities
   d. its effect on existing competition, and new competitions that will result from business success
   e. the potential for market acceptance.

■ Discuss the concept of a product life cycle.

In attempting to determine the feasibility of a prospective business venture in lessons 3 and 8, we read about one element of product/service strategies—how to direct those strategies toward consumers to positively affect their behavior. There, we identified the key concepts of consumer behavior: the psychological concepts of needs, perceptions, motivations, and attitudes in projecting the merit of a proposed business venture. Now it's time to apply those concepts to the development of a product strategy for an entrepreneurial business.

OVERVIEW

People buy things because they *need* them—or because they *perceive* a need for them. They may need your coffee for physiological reasons—it's the only thing that helps them wake up in the morning. Or for social reasons—serving a good cup of coffee or the perfect pot of tea is important to them and their friends. Or there may be some psychological or even spiritual underpinning to their need for your products. It's up to you to determine which of these needs is greatest among your target markets, and then to appeal to that need when presenting your marketing message.

Then you'll need to look at customer *perceptions* of your products—whether they perceive your products to be high-quality, fairly-priced, reputable, and otherwise attractive. If customers perceive your products to be what they prefer, they'll be more likely to buy them.

Another psychological concept that comes into play is *motivation*. By telling prospective customers that your coffee is water-decaffeinated, and therefore healthier for them, you motivate them to choose your product over someone else's. By offering a better product at a lower price, you reinforce that motivation.

Then there are *attitudinal* influences. Your customers' attitudes—toward your products, toward you and your employees, even toward the shopping center in which you locate your store—will influence their purchase decisions. It's your job to make sure that their attitudes toward your store, and its products and services, are positive.

Finally, such factors as *social heritage*, *social class*, *reference groups*, and *opinion leaders* will influence prospective customers' purchase decisions. If drinking tea is a family custom; if their social circle agrees that gourmet coffees and teas are the only ones worth drinking; if their family, co-workers, and neighbors agree that buying at The Coffee Bean is the smart thing to do; and if their cooking class instructor recommends The Coffee Bean to them ... chances are your prospective customers are ready to buy!

What you've got to do is play to these psychological influences—build themes into your marketing messages that help your target market identify your store as the one that offers the products they want and need. Do that, and you've done what the professionals do: you've translated consumer behavior concepts into product strategy.

Product/Service Strategies   Whether you're planning to market a product or a service, you'll need to develop a marketing strategy. Some of your strategy development will focus on the differences between products and services.

How do the two differ? First, a product is tangible, while a service is impossible to hold in your hands. A product is produced at one time and consumed at another, while the production and "consumption"—or delivery—of a service is usually simultaneous. And a product is usually standardized, while a service can be customized to fit the highly personal needs and preferences of its buyer. Clearly, then, the way you'd market a product can be quite different from the methods you'd employ to market a service.

To simplify the discussion of product strategy development, we'll define a "product" as the total "product offering" presented to customers in a transaction involving either goods or services. That would include the product or service, as well as its packaging and any ancillary benefits offered, such as product warranties or follow-up service.

Marketing Definitions You'll learn some new terms in discussing product strategy—including the terms product mix, product line, product item, and product mix consistency. Here's how to think of each one.

■ The *product mix* is a collection of product lines owned and marketed by one company. For example, if you manufacture and sell shampoo, conditioner, hair spray, and hair mousse, that's your product mix.

■ A *product line* consists of all individual product items that are related—for example, your aloe-and-lanolin shampoo and your ten competitors' aloe-and-lanolin products.

■ A *product item* is one item in your mix—your extra-hold hair spray or your gentle formula mousse.

■ *Product mix consistency* refers to the similarity of items in a product line. If your product mix is absolutely identical to that offered by your competitors, you'll have to compete on another basis—perhaps price or ease of use. If your product mix offers several products the competitors haven't developed, you've got an added advantage.

Look at the products or services you're offering to determine how you can set yourself apart from the competition. And then use those differences in executing your product marketing strategy.

Product and Market Strategies Small businesses usually select from eight specific product strategy alternatives, and they usually pursue the strategies in order. Sometimes you might decide to pursue more than one of the strategies at the same time, but that could make it more difficult for the new business owner to succeed with each strategy. Here's how to look at each strategy:

1. *One product/one market.* You're a solo practitioner advertising consultant. You offer creative and production services to the health care industry in your town. Growth will be achieved by selling more ad services to existing clients, by signing up new clients, and by convincing existing clients to use advertising for additional purposes. For example, the local hospital comes to you first for nurse recruitment ads. When those are successful, you convince them to develop ads targeting local residents for cancer and high blood-pressure screening.

2. *One product/multiple markets.* When your ad services business has successfully saturated the health-care market, you start looking to child-care service providers as clients for your advertising services.

3. *Modified product/one market.* You've done all you can in the area of print advertising for local health care providers, so you begin to offer broadcast ad creative and production services—taking the same ad campaign ideas and converting them for broadcast over local radio and television stations.

4. *Modified product/multiple markets.* You take the idea of broadcast advertising to additional markets—maybe to child-care providers, maybe to local political candidates who have had you develop some print ads for the upcoming election.

5. *Multiple products/one market.* As your business grows, you see the advantages of offering additional services. You team up with a public relations consultant and market that person's services to the health care market.

6. *Multiple products/multiple markets.* Again, you've teamed up with that PR pro, and you market his or her services through your firm to other target markets.

7. *New unrelated product/one market.* Although it's not your original line of business, you've recognized that your clients—with whom you're messengering packages back and forth almost every day—have a need for a quick, reliable messenger service. Since you've already dedicated one employee to the pick-up-and-delivery needs of your clients, you offer a delivery service to them—for pick-ups and deliveries at any location, not just between your office and theirs.

8. *New unrelated product/new market.* When that messenger service takes off, you start offering it to the entire town, not just to your own clients. You're now in two distinct businesses: advertising/public relations services and messenger services.

Strategy Management Tools You'll look to two tools to manage your product or service marketing strategy: the product development curve and the product life cycle. The product development curve is the three-step process you'll use to develop a new product. In the first step, you'll do whatever research and investigation you need to do to refine your product idea.

In the second step, you'll analyze the information you've gathered and screen your ideas. The kinds of questions you're likely to ask here: How does this new product idea relate to my existing product mix and to competitors in the product line? Is it needed—or wanted—in the marketplace? Can I afford to develop it? Will I be able to price it effectively? And can we handle the manufacturing? Do we have the people, the equipment, and the facilities to manage the job successfully?

In the third step, you'll narrow your ideas down to a single product for development and testing. Here, you'll make the decisions concerning brand name, packaging, pricing, and promotion; while you prove the product's ability to do the job and conduct test marketing to prove its salability.

Then, you'll need to determine the product life cycle for your new product, because your promotional, pricing, and distribution policies will have to mesh with that life cycle. If it's a "fad" product—such as the "Koosh" balls that found their way onto every playground a few years ago and are now stashed in the bottom of toy chests across the country—you'll want to go in big and fast with the product, hitting as many markets as quickly as you can and pricing the product as high as possible. Later, when the fad begins to weaken, you can cut prices drastically to sell off remaining inventory.

On the other hand, if your product is a high-status, fad-resistant commodity—a classic designer watch, perhaps—you can market your products selectively, to just a few choice jewelry stores and upscale chains, and price it high. And, assuming public tastes don't change and the economy continues to support purchases of status merchandise, you can keep the prices high and the distribution limited for a long, long time.

The Total Product Offering   The final step in preparing your marketing strategy is making sure you've completed that "total produce offering" your customers will expect to receive. You'll want to give your product a brand identity that appeals to customers, is easy to say and easy to remember, can be legally protected, has promotional possibilities, and might be applied to related products at a later date.

You'll want to package it attractively and appropriately. And you'll want to label it properly—both from a legal standpoint and in terms of the information customers will need to properly use your product.

Finally, you'll want to determine your warranty policies, so you can provide customers with a clear picture of how your company will stand behind its products or services.

ASSIGNMENTS

■ Before you watch the video program, be sure you've read through the preceding overview, familiarized yourself with the learning objectives for this lesson, and looked at the key terms below. Then, read chapter 12 of Longenecker, Moore, and Petty, *Small Business Management*, "Customer Loyalty and Product Strategy."

■ After completing these tasks, read the video viewing questions and watch the video program for Lesson 13, *The Right Mix*.

■ After watching the program, take time to answer the video viewing questions and evaluate your learning with the self-test.

■ Extend your learning through the applications, exercises, or field experiences this lesson offers.

KEY TERMS

Perceptual categorization Process consumers use to categorize new products/ services by grouping them, either favorably or unfavorably, with other known products/services.

Attitude Lasting opinion based on a mixture of knowledge, feeling, and behavior.

Psychological factors Psychological factors that affect one's purchase decisions including needs, perceptions, motivations, and attitudes.

Sociological factors Environmental factors that affect one's purchase decisions including culture, social class, reference groups, and opinion leaders.

Culture A group's social heritage.

Social class Divisions in society that suggest different levels of prestige.

Reference groups Groups to which a person belongs that influence his/ her opinions, purchase decisions, etc.

Opinion leader A group member who plays a leading role in group or individual decisions due to his/her knowledge, visibility, or exposure to mass media.

Product	The goods or services sold to a consumer, along with the "product offering" presented by the seller.
Product mix	All products within one company's ownership and marketing control.
Product line	All individual products of the same type (each product may be produced by a different company).
Product item	One specific product in a company's product mix.
Product mix consistency	How similar product lines are to one another.
Product strategy	How a company develops its product components to create a good marketing mix.
Product development curve	Process through which a company goes to develop a new product; includes research, analysis, product development, and product testing.
Product life cycle	Measure of how long a product is likely to remain successfully on the market; how quickly it will achieve peak sales and how quickly sales will drop off.
Warranty	A promise that a product will perform as expected or that a service will be provided as expected.

VIDEO VIEWING QUESTIONS

1. What justification does the video provide for focusing on customer service and satisfaction as the basis for product/service strategies?

2. Explain what Joseph Mancuso is referring to when he talks about a "counter cyclical niche."

3. When the saturation rate has been reached in a product life cycle or market life cycle, what does Jon Goodman advise?

4. What specific product/service strategies has M. L. Leddy's Boot & Saddlery implemented to sustain its "quality" niche.

5. How has the focus of Sunny Bernstein's business shifted over the years? Which service strategies have changed; which have remained constant?

6. Provide examples of how Patty Newkirk gauges and responds to customer attitudes and desires.

SELF-TEST

1. The stages of consumer decision-making include all of the following *except*
   a. need
   b. information search and evaluation
   c. purchase decision
   d. post-purchase evaluation

2. The key psychological concepts related to consumer buying decisions are
   a. perception, motivation, needs, and attitudes.
   b. problem recognition, motivation, and action.
   c. problem recognition, motivation, action, and post-purchase evaluation.

3. Narrowing your analysis of the cultural forces that may affect a buying decision to a smaller group is called
   a. subgroup analysis.
   b. cultural definition.
   c. subcultural de-massification.
   d. subcultural analysis.

4. Occupation, possessions, source of income, and education are indicators of
   a. opinion group status.
   b. social class.
   c. purchase tendencies.
   d. cultural identity.

5. The post-purchase evaluation process takes place to
   a. help the consumer determine how to use a product.
   b. confirm that the product reached its target market.
   c. help the purchaser reduce cognitive dissonance.

6. One chief difference between a product and a service is that
   a. a product is manufactured at one time and sold or used at another.
   b. a product can benefit from advertising, while services rely on direct marketing.
   c. a product is less standardized than a service.

7. The riskiest of all product strategy alternatives is
   a. one product/multiple markets.
   b. new unrelated product/new market.
   c. modified product/one market.
   d. multiple products/one market.

8. Valuable concepts for managing the product mix are
    a. the product offering and consumer behavior concepts.
    b. the product development curve and the product life cycle.
    c. needs, perceptions, motivations, and attitudes.
    d. research and development and the product life cycle.

9. Phases in the product development curve include
    a. staffing, research, and marketing.
    b. branding, packaging, labeling, and warranty.
    c. introduction, growth, maturity, and decline.
    d. idea accumulation, analysis, product development, and testing.

10. To offer consumers a total product offering, you must offer them
    a. favorable promotion, pricing, and distribution policies.
    b. a product, attractive & functional packaging, clear and appealing branding, complete labeling, and a good warranty.
    c. the product they want at the lowest price.
    d. the retail outlet that they prefer.

EXTEND WHAT YOU HAVE LEARNED

1. As a small business owner, or an employee of a firm, what is there about your company's product or service that attracts customers and influences them to purchase that which you offer? What do you receive the most complaints about? What specific actions could you take to enhance the appeal of your product or service?

    _____

    _____

    _____

    _____

2. Plot out the logistics for accomplishing two of the product/service strategies listed below:

    — introduce a product or service your company is currently offering to a new market

    — modify an existing product or service for your existing customerbase

    — modify an existing product or service and offer it a brand new market

— introduce a new but related product or service to your existing clients

— introduce a new but related product or service to a new market

— introduce a new, unrelated product or service to your customers

In each case indicate the relationship of the product or service you are introducing to your existing lineup and project the costs of development and introduction. Assess the impact this new line will have on personnel and facilities, how you believe your competitors will respond, and the line's potential for market acceptance and financial return.

After you have completed your analyses, place the options side by side and compare the two. Does one option offer more potential than another? Would it be wise for you proceed with either strategy? Why or why not?

_____

_____

_____

_____

3. Let's assume for the moment that you've decided to go forward with one of the product/service strategies you just developed, and need to name it. Think of some possible names for this new product or service. Select a name that:

is easy to pronounce _____

is descriptive _____

can be legally protected _____

has promotional possibilities _____

could lend itself to several product lines _____

If your new item is a product, what type of packaging would make your product distinctive and enhance its sales?

_____

_____

_____

_____

Lesson 14

What the Market Will Bear:
Pricing Products and Services

LEARNING OBJECTIVES

Upon completing your study of this lesson, you should be able to:

■ Discuss the importance of pricing and price image.

■ Indicate how cost, demand, and competitive factors influence pricing decisions.

■ Explain the significance of a break-even analysis in pricing and know how it is calculated.

■ Describe techniques that can be used to develop an appropriate price for a product or service.

■ List and compare five different pricing strategies that are used by small businesses.

■ Recognize the factors that affect the decision to grant credit to customers, and the variety of credit options that are available.

Pricing is both an art and a science. There's an intuitive element to pricing in which you look at the market, measure the value of your own products or services in relationship to that market, and try to guess just how much the market will pay for what you have to offer. And there's the more precise business analysis that tells you what prices you *must* charge to realize a sufficient profit and maintain your business.

In this lesson, we'll take a look at both the pricing process and the credit policies you'll need to consider in establishing a new business. Because credit—whether it's the credit you obtain from suppliers or the credit you extend to customers—plays a key part in determining how you set prices.

OVERVIEW

When we talk about the price of goods or services, we're talking about the amount the business owner is willing to accept in exchange for the products or services he or she sells. When we talk about credit, we're talking about an agreement between buyer and seller, in which the seller agrees to furnish goods or services to the buyer before the buyer pays for them. In exchange, the buyer either pays within a specified time period or agrees to pay for the merchandise at an additional cost and on an agreed-upon schedule. Both the pricing and the credit decisions you make will affect how much revenue your business will receive and how steady your cash flow stream will be.

It's far better to take a good, hard look at pricing and credit issues before you open your door than to set prices that are too low or credit terms that are too generous, and later find yourself having to tighten up. Customers don't mind a conservative credit policy, and they don't mind paying a bit more for a good product (when they perceive some additional value in doing so), but they *will* mind if their flexible credit terms suddenly become rigid or your prices suddenly take a leap skyward.

The revenue your business can enjoy will depend on two things: how much you sell and how much you charge for it. Even a small incremental change in the price of goods or services can have a major impact on overall revenues. Here's why.

If you raise prices—even slightly—and the price increase causes you to lose a large number of customers, you'll lose a great deal of revenue. The price change has an *indirect*, but significant, impact on revenue. By the same token, if you set prices too low, you may lose money by not pricing your product at an acceptable, but higher rate. In this case, your pricing error has had a *direct*, but again, significant impact on revenue. So how do you deter- mine the optimum price for your products? First, you look at your costs.

Calculating Your Costs The total cost of your products or services is composed of the price you paid for what you offer, plus the cost of selling them (such things as your time, advertising, and promotion expenses), plus your overhead (everything from supplies and utilities to taxes and salaries). You'll want to analyze your expenses first in terms of two types of costs: variable and fixed.

Total variable costs are the costs that increase as your sales volume increases. Open up a home-baked cookie store in the local shopping center, and your total variable costs—for flour, chocolate chips, eggs, oil, butter, merchandise bags, napkins, paper cups, straws, and so on—will increase as you sell more cookies, milk, and coffee.

Total fixed costs are the costs that remain constant, no matter *how* many cookies you bake! They cover such expenses as the ad campaign you initiated when the store opened; the ovens, sinks, and counters you installed; the coffee maker and the refrigerator you purchased.

The "average pricing" method may not be the best approach to setting prices, although many new business owners employ this process. They fail to distinguish between variable and fixed costs; simply dividing their total cost over the previous period by the amount sold during that time, and using that cost to set the current price. But if demand slips in the coming period, that price may not be high enough to allow them to recover their fixed costs—even if variable costs decline due to the drop in sales.

Other Pricing Factors Among the other factors you need to consider in setting a realistic price for your goods or services are demand and elasticity. If your chocolate chip cookies quickly achieve renown in your community . . . if they have everyone for miles around talking about how sinfully delicious they are . . . then the demand factor will work in your favor. Your products will be in demand.

You might even be able to sell them on a *prestige pricing* basis, which sets a high price for a product that is perceived to be unique or of particularly high quality. Prestige pricing works best in higher-income communities, or for products about which consumers know relatively little. In this instance they look to goods with higher prices for an assurance of quality.

If you're the only home-baked cookie shop in town, you'll probably enjoy what is called *inelastic demand*. Simply put, if you raise prices revenues will increase, and if you lower prices revenues will decrease. With a lock on the market—or with a product that is clearly superior to the competion—you'll sell what the market wants to buy, regardless of price.

But if you're one of four or five cookie outlets, and all of them offer a tasty, high-quality product, you'll probably find yourself in a market with *elastic demand*. If you raise your prices above the competition, your revenue will decrease. If you keep your prices lower than everyone else's, your revenues will increase.

Break-even Analysis Another way to determine the best price to charge is the break-even analysis. There are two stages in this process, which is fully graphed in the textbook:

■ *The cost break-even.* This calculation identifies the quantity at which your product or service, if sold at a certain price, will bring in enough revenue to allow you to begin showing a profit.

■ *The cost-adjusted break-even.* This calculation adds a demand curve to the analysis, to show the quantity demanded and the total revenue to be generated for that quantity at various price levels. This provides a more realistic estimate of the profits you can expect to receive if you sell at a certain level and for a certain price.

The Next Step: Setting Prices Assume you've done your demand and elasticity analysis for the cookie shop, and you've run the numbers on your cost-adjusted break-even analysis. Those studies have shown you that the break-even price for a single cookie is 70 cents. It's time now to set your prices. Typically, the new business will employ one of five pricing strategies: penetration, skimming, follow-the-leader, variable, or flexible. Here's what they'll mean to your new cookie shop.

Penetration pricing is a likely choice for a new cookie shop. Although your break-even price is 70 cents, you might offer a "getting to know us, getting to love our cookies" introductory price of two for $1.25. You'll give up a bit of profit at the outset to penetrate your market more quickly, and—thanks to your delicious products—make converts of every new customer.

You're not as likely to select *skimming* as your pricing option, since it involves setting slightly higher prices for a popular new product and reducing the price as demand settles in at a lower level. This is a good tactic to use if you have high initial startup costs which must be recovered quickly. It's more appropriate in industries where technological development costs must be recovered quickly, after which prices can come down to a more competitive level.

If you're the fifth cookie shop to open, and the biggest and most successful store in town is selling cookies for 75 cents each, you're likely to adopt *follow-the-leader* pricing and keep your prices to 75 cents or less.

If you want to appeal to specialized market segments—business customers shopping for special gifts or area restaurants interested in serving your cookies as a dessert option—you might want to offer *variable* pricing. You'll sell cookies to the general public for, say, 75 cents, but you'll offer a discount per dozen to the business customers, and a volume-discounted price for the restaurant.

Or you'll opt for *flexible* pricing—watching the cost of your raw materials, keeping an eye on your competitors, and varying prices to suit the moves on those two fronts, as well as offering specials and other incentive pricing options to your customers. On most days, you'll stick to the 75-cent-a-cookie range, but occasionally you'll extend your two-for-$1.25 special, or even offer a "back to the '60s" 60-cent bargain price.

And if things get slow—maybe it's hard to sell the last few dozen cookies at the end of the day—you might even be willing to sell those cookies for less than their total cost, but at a price high enough to recover your selling and overhead costs. Maybe cleaning out each day's inventory with a last-hour-of-business 3-for-a-dollar deal will make sense over the long haul.

Retailing Markups There's one other issue to consider if you're a retailer buying your merchandise from a wholesaler and reselling it to the public. To determine the proper markup for your goods, you'll need to add allowances for operating expenses, profit margin, and a cushion for any potential price reductions to the price you've paid for those goods.

And be sure to review the local, state, and federal laws concerning price fixing. It's usually not an issue for small companies, since price fixing laws were passed to protect consumers and small businesses from the price control efforts of key players in an industry or business area. Just be sure you're not violating any of these laws. Check, too, to see if your state has any pricing legislation on the books which requires you to base the price of your goods or services on their cost to you.

Finally, if you offer a multi-product line of related products, be careful about your pricing lines. If the price of one line is too close to the price of another, sales of one line may cut into sales of the other.

The Credit Question Clearly, extending credit has certain benefits. You attract new customers and you encourage existing customers to buy more goods, or to buy more frequently. But extending credit also opens your business to risk. If too many of your credit customers are late paying their bills—or fail to pay them altogether—your cash flow could be seriously impaired. And you could end up spending a great deal of time and money going after the delinquent accounts.

In judging a prospective credit customer, think of that person or company in terms of the five C's of credit: character, capital, capacity, conditions, and collateral. Is the borrower credit-worthy? Does he or she have the capital available to honor the obligation? Does the borrower have the capacity to meet the debt—is there a strong history of responsible business behavior? Do current business conditions suggest that the customer will continue to be able to pay, or are market trends in his or her industry heading downward? And can collateral be provided as security against non-payment?

To find out whether a credit candidate should be approved, there are several good information sources. Take a look at the applicant's own credit history—how fast does he or she pay? Review the applicant's financial statements and an up-to-date credit report, and talk to his or her banker. And check with any credit bureaus that may have a record of this customer's payment history with other businesses.

Is Credit Right for You? Before you extend credit, decide if it's appropriate for your business. Are you selling durable goods or perishables; products or services? If it's a long-lasting product, your competitors are likely to extend credit for its purchase, so you'd better do so, too.

If it's a box of gourmet candies or a professional service—something that the customer will use right *now*, and not think much about again—you're wiser to require immediate payment, or at the most offer bank-card credit. If the buyer defaults, the issuing bank will pursue collections. You'll pay a fee to the credit card issuer for that service, but you won't be at risk for the sale.

Look, too, at your customers' income levels. If they're doing relatively well, they're likely to have the resources to honor their financial obligations. If they're struggling college students, extending credit could be a bit riskier.

Finally, take a good hard look at your own operation. Can your really afford to extend credit? Do you have the working capital to carry customer debt and still meet your own expenses? And will you institute the proper systems—review of credit applications, credit limitations, billing procedures, collection on past-due accounts, and aging of accounts receivable—to ensure that your bad-debt ratio remains relatively low?

Types of Credit Consumer credit can be offered in several forms. First is the open charge account, such as a department store credit card account, in which the buyer may make relatively small purchases and will be charged no interest if the balance is paid in full each month.

Second is the installment account, used most often for automobiles and major appliance purchases. Here the buyer is responsible for a long-term repayment schedule. A down payment is often required, and finance charges are assessed.

Third is the revolving charge account most often found on bank credit cards. A variation of the installment account, the revolving charge gives the buyer a line of credit against which purchases can be made at any time. The buyer must pay at least a certain percentage of the balance each month and interest is charged for unpaid balances. Often the bank charges an annual fee for the account.

On the trade side, many businesses offer trade credit to their customers. This usually takes the form of a discount for prompt invoice payment, with the entire undiscounted amount due within a longer period of time. The most common terms are a discount if paid within 10 days and the entire amount due within 30 days.

ASSIGNMENTS

- Before you watch the video program, be sure you've read through the preceding overview, familiarized yourself with the learning objectives for this lesson, and looked at the key terms below. Then, read chapter 13 of Longenecker, Moore, and Petty, *Small Business Management*, "Pricing and Credit Strategies."

- After completing these tasks, read the video viewing questions and watch the video program for Lesson 14, *What the Market Will Bear.*

- After watching the program, take time to answer the video viewing questions and evaluate your learning with the self-test.

- Extend your learning through the applications, exercises, or field experiences this lesson offers.

KEY TERMS

Price	Amount seller is willing to accept for sale of goods or services.
Credit	Agreement that buyer will pay seller at a later date, on specified terms, for goods or services accepted from seller.
Total cost	Overall cost of providing a product or service; includes seller's cost of obtaining or producing the item to be sold, the cost of selling it, and general overhead.

Total variable costs	Costs that increase as sales volume increases.
Total fixed costs	Costs that remain fixed regardless of sales volume.
Average pricing	Pricing that divides total cost by quantity sold; disregards the difference between fixed and variable costs.
Demand factors	Factors that affect demand for a product or service, they include product appeal and prestige pricing.
Prestige pricing	Setting a product or service price at a high price to convey the image of high quality and uniqueness.
Elastic demand	Condition in which an increase in the price of a product or service causes total revenue to decline, and a price decrease causes revenue to increase.
Inelastic demand	When an increase in the price of a product or service causes revenue to increase, while a decrease in price causes revenue to decline.
Penetration pricing	Setting prices low at first to penetrate the market; prices will increase after a market is established.
Skimming pricing	Setting prices high at first to appeal to early buyers' interest in product or service prestige; prices will decrease later to expand market appeal.
Follow-the-leader pricing	Matching pricing strategy to that of the major market force in your industry.
Variable pricing	Offering different pricing policies to different groups of customers.
Flexible pricing	Allowing prices to adjust to market conditions and competitors' actions.
Price line	Range of several distinct prices at which various qualities of merchandise of the same type will be sold.
Consumer credit	Credit given by retailers to consumers.
Trade credit	Credit extended by manufacturers or wholesalers to other business firms that are their customers.
Aging schedule	Billing system in which accounts receivable are divided according to the date on which they are or were due; helps a business identify problem accounts.

Bad-debt ratio	Expense ratio that measures how many of a business's credit customers are problem payers, by dividing the amount of bad debt by total credit sales.

VIDEO VIEWING QUESTIONS

1. As you listen to the comments of experts that appear in this program— Chellie Campbell, Gerry Foster, Jon Goodman, and Farid Haqq—think about the ways in which cost, demand, and competitive factors influence pricing decisions. In what kinds of circumstances would one element exert greater weight than the others?

2. Relate the various pricing techniques that are described in the video to experiences you have encountered as a business owner, manager, or consumer. If you had been asked to comment about the techniques that can be used to develop appropriate prices for products and services, what would your advice have been? To what degree is pricing intuitive?

3. Do you agree that the extension of credit is a necessary part of today's business environment? How do your experiences compare with those noted in the video?

4. It is difficult to price a service that is nice to have, but not totally necessary—a service for which there is no close parallel. How did Vivian Belmont solve this problem for Enchanted Parties? What did she find out regarding what her market would bear?

5. Why do you think Andrea Totten is able to command the price she gets for quilts?

6. How does Chan Thai gain the competitive edge over his rivals in setting prices for produce at his Sunland Fruit Market? In marketing, what is this strategy called?

SELF-TEST

1. The revenue of a small business is a direct reflection of
   a. marketing strategy and sales volume.
   b. sales volume and product price.
   c. marketing strategy and advertising activity.
   d. price per unit and net profit.

2. Average pricing can cause problems because
    a. it ignores the impact of total cost.
    b. it ignores the impact of market size.
    c. it ignores the impact of fixed costs.
    d. it ignores the impact of variable costs.
    e. both c and d.

3. A business can set a higher than average price for its products when
    a. it offers clearly superior products or services.
    b. it is competing with several other businesses.
    c. it offers service, credit terms, and delivery arrangements that parallel its competitors.
    d. it wants to make a quick profit.

4. Prestige pricing works best in markets
    a. where customers seek top value for the dollar.
    b. where customers are middle-income.
    c. where customers have a high level of product knowledge.
    d. where customers tend to be high-income.

5. If you raise your prices and your revenues decline, demand for your products is
    a. independent of price.
    b. inelastic.
    c. elastic.
    d. prestige-based.

6. Setting your prices according to current market conditions and competitors' actions is called
    a. variable pricing.
    b. follow-the-leader pricing.
    c. skimming pricing.
    d. flexible pricing.

7. Setting your pricing artificially low at the outset to build market share is called
    a. penetration pricing.
    b. flexible pricing.
    c. variable pricing.
    d. skimming pricing.

8. To calculate a markup, a retailer must add up
   a. variable costs and fixed costs.
   b. operating expenses, profit, and anticipated price reductions.
   c. original cost, selling price, and taxes due.
   d. operating expenses, profit, and original cost.

9. A bank credit card is an example of
   a. an open charge account.
   b. trade credit.
   c. a revolving charge account.
   d. an installment account.

10. The five C's of credit are
    a. cost, capacity, conditions, creditworthiness, and capital.
    b. character, capital, capacity, conditions, and collateral.
    c. competence, credit history, cost, character, and collateral.
    d. character, capital, capacity, credit history, and conditions.

EXTEND WHAT YOU HAVE LEARNED

1. Develop a break-even chart for product(s) or service(s) your company offers. Allocate the fixed and variable costs as precisely as you can, taking into consideration any recent changes that would be significant.

   Total Fixed Costs (F) = $_____
   Variable Cost per unit (V) = $_____
   Selling Price per unit (P) = $_____

   $$\frac{_____}{\text{(F)}} \div (\underset{\text{(P)}}{_____} - \underset{\text{(V)}}{_____}) = \text{Break-Even Point in Units}$$

   Does the price schedule under which you are now operating provide you with enough profit margin? What would a sudden change, minor or major, do to your customer base?

   _____

   _____

   _____

   _____

2. The costs of producing a product vary with the level of output, the variable costs increasing on a "number of units x the cost-per-unit basis," while the fixed costs remain the same. (It should be noted that although the "fixed" costs seem to remain the same, the fixed-cost allocation per unit actually decreases as more units are produced. Why is this true?)

    As the price of a product is changed, the volume purchased normally changes as well. Suppose your fixed costs for manufacturing a cleaning compound used in heavy industry is $20,000, and that your variable costs are $6 per unit. You know that you can expect to sell 40,000 units if you price the compound at $6 a pint. If you charge $10 per pint, you estimate that the market for your product will decrease by 10 percent. A $12 charge would decrease the orignal market by 20 percent. Calculate the profit margin in each of these instances, and suggest a course of action.

    _____

    _____

    _____

    _____

    _____

    _____

3. If you currently own a business that offers credit, or are anticipating the acquisition of a firm that will need to provide credit options to be competitive, outline a credit policy that protects your cash flow, but provides the necessary purchase incentives to customers.

    _____

    _____

    _____

    _____

    _____

    _____

Lesson 15

Out From the Crowd:
Promotional Strategies

LEARNING OBJECTIVES

Upon completing your study of this lesson, you should be able to:

■ Recognize the importance of promotional planning in establishing and maintaining the image of the firm.

■ Determine the appropriate promotional mix given the goods or services a firm produces and the market it serves.

■ Discuss various methods a small businessperson can use to establish a realistic promotional budget.

■ Establish an advertising budget and program for a small business that is consistent with the role and purpose of advertising.

■ Recognize when and where sales promotions can be used effectively, and the various tools that can be employed.

■ Describe the role of sales personnel in promoting a firm's image.

You might have the best product or service to come along in a month of Sundays, but if the world doesn't know it exists, it won't matter. Without promotion—whether it takes the form of personal selling, advertising, or sales promotion activities—you're likely to have a hard time making a profit on that new product or service.

Budding entrepreneurs often labor under the mistaken assumption that *any* promotional activity is expensive and, therefore, out of reach for the new firm. But not all promotions are expensive. In fact, there are many things the new business owner can do without spending a great deal of money. That's what we'll talk about in this lesson.

OVERVIEW

By engaging in a bit of creative thinking, most entrepreneurs—even the most cash-strapped—can devise a promotional strategy to help their businesses. If you haven't got enough money for advertising, maybe a carefully targeted direct mail campaign will do the job. Or you can link up with a supplier or distributor and "piggyback" your marketing message on one of theirs, for less than you'd spend to market alone. Maybe it's a matter of hitting the bricks, and doing some one-on-one personal selling to your business prospects—a process that's quite common in the service sector of the business economy, where personal relationships do as much to cement a business arrangement as the nature of the service being offered.

You can even use ordinary business events to help market your firm. One southern California public relations consultant took advantage of a move from one office to another to send out eye-catching postcards instead of more conventional "we're moving" notices. The postcards showed the consultant hard at work . . . inside a packing crate, with computer, phone, paper, and reference books close at hand . . . to remind her clients and prospects that not even a move would keep her from providing the prompt, responsive service they'd come to expect from her firm.

Later, when the installation of a new telephone line for a fax machine necessitated the removal of a tree, the PR consultant kept her clients posted on the progress via humorous mail updates from her tree trimmer, aptly dubbed Paul Bunyan. Not only did she demonstrate to her clients that she was concerned about providing good service, but she also provided them with a glimpse of the creative energy she'd expend on their projects by using a bit of it on her own.

Those communications only required postage costs and some minor print production expenses, but they kept the PR consultant in contact with her client base and brought in a number of new assignments.

What promotion boils down to in the end is one thing: effective communication. Good promotion will do two things. It will *tell* people about your product or service, and *persuade* them it's a product or service they want and need. Both the telling and the persuading are acts of communication.

The Three Promotional Strategies   The three promotional strategies that work best for small businesses are personal selling, advertising, and sales promotion. Depending on the kind of business you're in, the promotional activities undertaken by your competition, the amount of money you can spend, and the nature and location of your target audiences, you'll need to choose from among those strategies.

You can employ a combination of the three. That's called creating a *promotional mix*—using different promotional strategies in different marketing situations to achieve the same end result: increased sales and profits.

Entrepreneurs typically use one of four methods to determine how much to spend on promotion. They are:

■ *Percentage of sales*—a simple method which sets aside a specific percentage of each sales dollar for promotion. That's great when sales are strong, but when sales slow down, so does your promotion budget—at a time when you may need promotion the most.

■ *What can be spared*—a cautious approach which says "I won't spend it unless I've got it," and which usually results in *nothing* being spent, since you can *always* find other needs for the cash.

■ *As much as the competition spends*—that's great if you're a local ice cream parlor facing only the competition from other local ice cream shops. But what if you're a local outfit going up against Baskin Robbins? Can *you* spend what *they* spend in your market? Unlikely.

■ *What it takes to do the job*—here you'll need to analyze the marketplace and study your promotional alternatives to come up with a plan that will get your message out to your target audiences. This will tell you what *really should* be spent on promotion—but it doesn't mean you'll be *able* to spend that amount.

So what does the wise entrepreneur do? The best strategy: use all four. Take each of the approaches into account when planning your promotional campaigns. Spend a percentage of sales when you can afford to—and when it's needed. Spend only what is left over when times are tight. Keep up with the competition when you're on a level playing field, but compete with the big guys only on special promotional efforts. And find out what your optimum promotional campaign would cost, and what it would entail, and do as much of it as you can!

Personal Selling Personal selling is one-on-one interaction with your customer or prospective client. To succeed at personal selling, you must believe completely in your product or service and you must know everything there is to know about it. If you don't know *all* the answers, you'll be perceived as little more than an order-taker. And your credibility will suffer as a result.

Not only must you know the product or service well, but you must also be absolutely honest about its strengths and weaknesses. It's okay to minimize the impact of a negative with information on how you handle that particular problem, but you must let your customers know that you're aware of the weaknesses of your product as well as its strengths. That honesty will go a long way.

You can prospect for new customers or clients in a variety of ways: through personal referrals, impersonal referrals (including researching media publications, public records, organization directories, etc.), contacts that you initiate (for example, telephone or mail surveys), and contacts that prospective customers initiate (response to an ad, a reply card, an article in the newspaper, etc.).

However you go about the prospecting process, you've got to be fully prepared for the next step: the presentation. Practice your presentation, and practice responding to critical questions you might encounter. Be ready for the objections and the "I'm not ready to buy now's" that you're sure to hear in almost every presentation. Learn how to listen to your customers, and how to ask questions of them, to help you do a better job of responding to their needs and their preferences.

Most important, learn how to customize each presentation to fit the special situation each customer presents. Just as your product or service has unique benefits and attributes, so do your customers differ from each other in their interests, needs, limitations, and preferences.

In addition, make sure to carefully schedule your personal selling efforts. All too often, people look on these activities as no-cost ventures, when in reality the time we spend preparing and undertaking them costs a great deal. It's an investment in your business—that's true—but it's still important to budget your time and resources wisely.

Advertising   When you advertise your product or service, you're making what really is an impersonal sales presentation. You're using mass media—print, broadcast, or perhaps even billboards—to get your message across to a broad target audience. Advertising makes sense when your target market is geographically dispersed and mass media is the best way to reach it with your message. That fact holds true regardless of your media choice.

There may be times when advertising makes sense for the entrepreneur on a tight budget. If your firm offers a professional service and individuals attending a particular industry convention are a high-priority target for your service, advertising in the convention issue of the biggest industry trade publication may be a good idea. Or you may want to advertise when you're introducing a new product, or launching a special sale or holiday promotion.

These kinds of events could be important enough to warrant the extra expenditure.

In general, however, it's wise to minimize advertising expenditures when a company is in the early stages, since the cost of regular, ongoing advertising can be quite high. And it's only through repeated presentation of an advertising message, researchers tell us, that a marketing message can have the desired impact on its audience.

When you do advertise, choose the medium that best reaches your target market without over-reaching it. Study each advertiser's demographic information to find out if their audience is the one you want to reach—and advertise only through those media that meet your criteria.

In terms of ad content, you're more likely to do product advertising, rather than institutional advertising, especially in the early years. Your focus should be on selling your products or services in the early going. You'll have plenty of time later to develop ads that present a message about the kind of company yours is.

Sales Promotion Activities   The third promotional avenue open to entrepreneurs is sales promotion. This category covers everything from contests and premiums, coupons and free samples, to exhibits and product demonstrations—and much more.

If you own a small oil company that has just developed a reduced-emission gasoline, and you're looking for a way to build market share in a particular community, you might devise a sales promotion activity in which local residents receive a $5-off coupon on a 10-gallon fill-up with the new product. Your local dealers will enjoy the added business, and you'll have a chance to attract new customers to your new product.

If you're opening a new cookie shop, you might find yourself doing what Debbi Fields did—walk through the shopping district that surrounds your new store and hand out free samples. If your cookies are good enough, people will follow the cookie crumbs back to your door, and sales will skyrocket.

Publicity also falls under the category of sales promotion, because it can often have a significant, if indirect, impact on sales. Because publicity seems to be "free"—you don't pay for that glowing account of your new company that appears in the local newspaper—people tend to forget that there are costs involved in attracting the media's attention, and that there are no guarantees.

In truth, publicity does cost. You can't "buy" editorial space like you buy advertising space; you present your story to the press and hope the press likes it enough to run it. And it takes someone who knows how to work with the media and understands the media's needs, likes, and dislikes, to present a company's story to the press. So spending a little money on professional public relations services can be far better for the organization over the long haul than trying to do a job you're not prepared to do—and offending the media in the process.

ASSIGNMENTS

■ Before you watch the video program, be sure you've read through the preceding overview, familiarized yourself with the learning objectives forthis lesson, and looked at the key terms below. Then, read chapter 14 of Longenecker, Moore, and Petty, *Small Business Management*, "Promotional Strategy."

■ After completing these tasks, read the video viewing questions and watch the video program for Lesson 15, *Out From the Crowd*.

■ After watching the program, take time to answer the video viewing questions and evaluate your learning with the self-test.

■ Extend your learning through the applications, exercises, or field experiences this lesson offers.

KEY TERMS

Promotion

Communication between seller and prospective buyer about the product or service offered and the reasons the buyer should want it.

Promotional mix

The appropriate combination of personal selling, advertising and sales promotion for a product or service; combines personal and impersonal selling activities.

Personal selling

One-on-one, in-person communication about a product or service and the company offering it.

Prospecting

The process of identifying potential customers and targeting communications to reach them.

Marketer-initiated contacts Communications that originate with the seller of a product or service.

Customer-initiated contacts Communications that originate with the prospective buyer of a product or service.

Advertising Impersonal presentation of a sales communication for a product or service that uses mass media as a communications channel.

Product advertising Advertising that makes potential customers aware of a product or service.

Institutional advertising Advertising that is designed to keep the public aware of a company and its good image and reputation.

Sales promotion Activity that encourages potential customers to buy something while offering them something of value in return.

Publicity Communication about an organization and its products or services that is not paid for directly (as is advertising).

VIDEO VIEWING QUESTIONS

1. How does the type of customer and product, and the location of the market, determine the emphasis that is placed on the role of advertising, personal selling, and sales promotion in communicating information about a product or service?

2. Link examples of the promotional mix featured in the video to the decision processes that prompted their selection.

3. According to Judith Framan, Cathy Walters, and Ken White, how does the small businessperson derive the most from his or her promotional dollar?

4. Given the shoe-string budgets with which many small business owners operate, there is a particular need for ingenuity and creativity in the development and implementation of promotional strategies. Focus on the three businesses featured in this lesson—Earthstone Wood-Fire Ovens, Kichatna Designs, and Laser Design—and answer the following questions:

   — What tactics did their owners use to promote their products or service?

— From what you heard and saw, how well do you think their strategies worked?

— Without increasing their promotional expenditures, what other elements within the promotional mix could they have used that, in your opinion, would have broadened their message and resulted in increased business?

SELF-TEST

1. According to the text, the mixture of promotional methods a company selects is determined by *all but one* of the following factors:
    a. The geographical nature of the market
    b. The "personality" the company wants to project
    c. The target customers
    d. The characteristics of the product

2. Which of the following is *not* among the most common methods of budgeting funds for small business promotion?
    a. Using a percentage of sales
    b. Deciding how much can be spared
    c. Doubling the competition's budget
    d. Determining what it will take to do the job

3. A promotional mix is
    a. a blend of marketing and advertising.
    b. a combination of personal selling and institutional advertising.
    c. a blend of personal and nonpersonal selling.

4. If your product is an expensive, high-tech piece of equipment used only in the aerospace industry, it will require
    a. a high level of personal selling.
    b. an extensive trade-publication ad campaign.
    c. heavy promotion and publicity activities.

5. When retaining an advertising agency, you want to make sure that its work will
    a. effectively "hype" your product or service.
    b. help you achieve a return that is greater than your advertising expenditure.
    c. reach the entire community in which you do business.

6. If you monitor industry trade publications for companies that might be moving and, therefore, in need of your company's moving and storage services, you're obtaining

   a. inside information.

   b. marketer-initiated contacts.

   c. customer-initiated contacts.

   d. impersonal referrals.

7. If your ads include a reply card for prospective customers to send in for additional information, you're practicing the prospecting technique known as

   a. personal referrals.

   b. demonstration.

   c. asking questions.

   d. customer-initiated contacts.

8. Acknowledging a prospect's objection to your product or service and identifying a compensating benefit is called

   a. positive conversion.

   b. listening and responding.

   c. "boomeranging" the objection.

   d. hearing the prospect out.

9. To be successful, advertising content must be based on

   a. the strongest selling point of the product or service.

   b. a coherent theme for copy and visuals.

   c. products rather than institutional image.

   d. product quality and efficient service.

10. Sales promotion techniques

   a. can stand alone as a company's promotional mix.

   b. should be combined with advertising and personal selling.

   c. exclude publicity from the promotional mix.

EXTEND WHAT YOU HAVE LEARNED

1. Develop a cost-effective promotions campaign for your business utilizing a broad-based promotion mix that includes advertising, personal selling, and sales promotion.

_____

_____

_____

_____

2. Develop a training package for coaching those who are engaged in personal sales for your company. What elements would you include? If you were to describe in just a few words the attitudinal or client- focused approach you would like your employees to assume, what would you say?

_____

_____

_____

_____

3. For the next month, be particularly sensitive to advertisement, sales promotion, and personal selling techniques that you feel are particularly effective. Keep a clip file of examples plus narrative descriptions of commendable personal selling techniques you encounter. In each instance, indicate why the promotional device worked for you. If possible, talk to the a manager from one or two of the businesses whose advertisement or sales promotion you admired to see if they are achieving the results they anticipated from the campaign.

_____

_____

_____

_____

Lesson 16

Going Places:
Distribution Channels and International Marketing

LEARNING OBJECTIVES

Upon completing your study of this lesson, you should be able to:

■ Compare the various channels of distribution that are available to small business owners, and the advantages or disadvantages of each.

■ Indicate the factors that should be considered in selecting distribution systems.

■ Describe the scope of physical distribution, from transportation and storage to materials handling and delivery.

■ Discuss the potential of international distribution for small business owners.

■ Suggest ways in which the small businessperson can research and evaluate foreign markets, and obtain assistance in deciphering export regulations and negotiating trade agreements.

When commerce was in its infancy, distribution channels were simple and direct. The potter crafted a pot, the farmer grew some corn, and the two negotiated a trade. Each one delivered his goods directly to the other, the end user.

In some instances today, that distribution channel still operates. Think about the roadside produce stand, run by the farmer on whose land it sits— selling produce directly to the families that will take it home and cook it that evening. Or Mom's Diner, that fabled eatery where Mom stands before the stove, dishing up her home-cooked chicken and roast potatoes and serving it to her happy customers.

More often, however, distribution channels are far more complex. The end user never meets Mom, much less the farmer who grew her potatoes. Deciding how to distribute goods or services can present a real challenge to the novice entrepreneur. This lesson will help put that process into perspective.

OVERVIEW

A distribution plan ensures that the products or services offered by a company reach the people who want to purchase them. It can provide a strategy for the local printing company to deliver its services to just one corner of a major city—or offer a system for worldwide distribution of a variety of consumer products for a major food and sundries conglomerate. Every company should have a distribution plan to help guarantee that its products or services are reaching as many potential markets as possible.

The distribution process involves two issues: physically getting products or services to their markets, and establishing any necessary middleman relationships to get the job done.

Channels of Distribution Two types of distribution channels exist—direct and indirect. As we've already discussed, *direct distribution* involves no middlemen. The producer delivers a product or service directly to the end user. Think of someone who goes door-to-door selling her own handmade wares—or who sells them via her own mail-order catalog—and you're thinking about a businessperson who uses a direct channel of distribution to market her products.

Indirect distribution can involve one or more intermediaries. The most common form of indirect distribution is producer (or manufacturer) to wholesaler to retailer to end user. But there are many variations on that theme, including sales representatives, manufacturers' representatives, distributors, commission agents, and more.

Sometimes a company will discover that one distribution channel reaches one of its target markets, but that another one is needed to reach a different target. When that happens, the smart business owner will establish a *dual distribution system*, reaching each of his key markets through the most appropriate distribution channel.

A common concern of entrepreneurs who find they must establish distribution relationships with intermediaries is that the intermediaries represent a business expense. That's true—but what you have to recognize is that, if the intermediary can do the marketing job more effectively and more efficiently than you can, it's worth taking on the added expense. Because, in the end, it will result in additional sales, which should more than compensate for the intermediary expense.

Functions of the Intermediary Intermediaries can provide a number of benefits to the company producing goods or services. Chief among them:

- *Breaking bulk*—Taking large quantities of a product and breaking them into smaller amounts for sale to individual customers. If you're a running shoe manufacturer, you may need to manufacture and sell in large quantities to realize the required rate of return, but individual sporting goods stores can't buy in large quantities. An intermediary can buy a large quantity of product from you and resell it to small stores in the quantities they desire.

- *Assorting*—You manufacture only the running shoes, but those small sports shops want related products as well—socks, shorts, headbands, wrist wallets, and so on. Your intermediary puts together an entire product line and offers it to small stores, selling your product along with all the rest.

- *Provide information*—If you choose your intermediary wisely, he'll be able to tell you how strong business is in the sporting goods market, which products are hot and which ones are dying off, and how well your products stand up against the competition in terms of price, quality, and in-store presentation. Good intermediaries are a great information resource.

- *Shift risks*—Depending on the kind of intermediary relationship you establish, you may be able to shift some of the risk of selling your products to them. Intermediaries known as *merchant middlemen* buy products from the producer before reselling them to retailers or end users. If you're working with an agent or broker, you retain title to your products until the agent or broker arranges a sale.

Choosing a Distribution System After studying how your competition handles distribution of its products or services, you'll want to ask yourself three questions before choosing the best distribution system to reach one of your target markets.

First, compare distribution costs for direct distribution with any indirect distribution system you're considering. Then, if the cost of indirect distribution is higher than your costs for direct distribution, ask yourself if you'll reach a larger market by using the indirect distribution system. If you will, it may be worth the extra cost.

Third, ask yourself if you can accept the loss of some control over your products or services and how they're marketed. Since you won't be the one dealing directly with the end user, you can't control how your intermediary will do the job. You can suggest, and you can guide—but you can't control. If you trust the intermediary to represent you effectively and with the level of professionalism you'd present yourself, giving up the control in exchange for a wider distribution range is probably a good idea.

Physical Distribution   Once you've chosen your distribution channels, you'll have to make the decisions about physical movement of your products to market. Depending on what you're shipping, where it has to go, and how carefully it must be handled en route, you can choose from among three basic transportation systems.

If shipments are relatively small and they tend to be irregularly scheduled, you'll probably opt for a *common carrier*—a transportation supplier that offers its services to the general public on a first-come, first-served basis.

If you want regularly scheduled shipments, you might prefer to sign a contract with a *contract carrier* that will provide you with regular shipments at a predetermined price.

And, if you must maintain control of your shipments, if you're delivering goods to a relatively small geographic area, or if you have enough shipping demand to warrant the expenditure, you might choose to be a *private carrier*— shipping your own goods through your own transportation system.

In terms of warehousing, if you have a lot of merchandise to warehouse and can't afford the warehousing costs, you might want to choose a *merchant wholesaler* as your chief intermediary. Merchant wholesalers buy your goods and store them in their own warehouses while reselling them to their customers.

Finally, take a close look at delivery options, and establish terms that make sense, both to you and to your customers, and compare favorably with the competition's. Decide if you'll pay all freight costs or if your buyers will. Determine who chooses the transportation method and carrier, and who bears the risk of damage in transit. And then remember to factor the costs of any transportation services or guarantees which you provide into your prices.

International Distribution   If there's a market for your products or services in other countries—a possibility that grows stronger every year with the growth of the international marketplace and the breakdown of political barriers to cross-national trading—you'll want to consider the possibility of international distribution. There's no need to wait until the domestic market is saturated with your products or services, if there's a good distribution channel and a strong market for your products elsewhere.

Before embarking on international distribution, study your target markets carefully, to be sure your product or service is appropriate in each market and to learn all you can about the culture and business practices of each country. Your market niche may be quite different in other countries than it is back home, so study the potential competition to decide how you can best position your company.

To research international markets, colleges and universities are outstanding resources, as is the Federal government, which is working hard to support exports of products and services to other countries.

Study the specialized distribution channels available to companies undertaking international marketing. In addition to the sales reps, agents, commission agents, and other intermediaries you might find in domestic situations, you also can consider a variety of specialized options. Those options include the licensing of a foreign manufacturer to make and market your products in the foreign market, joint ventures with companies based in the target country, and establishment of wholly-owned subsidiaries of your company in the other country.

You can also work with export management companies, export merchants, or export agents in this country who are active in the countries you've targeted for marketing activity.

Finally, be sure you're familiar with any trade agreement restrictions between the United States and countries in which you're considering undertaking a marketing effort.

ASSIGNMENTS

■ Before you watch the video program, be sure you've read through the preceding overview, familiarized yourself with the learning objectives for this lesson, and looked at the key terms below. Then, read chapter 15 of Longenecker, Moore, and Petty, *Small Business Management*, "Distribution Channels and Global Markets."

■ After completing these tasks, read the video viewing questions and watch the video program for Lesson 16, *Going Places*.

■ After watching the program, take time to answer the video viewing questions and evaluate your learning with the self-test.

■ Extend your learning through the applications, exercises, or field experiences this lesson offers.

KEY TERMS

Distribution	Moving products or services from producer to consumer, either directly from one to the other or through intermediaries.
Physical distribution	The actual movement of products.
Channel of distribution	The intermediary network through which products or services are sent from producer to consumer.
Direct channel	A distribution channel in which there are no intermediaries.
Indirect channel	A distribution channel with one or more intermediaries.
Dual distribution	A distribution system in which a producer of goods or services uses both direct and indirect channels to reach different target markets.
Breaking bulk	Process in which an intermediary splits large quantities of product into smaller units for resale.
Assorting	Process in which an intermediary assembles lines of goods into a heterogeneous assortment for resale to retailers who need all the goods and wish to buy them from one source.
Agent	An intermediary who works to sell the products or services offered by a company without buying them from the company; the products move from producer to reseller or consumer only if the agent succeeds in selling them. Risk of selling products or services is not shifted to the agent.
Broker	Like the agent, an intermediary who works to sell a company's products or services without taking title; risk is not shifted to the broker.
Merchant middleman	Intermediary who takes title to products or services produced by a company and attempts to resell them; risk is shifted from producer to middleman.
Common carriers	Merchandise transporters whose service is available to the general public.

Contract carriers	Merchandise transporters who offer their service on a contract basis.
Private carriers	Producers who own their own means of transportation.
Licensing	Giving another company the right to produce one's products or services; often a means of distribution in foreign markets.

VIDEO VIEWING QUESTIONS

1. How can marketing research be used to determine where people will buy a product or service?

2. Once the patterns of distribution are determined, then how are the physical channels of distribution brought into play? How does this differ for the various products and services that are illustrated in the video program? Does the fact that the business is involved in a retail, wholesale, manufacturing, or service operation tend to make a difference?

3. According to Wesley Buford, Jack Nadel, and Mary Ann Shemdin, is it realistic to think that a small business can compete for world markets? Given the difficulty of interpreting foreign laws, cultural differences, and political vagaries, and finding the appropriate contacts, how do they suggest small business owners get started in the international arena?

4. Robin Rose has selected a number of different distribution channels for her ice cream and chocolate products. List the different approaches she uses and indicate whether or not you believe a multi-faceted approach makes good business sense.

5. Discuss the strategies used by Beauchamp Distributing Company in delivering product to an area that was considered too dangerous by most businesspersons. How well did his tactics work?

6. Held and Associates is in the business of transporting goods, particularly to international markets. As a small business owner, what insights did you gain from Richard Held and Vicki VanDenburgh?

SELF-TEST

1. Distribution involves
   a. movement and sale of products or services.
   b. movement and delivery of products or services.
   c. physical movement and intermediaries.
   d. logistics and delivery.

2. If you sell your products to a middleman who resells it to a retailer, you are using a
   a. direct channel of distribution.
   b. indirect channel of distribution.
   c. sales representative.
   d. marketing agent.

3. You decide to sell your products via mail order to end users, as well as to distribute some through a manufacturers' representative who handles products in your industry. You are using
   a. indirect channels of distribution.
   b. direct marketing methods.
   c. a mixed distribution system.
   d. a dual distribution system.

4. Among the chief benefits of working with intermediaries who take title to your product or service is
   a. shifting of risk from producer to distributor.
   b. their ability to provide you with greater profit.
   c. the credibility you gain from appearing to be a larger organization.

5. The three key issues in choosing a channel of distribution are
   a. choice, channel, and competition.
   b. cost, coverage, and control.
   c. channel, cost, and competition.

6. The four key issues to consider when deciding on a system of physical distribution are
   a. competition, handling, control, and timing.
   b. efficiency, appearance, convenience, and cost.
   c. transportation, storage, handling, and delivery.

7. The delivery term F.O.B. refers to
   a. free on board.
   b. first on board.
   c. freight on board.
   d. freight of buyer.

8. If you permit a foreign company to use your designs, patents and trade-marks in producing and distributing your product in the other country, you have sold that company
   a. distribution rights.
   b. production rights.
   c. marketing rights.
   d. licensing rights.

EXTEND WHAT YOU HAVE LEARNED

1. What do you see as the strong and weak points of the distribution channels your company is currently using? What additional channels would you recommend for consideration?

   _____

   _____

   _____

   _____

   _____

   _____

2. If you are not currently employed, select a small business in your area. Observe their operation, and ask the owner/manager to respond to the questions above.

   _____

   _____

   _____

   _____

   _____

   _____

3. If, within reasonable driving distance, there is an international trade center—or if your local Chamber of Commerce or college provides consulting services to small business owners considering the global community as the ultimate destination for their goods and services—spend some time learning about the international marketplace. Prepare your questions in advance of any scheduled meeting; take notes to assist you in constructing an international marketing plan.

_____

_____

_____

_____

_____

_____

_____

A Vintage Blend:
The Foris Vineyard Story

Whoever suggested that if you build a better mousetrap the world will beat a path to your door left one key component out of his equation for success. That one little something: marketing. It doesn't matter how good your mousetrap is if no one knows it exists, or if no one knows how good it is . . . or if those who *do* know about it can't find it in the local hardware store.

Making sure the world hears about your product or service—and making sure folks hear the right things—can make the difference between success and failure for the entrepreneurial firm. And no one knows that better than Ted and Meri Gerber, owners of the young, growing Foris Vineyards in Cave Junction, Oregon.

Foris Vineyards It's every city slicker's dream at one time or another to break away from the rat race, buy a piece of land out in the country, and build a new life on the farm. For the Gerbers, it's been a reality for nearly two decades. But not an easy reality. Starting a vineyard from scratch is a long, arduous undertaking—both from a physical and an economic standpoint.

The Gerbers moved to southern Oregon in 1973, hoping to raise their children on the 80-acre farm they'd bought. But uncertain weather and the harsh reality of farm economics—not to mention a love of wine—quickly led the Gerbers to a new idea. They'd grow wine grapes.

No matter that they'd be the first to try growing the crop in the Illinois Valley area. And no matter that they knew nothing about grape growing. Field trials run by Oregon State University suggested that their land might be good for grapes. And the ins and outs of grape growing—well, they'd learn all that.

The Gerbers started out small, planting just five acres with pinot noir and gewurztraminer to see if the two varieties could grow in the tricky Cave Junction climate. And they did. The area's big day-to-night temperature swings actually improve the character of wine grapes—with the hotter days enhancing sugar development and the colder nights keeping the flavor in. But spring frosts were a problem, which the Gerbers solved by installing the region's first vineyard sprinkler lines.

Since it takes years for a vineyard to begin producing commercial quantities of grapes—for Foris Vineyards, it was 13 years from first planting to the sale of the first bottle of Foris-labeled wine—the Gerbers supported themselves by growing more conventional crops in the early years and by selling grapes to other vintners as their crop yield increased. Even today, Meri Gerber uses a sideline business—designing, creating, and selling grapevine wreaths to winery and mail-order customers—to help fund expansion of the business.

Finding a Market Once the initial challenge—getting grapes to grow—was overcome, the Gerbers quickly confronted their second hurdle: identifying and reaching their target market. In the early years, they simply sold their grape crops to other Oregon vintners. But when they saw their grapes being used in award-winning wines, and when they encountered some difficulty in marketing all of their grapes to others, the next step was clear: they'd begin producing, bottling, and marketing their own wines under the Foris Vineyards label, first in their own on-site winery and later through intermediaries.

Theirs, Ted Gerber said, is a two-industry business. "The vineyard is farming, and the winery is somewhat a factory or a processing plant for the farm product. It was . . . necessary to get our vineyard established before we went into the winery."

Fortunately for the Gerbers, they recognized the value of marketing right from the start. "You can have a great wine," Ted said, "and if your marketing is poor, you'll go broke; and you can have poor to average wine, and if your marketing is good, you might be able to make a living. So marketing's essential, but it's usually the thing that's forgotten."

The Gerbers made a conscious decision not to compete with the "big guys" and not to target major U.S. markets. "You're not really competing with them [Gallo, Mondavi, etc.], because they have a whole different marketing scheme," Ted explained. The majors can win the war on pricing, so smaller vintners must compete on the basis of quality. And consumers interested in quality don't shop for wines at supermarkets—they discover them at top-notch restaurants and in gourmet wine shops. So Foris Vineyards focuses its marketing efforts on those audiences, seeking out opportunities to talk one-on-one with restauranteurs and wine shop owners—and forsaking the notion of supplying wines to grocery chains, either locally or farther afield.

The company has concentrated its efforts on what Ted calls "secondary markets"—cities like Minneapolis instead of Chicago, or Charlotte, N.C., instead of New York City. "You just pick a few areas and you go . . . and you work the market. You let people know who you are, so there's more than just a bottle with a label—there's a person behind it, and people can connect your story with the wine."

And, when the time was right, Ted provided Foris Vineyards products to a distributor. "You can't hit every retailer alone, so you need distributors. There's less of a margin but you move more product."

Creating a Marketing Strategy But even before the Gerbers could hit the road with the story of Foris Vineyards, they had to start marketing at home. Targeting the right markets, and reaching those markets with the appropriate kinds of messages, was the key to Foris Vineyards' early success. They used a number of tools—none of them expensive, and most of them quite effective.

In the wine business, Ted explained, "it takes years of building relationships with people who are in the distribution and the sales end, and also just word of mouth—that's one of the best advertisements a person can have, and that takes years." One way to build word-of-mouth, the Gerbers reasoned, was by operating a tasting room at their winery. "We're probably one of the few wilderness wineries, if you will, and we try to let people know that if they want to see a very rural scene . . . our winery's a nice place to come to. If we can get people to come here, they'll go back and tell their friends."

Mail order business has picked up as a result of the tasting room operation, too. "After you build a mailing list and word of mouth through friends," Ted said, "you can get to more people. But it's years of building."

The best marketing tool, Ted declared, is winning medals at competitions. "If a wine has won lots of medals, you might start thinking maybe this is a very good wine." And that helps sell product. Attending wine competitions, seminars, and tastings has an added advantage, Ted said. "If a broker from New York City comes and tastes your wine, he'll go back and talk about it, and if you get good press, your phone starts ringing—people want to carry your wine."

Pricing comes into play, too. If your wines are competitively priced, explained Ted, and if people have tasted them over the years and found themto be good, a client base can be established for the new winery.

The right product mix also factors in. With red meat a less popular choice as an entree, red wines are less popular, too. So emphasizing the production of lighter wines, those that go well with fish and poultry, is a wise move in today's market.

No Room for Advertising But is there any room in Foris Vineyards' marketing strategy for advertising? Not much. "I think as you grow, you do more advertising," Ted said. "Right now, we do a few small print advertisements with the local music festival or the Peter Britt Festival or the Shakespeare Festival. We advertise in their bulletins to get people to come to our winery, which tags along with the word-of-mouth idea. But print media is too expensive for a small winery. It's much better to spend your advertising dollars on trips and giving wine away in tastings than it is to buy print media."

What really counts, Ted Gerber says, is quality. "Taking care of the vineyards is the first thing that makes a good wine . . . and taking care of the wine—doing the things you need to do in the winery when they need doing—is the second key. And the last key is giving the perception that there's quality in the bottle, and that's marketing."

APPLYING THE CONCEPTS FROM LESSONS 13–16

Before you watch the video program for Lesson 17, *A Vintage Blend*, review chapters 12–15 in the text. Then answer the following questions:

1. Relate the multiple aspects of developing and implementing a marketing plan to the Foris Vineyard operation.

2. Is advertising essential to an effective marketing campaign? Why or why not? What else could Foris's owners do to attract customers?

3. If your target market were composed of small, distinctly separate sub-markets, what marketing tools would you use to reach those sub-markets?

4. Ted Gerber believes that even a strong marketing campaign can't compensate for a poor product. Do you agree? Why or why not?

5. How can a small company succeed in a market dominated by much larger companies?

6. Why would third-party endorsements (awards, news coverage, editorials) influence people to try a product or service? How might you seek out those kinds of recognition for a new company, product, or service?

7. If you don't have a lot of money for advertising, how might you maximize the impact of your expenditures?

Lesson 18

Making the Pieces Fit:
Managing a Small Business

LEARNING OBJECTIVES

Upon completing your study of this lesson, you should be able to:

- Recognize the distinct aspects of managing a small business.

- Relate basic management functions to the leadership of a small business operation.

- Compare the management of small retail stores, franchises, service firms and manufacturing plants.

- Examine alternative styles of leadership and how they affect employee productivity and satisfaction.

- Describe the role of human relationships and communication in a small business.

- Explain the importance of formal planning in a small organization, the value of involving employees in the process, and the kinds of plans that are critical to a small business.

- Recognize the importance of revising and updating plans and the organizational structure as the economic climate, goals, and resources change.

- List sources of assistance outside the organization that might be called on to give support to the manager of a small business.

Managing a business—small or large—requires certain skills. And, although there's usually a difference in the level of sophistication between small and large businesses, both demand a great deal of attention.

Many businesses sputter along for years, never achieving their full potential but somehow managing to avert disaster. To help a business reach its true potential, its owners must give the business, and the people who work in it, a clear sense of direction and purpose. Developing a strategy for doing so is the topic of this lesson.

OVERVIEW

Normally, when an entrepreneur sets up a new business, its management practices are relatively simple. New organizations today may use computers from day one—traditionally a sign of the larger, more complex organization—but in most other respects, the new firm is likely to have the features of an entrepreneurial enterprise. Just what are those characteristics?

First, there's not enough money to do everything the way you'd like to do it. You may not be able to do the kind of research you'd really prefer to do, so a less scientific form of analysis must suffice. Or perhaps you can't hire all the experts and specialists you want on staff—so you find a number of individuals doing double, and even triple duty, and you rely on outside consultants and services for some of the work you'd rather handle in-house. And you may not be able to offer your employees the kind of formal training programs that larger companies offer. For the time being, they've got to learn by doing.

The distinction is pretty clear. Money dictates a great deal about the structure of the young organization, and it determines a great deal about what that organization can offer its employees.

What's harder to distinguish are the transitions that an organization goes through as it grows. There are four key stages to watch for.

■ *One-person operation*—Some, but not all, new organizations start this way. Clearly, there are no problems in terms of delegation of authority or chain of command. And if the business owner needs training or research, he or she can decide to sign up for training or commission the research—just as long as it's affordable. There's no one else around to tell the owner it can't be done.

■ *Entrepreneur as player-coach*—When the business begins to grow a bit and the owner brings in a few employees, the second stage has been reached. Here, the owner must remain involved in the day-to-day work, because the company isn't yet large enough to permit him or her to move primarily into administration and management. But the owner also has a new role: that of coordinating the work done by every other employee, and making sure each person's work contributes to the organization's overall goals.

■ *Intermediate level of supervision*—Here, the organization has grown enough to require levels of management. The owner no longer can supervise every employee directly—there are too many, and their jobs may be too specialized. The company needs managers, who report to the owner and supervise other employees. The big hurdle for the owner in reaching this level is delegation—learning how to let go of some control over the organization's day-to-day operations and sharing that control with his or her managers.

■ *Formal organization*—Finally, the organization grows to the point where, not only are intermediate levels of management necessary, but so is the adoption of formal, written policies, procedures, plans, budgets, personnel practices, organization charts, job descriptions, control procedures, training programs, and more. In companies where computerization hasn't already occurred, computers are almost certain to be added to the mix at this point. The entrepreneur must be prepared to use skills that are vastly different from those that served him or her well as a one-person operator. The entrepreneur must move from being "doer" to being "manager."

Business experts tell us that if you don't take your company through these stages, you won't achieve your full growth potential. A large company in which the owner must approve every decision, even down to the number of printer ribbons to be purchased that month, simply won't move ahead as quickly as it could. Its owner will be too busy tending to details to look at the big picture.

On the flip side, a company that rushes through the stages and doesn't allow itself to develop fully at each juncture may find that its entrepreneur has been pulled prematurely from the "creative genius who came up with this great idea" role to become preoccupied with administrative decisions. When that happens, the great idea may not develop fully, and the company won't do as well as it could have.

Allowing the organization to change is a matter of flexibility. The founders of organizations are primarily creative, risk-taking, achievement-oriented, intuitive, and self-oriented people who tend to be emotional, personally involved, and somewhat autocratic; and who look at matters from a long-range perspective. They're "big picture" people.

On the other hand, professional managers—the people needed to take the company to its third and fourth stages—are primarily survival, power, influence, and organization-oriented. They're more analytical than intuitive; they would rather deal with short-range issues than matters of long-term concern.

There's more emotional involvement for the entrepreneur, but there's more concern over security and stability for the professional manager. So somehow the organization must mesh the distinctly different values and behavior patterns of these two types of individuals if it is to grow and prosper. Fortunately, it is possible to do so.

The Planning Process   Although it's the manager's job to plan—to take the business plan (which you learned about in lesson7) and bring it to life on a day-to-day basis—smart managers get their employees involved in the planning process. Not only will a better plan result, since the employees are closer to the work and closer to the customer, but the plan will also be more fully supported by the workforce. If they helped create it, it becomes theirs.

But watch out. Don't ask employees for their ideas and then ignore those ideas when putting the plan together. If you're going to ask for input, you've got to be willing to integrate it into your own thinking. Employees will quickly figure out if their views are valued, or if the consultation process is just window-dressing.

When your organization is small, planning can remain a relatively informal process. The same is true for organizations that face little or no competition and that have a secure outlet for their products or services. Many small, uncomplicated organizations function quite well with the plans filed comfortably in the owner's head. But as the organization grows and faces greater competitive challenges, formal planning—planning that is systematic, regular, and periodically reviewed—will be needed.

You'll need to develop a number of plans: the *long-range strategic plan* that sets the course for several years of activity; the *short-range plans* that direct your actions on a yearly and quarterly basis; *standing plans* that establish policies and procedures for repeat situations; *single-use plans* to guide actions through special projects or to establish operating budgets; and *functional plans* to help organizational units plan their operations.

Positive Leadership   Employees can't do their best if they don't know what they're working for—if they don't understand the organization's goals and accept them as their own. So it's the manager's job to motivate as well as direct employees, and it's the manager's job to see that employees have everything they need—both in a physical and psychological sense—to do their jobs well.

One important tool is personal contact. Maintaining contact with employees is easy in a small organization, but it becomes harder as the organization grows. As you grow, be sure to set up systems—monthly lunch meetings or business discussions with small groups of employees, two-way communications networks (for example, a newsletter with a response/question card, a suggestion box, or a phone-in question-and-answer system), employee recognition programs, grievance procedures, periodic performance reviews—all approaches that enable employees to ask questions, air concerns, and share in the development of the organization. Keeping communication lines open not only helps employees understand the organization they're part of, it also helps management impart its business philosophy and its values to the workforce.

Delegation is another important tool. Give as much responsibility and authority to your employees as you can. Let them make decisions about the things that affect them. Doing so will enable you to focus on *your* job, not theirs.

To help managers manage, make sure their span of control isn't too great. If a person manages a group of people whose jobs are distinct, technical, and demanding, you'll probably want to keep the number of people in that group down to six or eight. If, on the other hand, a person manages a group of people whose jobs are routine and largely the same, the group can be much larger.

Finally, a manager must inspire enthusiasm to be an effective leader. That isn't accomplished by being autocratic and dictatorial. It's been a long time since employers held a whip over their workers' heads. Holding a psy- chological whip over employees is no better. Look for ways to help people enjoy what they do at work; give them the power to control their own part of the business and they'll help you succeed.

Create a Clear Organization   One of the worst mistakes a manager can make in setting up an organization is to fail to clearly define organizational re- lationships. Here's an example. A director in a major U.S. cable television net- work was promoted to vice president of another department, and asked one of her managers to follow her there. He became manager of one of the units un- der her control, and assumed that he reported directly to her since nothing had been said about any intermediate level of authority. However, another manager—a "leftover" from the prior VP's staff—would periodically stick her head out the door of her office and ask the new manager, "How are things go- ing?" There was no official announcement of the relationship between the two managers, no staff meetings involving the two—just the occasional friendly inquiry.

Slowly, it became clear to the new department manager that the other manager thought she was supervising him. Still, the VP didn't say anything to make it official. The new manager finally had to go to his VP and ask her before learning that, yes, the other manager was his immediate supervisor. He no longer reported directly to the VP. That didn't do much for the new man- ager's morale, and it didn't do much to build his respect for the VP, either. She owed him a clear statement of the work relationship before asking him to accept the new job.

Identifying the *chain of command*—who reports to whom—is a crucial element in the development of an organizational structure. Make the relationships specific and clear, and avoid splitting an employee's allegiance between two supervisors. One of them is sure to lose out.

Case in point: the same manager who discovered he didn't report to the VP was asked to hire an acquaintance of the VP as a data entry clerk. Because of the clerk's close relationship with the VP, he would frequently go to the VP to have her overrule the manager when he was given work he didn't want to do. By allowing the clerk to bypass the chain of command, the VP created an impossible situation for her manager. He couldn't direct his own employee to do what needed to be done, because the *unity of command* in his department had been violated.

The rule is clear: a manager or owner cannot regularly ignore the chain of command. Occasionally, the chain can bend—but managers break it at their own peril.

Be sure, too, to keep the relationship between line and staff functions clear in a *line-and-staff organization*. *Line activities* (production, purchasing, marketing, etc.) contribute directly to production and sales objectives, while *staff activities* (personnel, public relations, accounting, etc.) support the line activities. Staff specialists should report to staff supervisors, but staff departments should exist to support the line operation.

Time Management Another crucial management issue is time management. When your organization is small, you'll find that you must attend to a wide variety of problems and consider a large number of questions every day. You're likely to put in long hours in the early months and years. Both of those facts can lead to inefficient use of time. To avoid this pitfall, it's important to:

- organize your work carefully,

- delegate duties to subordinates whenever possible (without overloading *them*, of course),

- periodically evaluate how you use time and deal with any problem areas,

- prepare a daily written activity plan, and set priorities for the activities to be undertaken that day,

- avoid procrastinating, and

- control the amount of time dedicated to meetings, by preparing agendas, setting time limits, and sticking to both.

Get Outside Help Finally, when you recognize that supplementing your own managerial wisdom would be a good idea, look for help outside. There's plenty to be found, particularly for new businesses. You might set up shop in a new business incubator (discussed in lesson 9), and take advantage of the management consulting services it offers. Or you might call on the Small Business Administration and its variety of support programs. One such program—the Service Corps of Retired Executives, or SCORE—is composed of a group of retired business leaders who offer their counsel, free of charge, to small business managers. The program is operated through the SBA.

Your own CPA firm—particularly if it's one of the larger national firms—may provide management advice. And there are a host of management consultants and other business experts—bankers, attorneys, suppliers, trade associations, Chambers of Commerce, even other business owners—who will be happy to help you succeed. Because if you succeed, they can continue to serve you. These people recognize that helping you can be a two-way street, so look to them when you need ideas or advice.

Turn to your Board of Directors or Advisory Board (a group that functions like a Board of Directors in terms of its advisory service, but has no liability for the organization's actions) for advice, too. And be sure that, when you establish your Board of Directors, you staff it with people who will tell you what you *need* to hear—and not just what you *want* to hear.

ASSIGNMENTS

■ Before you watch the video program, be sure you've read through the preceding overview, familiarized yourself with the learning objectives for this lesson, and looked at the key terms below. Then, read chapter 17 of Longenecker, Moore, and Petty, *Small Business Management*, "Professional Management in the Growing Firm."

■ After completing these tasks, read the video viewing questions and watch the video program for Lesson 18, *Making the Pieces Fit*.

■ After watching the program, take time to answer the video viewing questions and evaluate your learning with the self-test.

■ Extend your learning through the applications, exercises, or field experiences this lesson offers.

KEY TERMS

Professional manager   Person who uses formal systems of planning and control to run an organization or part of an organization.

Small Business Institute   Small Business Administration program that provides university-level consulting services to small businesses.

Service Corps of Retired Executives   SBA-sponsored program that offers consulting services of retired business leaders to small businesses.

Small Business Development Centers   Groups affiliated with colleges or universities that offer consulting, research, export, and minority services, as well as continuing education opportunities to small businesses.

Networking   Building mutually beneficial support relationships between individuals in related industries or business areas.

Long-range plans   Also called strategic plans, they help direct an organization's activity for several years.

Short-range plans   Plans that help direct an organization for shorter time periods; usually one year or quarter.

Budget   A short-term plan that helps define an organization's monetary plan for a certain period of time.

Business policies   Statements that guide management practice in areas where an issue may arise repeatedly.

Procedures   Step-by-step instructions for carrying out an activity.

Standard operating procedure   Standardized procedure for an activity that is frequently conducted.

Line organization   Organization in which each person has one supervisor to whom he or she reports.

Chain of command   Vertical channel for order-giving from superiors to subordinates, and a two-way channel for information flow in the organization.

Line-and-staff organization   Organization in which each person reports to one supervisor, but which also includes staff specialists whose job it is to support line operations.

Line activities   Work activities in an organization that contribute directly to production and sales objectives.

Staff activities   Work activities in an organization that support line efforts.

Unity of command   Ensuring that each employee receives instruction from only one supervisor.

Delegation   Giving employees the authority to make decisions about their own work.

Span of control   The number of employees under one supervisor's direction; should be limited to the number he/she can effectively supervise.

VIDEO VIEWING QUESTIONS

1. How do the entrepreneurial skills necessary to start a new enterprise differ from the skills required for the ongoing, capable management of a firm?

2. What differences are there between managing a small business and managing a large firm, according to program experts?

3. How do alternative styles of leadership affect employee productivity and satisfaction?

4. What is the role of formal planning and organizational strcuture in a business that is relatively small?

5. Although Merry Maids, Inc., is a franchise and, as such, provides training and management assistance to new owners; the daily responsibility for running a labor-intensive organization falls to people like Suzanne Young. Summarize the broad-based management functions Young must perform if her franchise is to be successful.

6. As you saw in this program, it is not easy to make the transition from entrepreneur to manager. Relate this specifically to the story of Kosti Shirvanian and Western Waste Industries. What suggestions would you offer Shirvanian, based on your own experience and what you have learned in this lesson?

7. Contrast the experience of Kosti Shirvanian with that of Bob Meichtry of Interior Illusions. How does a new manager, with his own administrative approach and leadership style, gain the loyalty and respect of staff?

SELF-TEST

1. Among the chief weaknesses of small-organization management is
   a. a lack of business experience among the managers.
   b. poor management practices.
   c. inadequate financing.
   d. a lack of structure.

2. If an entrepreneur hires a few employees and supervises each one directly, his/her business is in the
   a. third stage of business growth.
   b. first stage of business growth.
   c. fourth stage of business growth.
   d. second stage of business growth.

3. Formalization of management occurs in the
   a. fourth stage of business growth.
   b. third stage of business growth.
   c. second stage of business growth.
   d. first stage of business growth

4. A person who uses systematic and analytical methods in their work is known as
   a. a middle-level manager.
   b. an entrepreneurial leader.
   c. a professional manager.
   d. an organization founder.

5. One of the reasons entrepreneurs give for seeking outside counsel is to overcome management deficiencies. The other key reason is
   a. to counter a sense of isolation.
   b. to find ways to solve financial problems.
   c. to build a business network.
   d. to validate their business decisions.

6. Planning one's use of time should begin with
   a. a determination of objectives.
   b. eliminating practices that waste time.
   c. a time management specialist.
   d. a determination of time normally spent on various activities.

7. A document that expresses a firm's future plans in monetary terms is called
   a. a strategic plan.
   b. a short-range plan.
   c. a budget.
   d. the standard operating procedures.

8. If you want to tell employees how to approach a certain type of business issue and do so consistently over time, you would prepare
   a. a business practice guide.
   b. a standard operating procedure.
   c. a business policy.
   d. a procedure.

9. Performance reviews, bulletin boards, meetings, and suggestion boxes are examples of
   a. communications tools.
   b. business systems.
   c. operating methods.
   d. controlling devices.

10. An organization in which every person has just one supervisor to whom he or she reports is
    a. a staff organization.
    b. a line-and-staff organization.
    c. a line organization.
    d. a hierarchy.

11. A superior-subordinate relationship in which directions flow downward but communication is two-way is called
    a. a line-and-staff organization.
    b. chain of command.
    c. departmental organization system.
    d. unity of command.

EXTEND WHAT YOU HAVE LEARNED

1. For a period of several weeks, spend a few minutes at the end of each day analyzing the managerial functions in which you have been engaged during the day. Indicate on the chart below—and on duplicate copies you make prior to starting this activity—just how many hours or fractions of hours you spend each day on tasks that can be categorized as planning, organizing, leading/motivating, and controlling. The hours that you place in the "other" category are those in which you are engaged in doing rather than managing roles.

Activity	Sun.	Mon.	Tues.	Wed.	Thur.	Fri.	Sat.	Total Hours
Planning								
Organizing								
Leading/Motivating								
Controlling								
Other								

At the end of each week, total the hours in each category. Do the results surprise you? If you spent more hours in a category that seems to have been neglected, what difference do you think it would make to the business, both in the short term and the long term?

If you are not currently employed, ask the owner of a small business if he or she would keep track of their hours for a specified number of weeks. Provide them with the chart, and schedule some time to talk at the end of the activity. Ask them the questions in the paragraph above and record their answers. In addition to their response, indicate what you believe would happen if adjustments were made.

_____

_____

_____

_____

_____

2. Think of the many different kinds of plans your business has created, however long you have been in business. It all started with the business plan, a document that has been modified as your business has grown and changed.

   Give yourself a gift of four uninterrupted hours to review and organize the various planning documents that have been developed in recent years: the long-range plans, short-range plans, policies, and procedures. If some of the documents need revision or updating, set up a timeline by which the task will be completed.

3. Prepare an organizational chart of your business as it exists today. Analyze the structure and the working relationships. If you see flaws in the organizational chart, or envision ways in which the business might be structured more efficiently, draw a second chart that reflects your ideas.

4. Take advantage of the consulting services offered by such organizations and programs as the Small Business Institute and the Service Corps of Retired Executives.

Lesson 19

The Human Factor:
Individuals in the Organization

LEARNING OBJECTIVES

Upon completing your study of this lesson, you should be able to:

- Recognize the value of human resources in a small firm, and the importance of establishing sound personnel practices.

- Describe how job descriptions and job specifications affect the acquisition of appropriate employees for the organization.

- Give examples of sources a small business might use to find good employees, as well as recruitment devices that may attract applicants to small firms.

- List and describe the steps involved in the evaluation and selection process.

- Indicate why training and development is important, and suggest coaching techniques that can be used to improve performance.

- Compare compensation and incentive alternatives that small businesses employ.

- Examine the manager's role in dealing with employee discipline; in developing positive employee relations and a productive, supportive work environment.

- Discuss social and legal issues related to personnel management that affect small businesses.

When Jordan Marsh—one of the companies in the massive Allied Stores Corporation-Federated Department Stores, Inc. conglomerate that filed for bankruptcy in 1990—found itself struggling to sustain normal operations after its reorganization, chairman and chief executive officer Richard Van Pelt offered a piece of management wisdom to other business leaders. "The greatest asset I had at Jordan Marsh . . . was the human asset. Everything else was either mortgaged or sold."

If that fact is true of a major retailer, it's even more true of the small, startup enterprise. People can make or break an organization—in good times or bad. Making sure that the people you hire are an asset to the organization, and making sure you create an environment that allows them to feel valued, is the subject of this lesson.

OVERVIEW

If it is true, as many business leaders will argue, that you can't overcome inadequate human resources, even by boosting your financial or physical resources, then it's important to create an organization that works for the people who staff it. That's a far different notion than finding people who can "fit" into a particular niche in an arbitrarily structured organization. Flexing the structure of your organization around the people you find to run it will offer significant benefits in the long run—particularly for the small, startup firm.

Small firms *can* attract good people, and many of them do. But typically they don't do so by competing head-on with the benefits, fringes, and environmental amenities that larger competitors can offer. They simply haven't got the economic resources to do so.

So what does the smart small-business owner do to get the best people to work for him or her? Offer something the big guys can't offer—whether it's a bigger piece of a smaller pie, a more flexible work routine, more authority and autonomy, greater creative opportunities, or simply the more personal, friendly environment that often exists in smaller organizations. Any combination of these factors may entice a top-notch employee to your firm rather than to a larger competitor.

Since sales levels—particularly in smaller organizations—can be so directly affected by the attitudes and behavior of your sales force, it's critical that the organization find, hire, and retain the right people for the front lines. It's important, too, from an expense standpoint; typically, payroll is one of the biggest expense categories for an employer.

Among the chief advantages of joining a smaller organization, many people say, are the opportunity to obtain general management experience more quickly, greater potential for rapid upward mobility, greater freedom to do the job as you think it should be done, greater creative and learning challenges, and the feeling that your work makes more of a difference to the organization.

What's most significant about that list is the simple fact that money enters into the picture only tangentially—in terms of one's potential for movement up through an organization. So simply matching the pay offered by a bigger competitor isn't enough—and in fact, it may not even be what attracts someone to your organization. Simply put, you must create the kind of organization for which people want to work, and success will follow—for you, and for your people.

Finding Good Employees So how do you go about finding good people for your organization? There are several methods. If yours is a business with a number of unskilled, entry-level jobs, you may benefit from *walk-ins*—people who come to your organization looking for work. Even if you don't have an opening when a walk-in arrives, have the person fill out an application. That individual had the initi- ative to seek out employment, so he or she may be a self-starter, and that's an asset to your organization. But the quality of walk-ins can vary greatly, so you don't want to find yourself relying on the walk-in who comes through the door on the day you need someone. That person may not be as strong a candidate as the one who filled out an application last week or last month.

Schools are, obviously, another good source for both full- and part-time employees. If you're looking for people with a particular work skill, trade schools may be the answer; if you need unskilled, entry-level workers, the local secondary school may be a good place to start. And if you're looking for entry-level managerial employees, head to the college or university in your community.

Public employment offices are a third source of candidates for a variety of jobs, among them clerical, unskilled labor, production work, and technical jobs. Many factors can send an individual to a public employment office, and it's far more likely that a person ended up there because of a downturn at his or her prior place of employment than because of poor work performance. The question of prior work performance can, as we'll see later, be dealt with in the interview and qualification process.

Private employment agencies are another source of job candidates. Some collect their fees from the job candidates, but those that locate qualified appli- cants for jobs requiring a high level of skill and experience usually charge the fee to the employer. If your organization needs skilled people in specific areas—accounting, computer services, management and so on—it may be worthwhile to pay an agency fee, if it helps you locate more qualified people.

You might want to run *help-wanted ads* in your area newspaper, too—or post a sign in the window if yours is a retail establishment. Print ads are effec- tive if they set the organization apart from others, by expressing something about the distinctive qualities that make your organization a great place to work. If you run ads, be sure to have them written persuasively and profes- sionally.

If your need is temporary—whether due to seasonal sales peaks or the absence or departure of a key employee—you might find help at a *temporary employment agency*. They provide temporary help in a wide range of work areas—everything from nursing to sales, and accounting to engineering.

But probably the best leads to promising new hires will be your *current employees*. If one of your top employees refers someone, chances are that "someone" is another top worker. Successful people like to work with other successful people, so they're unlikely to recommend someone who won't match their level of commitment. In fact, many employers will say that current employees are, by far, their best source of new employee referrals, and many organizations encourage internal referrals by setting up reward systems for employees who recruit others into the fold.

Establishing Selection Criteria To determine the best candidate for a particular job, you've got to know what the job holder must be able to do to succeed in that job. That means analyzing the specific demands and activities of the job. The duties of each position are spelled out in the *job description*. The qualifications and requirements are listed in the *job specifications*. Once you have established these documents, you can look at your candidates—no matter how you found them—and have some sort of objective criteria on which to base your selections.

Probably the most important thing to remember when evaluating candidates is to look not for the person who most closely matches a particular set of educational or experience criteria, but for the person who has the greatest ability to do the job, and do it well. It may be frustrating to someone to be rejected for a job because he or she lacks a college degree in a particular field—but it's also foolish for the organization to fail to hire that person when he or she had the experience and the ability to handle the job. *Do* establish criteria—just be sure that they're appropriate, flexible, *and* legal.

Similarly, when looking at candidates for managerial or professional assignments, don't look just at the candidate's technical competence and educational background. Look, too, for indications of versatility—because that's an intangible young (and small!) organizations need. And versatility isn't something a person will demonstrate by meeting arbitrary criteria.

Evaluation Tools To evaluate employment candidates, it's important to use several tried-and-true tools: the application form, the job interview, reference checks, any appropriate testing, and pre-employment physicals.

Application forms help ensure that you get key information about every candidate you encounter, and they enable you to conduct a systematic collection of background information. Just be sure not to include any questions that will identify a person by race or religion, and be sure that all questions about a person's education are clearly job-related. These and other precautions we'll discuss later will help to keep you in compliance with Federal laws on employment discrimination.

The *interview* is the most important part of the employment process—and it's probably the most poorly-used tool. It gives the employer an opportunity to evaluate a candidate's professional appearance, job knowledge, intelligence, and personality; and it give the prospective employee a chance to learn something about the organization to which he or she has applied for work. Both parties should come to the interview ready to listen, and ready to ask pertinent questions.

It's the interviewer's responsibility to make sure the session goes well, by controlling the environment and keeping interruptions—if any are truly necessary—to an absolute minimum. And it's the interviewer's responsibility to put the job candidate at ease—it's not the right time to put people on the hot seat to see if they squirm.

An example: A young professional went on an interview at a major national firm in her city—a place where she very much wanted to work. She knew that someone with whom she had gone to graduate school was employed there—someone whose abilities and qualifications she questioned.

The interviewer conducted a reasonably pleasant, low-stress interview, and then asked the candidate the "hot seat" question. Did she know that other employee? Yes? What did she think of him?

What should she say? That she doubted his abilities? That would call into question the judgment of people in the organization she was trying to join. So she responded with a polite but vague comment about the young man, and was stunned by the interviewer's reply.

He said, "I'm surprised you feel that way. I just fired him."

If that didn't put a damper on the tone of the interview, nothing would. Years later, the woman felt angered by having been put on the spot, and continued to mistrust the interviewer—a person with whom she had many subsequent professional dealings. But she never went to work for him.

Another cautionary note about interviewing from the U.S. Equal Employment Opportunities Commission. Be sure not to ask any questions whose answers will reveal the applicant's national, ethnic or racial origins; any questions about a woman's marital status, the number and ages of her children, or about pregnancy or any child-bearing plans; or any questions about arrests and convictions unless your need for that information is clearly job-related.

Once the interview is over, it's time to *check job references* for the people you're most interested in hiring. Assume, of course, that any individuals listed as references are likely to give glowing recommendations—and use that assumption in two ways. First, pay attention if the reference *doesn't* offer up that glowing recommendation. That's a warning sign that something is amiss. But don't automatically blame the candidate—it could be a jealous associate trying to sabotage the candidate. Second, glowing recommendations aside, look elsewhere for confirmation of the candidate's qualifications. Check with the schools listed on a candidate's application to verify attendance and graduation. Talk with former employers who *weren't* listed as references. Conduct a financial, criminal, or credit check, with the assistance of the appropriate investigatory bureau if necessary. But remember that the candidate must be notified if you plan to conduct a credit check.

Conduct pre-employment *testing*, if it's appropriate, for jobs that lend themselves to objective test criteria. That may cover typing or computer proficiency, manual dexterity skills for production jobs, or even on-the-spot writing tests for people seeking jobs in the media or in a firm's communications operation.

Ask every candidate to submit to a basic physical exam, for which your organization pays—even if the job you're filling doesn't require it. It may cost a bit up-front, but it will alert you to any medical problems for which your insurance will have to pay, as well as to any physical limitations the candidate may have.

When They're on the Job Your responsibility for the hiring process doesn't end when you've offered someone a job and they've accepted. It extends to providing the proper orientation and training—on an ongoing basis—to help every employee do his or her best at all times.

Orientation is required for all employees, in all organizations, whether large or small. It may be a matter of the owner walking the new staffer around a small office, introducing him or her to the other employees—and it may be a full-blown, two- or three-day session, complete with presentations from senior executives and insurance providers. The length and complexity of an orientation session probably depends on the size of the organization. But all employees deserve an introduction to the new organization, if only to put them at ease.

Training can be used to prepare people for new jobs, improve their skills, position them for upward mobility, and update their knowledge in a technical area. Whatever the purpose of a particular training session, it's critical that the training be effective and professionally presented. Because, while good training can be a real morale-booster, poorly planned and executed training can have the opposite effect.

Whatever type of training you're conducting—JIT (Job Instruction Training) for the managers of nonmanagerial employees, or managerial or professional skills training programs for management staffers themselves—be sure that the reason for the training is clear to the employees who are involved, and be sure that they understand the impact that training may have on their careers.

Be sure that the people conducting the training really know how to teach, so that training sessions are beneficial to the trainees. It's hard for a student to tell a teacher, "You're not teaching me anything—you just keep doing it yourself," so make sure that trainers know how to involve people in the learning process. That's the only way the lessons will be internalized.

Another crucial tool for the ongoing management of employees is the policy manual or employee handbook. By producing this document, you set up systems that will regulate personnel relationships in your organization—something that helps ensure consistency and fairness in management.

Whether you develop and administer personnel policies as the owner-manager or you can delegate the responsibility to a part- or full-time personnel manager, this is an important step to take. By formalizing the work relationship (but remembering to allow for flexibility when it's appropriate), you'll help prevent such problems as high turnover, recruiting difficulties, low morale, and the loss of key people to your competition.

Finding Ways to Compensate People If you can't fully match your competitors' pay offers, your wage and salary scales must be at least roughly competitive, or you'll have trouble luring good people to your organization. Once you've achieved that competitive parity, you can look for other ways to set your firm apart.

Beyond the regular paycheck, you can offer financial incentives—bonuses, profit-sharing, stock options, commissions, and the like—to re-ward performance. But be sure to consult with a CPA or other consulting firm before establishing a profit-sharing plan, though, to ensure that it's one whose promises you can live up to.

Then there are fringe benefits: vacations, holidays, insurance, pensions, severance pay, etc. Don't play Mr. Scrooge here, even though the high cost of these fringes can be a problem. Look for innovative ways to solve the cost problem—preferred-provider organizations for health coverage, "cafeteria" plans that allow employees to choose among a group of benefits options, wellness programs that are relatively inexpensive and help keep medical costs down while improving both employee health and employee morale—the options are numerous.

Or maybe you can set up an ESOP—an Employee Stock Ownership Plan—to give employees the chance to buy a piece of the company. By giving them a stake in the operation, you help build commitment to your own success. And ESOPs give owners a convenient way to "cash out" when the time comes, without having to sell the company to outsiders who may not appreciate it the way you and your employees do.

Another way some employers are offering better benefit packages to their employees is to stop employing them, and turn over their employment to an employee leasing company. These companies—there are about 300 of them operating today—hire a company's employees, pay them, pay any applicable employment taxes, and file any required government reports in exchange for a fee that usually is between 5 and 10 percent of the company's payroll. The company where employees actually do their work still is responsible for recruiting, selecting, training, promoting, or firing its workers. But by hiring them through the leasing company, it can offer employees better benefit packages. After all, the leasing company "employs" many more employees than does any of its client companies, so it is eligible for much better group benefit programs.

Legal Issues A variety of legal issues will arise in the course of your business operations. Being aware of the basic issues involved is the key to avoiding major legal crises. Among the laws to which you must pay close attention are:

- The 1964 Civil Rights Act (amended by the Civil Rights Act of 1991), forbids discrimination on the basis of race, color, religion, sex, or national origin.

- Occupational Safety and Health Administration rulings, which demand that the workplace be free from any hazards that are likely to kill or seriously injure your workers.

- The Family and Medical Leave Act of 1993 requires firms with fifty or more employees to allow workers up to twelve weeks of unpaid leave for childbirth, adoption of a child, and other specified family needs. The company must continue health-care coverage during the leave and guarantee the employee the same or a comparable job on return to work.

ASSIGNMENTS

■ Before you watch the video program, be sure you've read through the preceding overview, familiarized yourself with the learning objectives for this lesson, and looked at the key terms below. Then, read chapter 18 of Longenecker, Moore, and Petty, *Small Business Management*, "Managing Human Resources."

■ After completing these tasks, read the video viewing questions and watch the video program for Lesson 19, *The Human Factor*.

■ After watching the program, take time to answer the video viewing questions and evaluate your learning with the self-test.

■ Extend your learning through the applications, exercises, or field experiences this lesson offers.

KEY TERMS

Management team   Individuals selected to head up key operating units of a company; their skills and experience should be complementary.

Walk-ins   People who come to a firm looking for work, the firm having conducted no recruiting activity.

Leased employees   Employees who do their work for a firm that has contracted with an employee leasing company to hire its employees and lease them to the actual employer; system enables employees to receive better benefits packages and employers to delegate administrative work to the leasing company.

Job Instruction Training   A system for effective non-managerial on-the-job training; helps managers who are not trained as teachers to train their employees.

Daywork   Compensation based on time increments.

Employee stock ownership plans   Plans that give employees a stake in the company, by offering them shares of stock as a fringe benefit; cultivates closer ties to the company and provides a committed cash source if the owner decides to "cash out" of the business.

Civil Rights Act of 1964 Prohibits discrimination on the basis of race, color, religion, sex, or national origin.

Occupational Safety and Health Act Requires employers to provide a safe workplace for their employees.

Family Medical Leave Act of 1993 Ensures employees of unpaid leave for childbirth or other family needs.

VIDEO VIEWING QUESTIONS

1. Just how important are human resources and personnel policies in firms with fewer than 100 employees?

2. How do job descriptions and job specifications assist in the acquisition of employees in small firms?

3. What kinds of incentives can a small business offer potential employees? Can a small business compete with larger companies?

4. Is training and development important in a small business? What about coaching and discipline? If your answer is "yes," to either question, indicate why.

5. What problems has Jim Carley encountered in attempting to fill positions at his three manufacturing plants?

6. How has its relationship to the community affected the available pool of employees for the Landis Department Store?

7. With candor, Drew Bernstein talks about the difficulties he has experienced in dealing with members of his staff. List the specific challenges he talks about, and some possible solution strategies that might be implemented.

SELF-TEST

1. The best source of new employees, many employers say, is
   a. other employees.
   b. schools.
   c. private employment agencies.
   d. help-wanted advertising.

2. The use of application forms helps an organization most by
   a. giving it information to research about applicants.
   b. getting a list of job candidates' prior employers.
   c. systematically collecting needed data.
   d. testing the employee's ability to spell and write.

3. Which of the following can be used legally as the basis for selecting employees?
   a. Gender
   b. Minority status
   c. Age
   d. Experience

4. To improve your interviewing skill, you should observe a number of principles, among them
   a. asking questions about the person's cultural heritage, to show interest in him/her as an individual.
   b. putting all of your attention into the interview and not allowing telephone or physical interruptions.
   c. checking on the candidate's relationship to the people listed as references.
   d. testing the candidate's vocabulary by using highly technical language in your conversation.

5. The law that prohibits employment discrimination is called
   a. the National Labor Relations Act.
   b. the Civil Rights Act of 1964.
   c. the Occupational Safety and Health Act

6. To help your managers do a better job of training their employees, you can institute a program known as
   a. job instruction training.
   b. skills dissemination training.
   c. manager training workshops.
   d. manager teachers' training.

7. If you handle all recruiting, selection, training, and retention or discharge activities, but another firm pays your workers and provides them with benefits, you are

   a. a secondary employer.

   b. an employee lessor.

   c. an employment manager.

   d. an employee lessee.

8. Among the key factors an employer should consider in developing a management training program is whether employees

   a. received enough education before joining the organization.

   b. understand the purpose and potential benefits of the training.

   c. at the management level can take the time off to participate in training sessions.

   d. employees participated in training sessions at other firms.

9. Compensation based on increments of time is called

   a. daywork.

   b. hourly wages.

   c. pro rata salary.

   d. profit sharing.

10. A good way to offer employees fringe benefits and keep overall costs down is to

   a. offer only the basic fringe benefits.

   b. match what your competition offers.

   c. offer a "cafeteria" plan for benefits.

   d. eliminate health coverage from the benefits offered.

EXTEND WHAT YOU HAVE LEARNED

1. Evaluate your company's performance in each of the following aspects of personnel management. For those categories in which you judged your record to be 3 or less, indicate in the space provided one reasonable action

that could be taken to improve the company's performance in this area of personnel management.

Personnel Management Function	5 Excellent	4 Good	3 Average	2 Fair	1 Poor	Suggestions for Improvement
Job descriptions/ specifications						
Recruitment						
Application forms						
Applicant interviews						
Reference checking						
Performance testing						
New employee orientation						
Job instruction training						
Periodic evaluation						
Wage or salary levels						
Fringe benefits						
Nonfinancial incentives						
Compliance with personnel laws						

2. As any experienced manager knows, working with employees requires a blending of skills . . . the perseverence of a career diplomat, the directness of an army field commander, the understanding of a counsellor, the motivational abilities of a coach. Knowing when to wear which hat is one of the tricks of the trade.

    The employee complaints that follow may be very familiar to you. In each instance, indicate how you would respond to an employee who makes the remark. Assume that the employee is a skilled technician the organization needs, and that you want to respond in a way that will be productive, both in the short term and long term.

    _____

    _____

    I'm overworked and underpaid!

    _____

    _____

I need something new to do. There's not enough challenge and variety in my job.

_____

_____

Management never keeps us informed about what's happening around here.

_____

_____

I stayed late every night last week just finishing what you asked me to do. I expect to be paid for those extra hours I put in.

_____

_____

Joe Smith doesn't do half the work that I do, and yet he's paid the same hourly wage that I am.

_____

_____

I'm not being given a chance to advance because of my ethnic background.

_____

_____

Lesson 20

Taking Stock:
Purchasing and Inventory Control

LEARNING OBJECTIVES

Upon completing your study of this lesson, you should be able to:

■ Recognize the stages of the purchasing cycle, and the importance of effective purchasing in the profitability of a small business.

■ Indicate the policies and procedures necessary to establish a sound purchasing system.

■ Discuss the importance of good relations with suppliers.

■ Recognize the objectives of inventory control.

■ Compare various inventory control methods and indicate how they can assist managers in controlling costs.

■ Assess the capabilities and limitations of a computer-based control system.

■ Compare the advantages and disadvantages of retail inventory valuation procedures.

If you've ever gone into a business for a particular item and found it out of stock, you know what effect that discovery had on you. You were disappointed, or frustrated, or even fed up—depending on how much you needed the item.

And if you returned to that business, only to find the item still out of stock, you probably left, determined never to return again. (About the only reason you might not react that way would be if you absolutely *had* to have the item, and that business was the only one around that carried it.)

Looking at that problem from the business owner's point of view is the focus for this lesson. Because only by establishing sound purchasing and inventory control policies and practices can you assure that your customers will get *what* they need *when* they need it. And that is the secret to sales success.

OVERVIEW

A great deal of money can be spent on the materials and merchandise you'll need to run your business. For many businesses—particularly in manufacturing and retailing—materials and merchandise can be one of the biggest items on a capital expenditure budget. And business experts have calculated that for every $1 of materials or merchandise held in inventory, it costs the holder between 15 and 20 cents in direct, out-of-pocket expense. That can add up.

The point is clear: not only does inventory cost money to acquire, but it also costs money to keep materials until they are used in the manufacturing process, or merchandise until it is sold to an end user. Among the factors contributing to that expense are interest charges, warehousing costs, bookkeeping costs, handling costs (what it costs to have your employees handle the goods while they're in your possession), damage or theft, and even the possible cost of obsolescence (the loss you'll incur if goods become out-of-date while you hold them). Determining the most cost-effective system of purchasing and managing inventory is a critical component of successful business operation.

And when it comes to inventory management, timing is of the essence. You must set up an inventory management system that gets goods to you at the best possible time. For a manufacturer, getting materials late means that the production process will be interrupted. A stock item missing from the shelves of a retail establishment may result in customer dissatisfaction and the loss of future revenue. On the other hand, getting materials too soon means that you'll spend money storing and keeping track of them, increasing the time it takes for you to recover the purchase cost.

The Purchasing Cycle There are several steps in the purchasing cycle for either materials or merchandise. Careful timing and management of each step will help ensure efficient inventory practices.

The first step for small business owners takes place when they *receive a purchase request* from an employee. If your operation is larger than a one- or two-person shop, you should prepare official purchase requisition forms, to help keep track of purchases and control their number and timing.

Second, you'll need to *locate the best sources of supply* for the materials or merchandise you need and obtain price quotes or bids from them. It's wise to be in contact with more than one source for each item you need, to protect you if there's a problem with your primary supplier.

There are additional advantages to dealing with several suppliers—doing so gives you price and delivery options, and it encourages suppliers to try harder to serve you well. But you must balance those advantages against the potential disadvantages—which include the possible loss of discounts for volume buying, less chance of help when you need a rush order, and less chance of financial aid from a supplier if you should need it. So weigh your options carefully, and decide on the merits of the particular situation whether it's more beneficial to buy from one supplier or several.

Third, you'll *issue a purchase order* for the supplier from whom you'll buy the materials or merchandise. That paperwork tells the supplier what you wish to buy, how much of it you need, what the agreed-upon price is, and what delivery and payment terms have been established. The P.O. is prepared in contract form, so it is binding on both parties

Fourth, you'll need to *maintain buying and warehousing records*, to make sure you know exactly how much you have on hand and how much is due to arrive.

Then you should *follow up* on the purchase order to be sure that what you've ordered will be delivered when it should be and in the proper quantity.

Finally, you'll *receive the goods* from your supplier, check their condition, and sign a receipt form to indicate your acceptance of the merchandise.

Purchasing Policies To help ensure that the purchasing cycle runs as smoothly as possible, it's wise to establish policies that will govern your firm's purchasing activities.

First you must determine your *make-or-buy policy*. Particularly if you're in manufacturing, it may be possible either to make or buy components you need in the manufacturing process. There are advantages and disadvantages to each option, so you'll have to make the decision after comparing such things as relative cost, available production capacity, assurance of supply, production coordination, equipment and space availability, staffing, and operating flexibility.

The practice of purchasing services that are outside the firm's area of competitive advantage is known as *outsourcing*. Just as it may make better business sense for a company to purchase from an outside source the nuts and bolts it needs to make widgets, it may also reduce costs by contracting with an outside source for such services as payroll or equipment repair.

You'll want to alert your accounts payable person, whether it's an in-house staffer or an outside bookkeeper, of your policy concerning *purchase discounts*. If you take purchase discounts that are offered by your suppliers—paying an invoice within the first ten days, for example—you receive a discount, which helps your balance sheet. The obvious question here: do you have the cash flow to cover the payment before you've sold the items and realized a profit?

Whether or not to *diversify sources of supply* is another issue to be considered. There are a number of reasons for a small business to concentrate purchases with one supplier. One supplier might be preferred because of the outstanding quality of their product. Or it may be impractical to divide small orders among suppliers. A small business might qualify for quantity discounts and/or special treatment by concentrating purchases with one vendor. Some firms, such as franchises, might even be linked to a specific supplier by the nature of their business.

There are equally compelling reason for diversifying sources of supply. Shopping among suppliers enables a firm to find the supplier with the best price, quality, and service. Knowing that competitors are getting some of its business, a supplier might try to induce a company to direct more business their way with better prices and/or service. Diversifying sources of supply helps protect a firm against interruptions caused by strikes, fires, or other problems a supplier might encounter.

Just remember to evaluate the advantages of buying from several suppliers with the benefits of directing all, or most, of your purchases to one supplier. And make the diversification decision on an item-by-item basis.

Building Rapport with Suppliers Once you know what you want, you can choose your suppliers by comparing their prices, the quality of their products, their location and its impact on ease of delivery, and any special services they might provide (credit, merchandising aids, sales promotion ideas, repair services, and the like).

To build a good relationship with your suppliers, you'll want to observe some common-sense rules. First, be as polite to your suppliers' employees as you'd like them to be to you. Pay your bills promptly. Don't cancel standing orders to gain a temporary advantage elsewhere. Don't give suppliers a hard time about their prices—negotiate fairly and then simply say "yes" or "no." If you say no, tell them why—again, nicely. If there's a dispute over pricing, work out an adjustment that is equitable to you and the supplier. And, if you've got an idea that can help a supplier save money or do his or her job better, offer it!

Maintaining Control of Inventory Inventory control is important, not just because it will tell you how much of something you have, but also because it will help you keep your business running smoothly, protect your assets against theft or deterioration, and minimize your inventory investment.

Business specialists have developed several systems of inventory control. Let's look briefly at three of them.

- *ABC inventory analysis*—In this system, you classify all of your inventory items into at least three categories. Items in the "A" category are the high-dollar, crucial items whose availability you must monitor closely, either because they represent major sales or because their lack would seriously disrupt your operation. Items in the "B" category are less costly or of moderate significance to your operation, so their availability can be monitored somewhat less diligently. And items in the "C" category are low-cost, low-significance—for example, rubber bands in a business office or printed matchbooks at a take-out restaurant. (If those run out, you can hand out plain matchbooks—or offer none at all—until a new supply arrives.)

- *Just-in-time (Kanban) inventory*—A precision system invented by the Japanese, this inventory system reduces inventories to a bare minimum and calls for ordering on a "just-in-time" basis. Lower costs result from the use of this system, but it must be carefully coordinated. In addition, you must be highly confident that your suppliers will be able to deliver when you need them to do so.

- *Economic order quantity*—By using this method, you take the question of carrying costs into account when deciding on your purchase timing. The quantity that is purchased is the amount that minimizes your total costs. The goal of this system is to avoid both high order costs and high carrying costs for inventory.

Keeping Track of Your Inventory Keeping tabs on all of the hundreds, and possibly thousands, of inventory items in one business is no small task. Witness the standard pattern of major retailers, who close their doors early on a given weeknight and round up their staffs for all-night inventory counting sessions. At least that was the pattern, before the advent of computerized inventory systems. Today, those retailers are likely to use both traditional and computerized systems to conduct an inventory accounting, since computers can only tell you if an item has been sold or used—they can't tell you if a particular item has been stolen or damaged.

The target for all inventory accounting systems—particularly for small businesses—is simplicity. Keep the system as simple as your business allows, so it doesn't start to run your life and the lives of your employees.

Make sure the system covers whatever needs to be accounted for, whether that is raw materials, supplies, work-in-process, finished goods, or merchandise bought from wholesalers that you're selling at retail.

You can choose from two inventory accounting methods: the *physical inventory method* (closing the department store and counting everything inside), to get a count of items on hand at one moment in time; or the *perpetual inventory method,* which uses inventory cards and requires that workers mark the cards every time an item is sold or otherwise removed from inventory. The latter system is good for small factories and warehouses, or for critical and expensive items, but it's hard to maintain—at least, without computers—when a business is larger or the number of items to be inventoried is great.

ASSIGNMENTS

■ Before you watch the video program, be sure you've read through the preceding overview, familiarized yourself with the learning objectives for this lesson, and looked at the key terms below. Then, read pages 444–451 in chapter 19 of Longenecker, Moore, and Petty, *Small Business Management,* "Quality Management and the Operations Process," and pages 520–522 in Chapter 22, "Managing the Firm's Assets."

■ After completing these tasks, read the video viewing questions and watch the video program for Lesson 20, *Taking Stock.*

■ After watching the program, take time to answer the video viewing questions and evaluate your learning with the self-test.

■ Extend your learning through the applications, exercises, or field experiences this lesson offers.

KEY TERMS

Purchase requisition Form which an employee must fill out to initiate the purchase of materials or merchandise.

Purchase order A binding contract which declares that a buyer will purchase certain items, in a particular quantity and at a particular price, from a seller who agrees to deliver those items within a certain time and at a certain quality level.

Make-or-buy decisions   Deciding whether to make a component needed in a firm's production process or to buy it from an outside supplier.

Outsourcing   The purchase of business services from outside providers that specialize in the required service.

Budget buying   Buying in anticipation of need, and adjusting purchases to fit production or sales needs at a particular time.

ABC inventory analysis   Method of inventory analysis that classifies inventory according to its importance to the operation or its value as a revenue generator; the more important the item, the more closely its supply is monitored.

Just-in-time (Kanban) inventory   Japanese system of inventory management in which items are ordered on a "just-in-time" basis, cutting inventory to the bare minimum and minimizing inventory costs.

Economic order quantity   Amount to be bought that minimizes total inventory costs.

Physical inventory system   System in which inventory of all items is counted by hand.

Perpetual inventory system   System that keeps track of inventory by using cards for each item, which are marked every time an item is used or sold; computers also can be used for perpetual inventory systems.

VIDEO VIEWING QUESTIONS

1. Simply stated, what is the goal of effective purchasing and inventory control?

2. According to Joan Hall, Ron Castell, and Ken Knicker, what factors should the small business owner take into consideration when selecting a new supplier?

3. What common mistakes do business owners make when they first start acquiring inventory? How does this affect cash flow? Their ability to satisfy customers and meet critical manufacturing deadlines?

4. What types of control systems can the small business implement?

5. James Kaplan, founder and CEO of Harlan Corporation, has been on both sides of the inventory equation, first as a supplier of spare parts and then as a manufacturer of towing tractors. What has he learned from both experiences? Contrast the methods of inventory control the company used in its early days to the approach that is used now.

6. In establishing Frame Art, how did Alfredo Zayden go about selecting his suppliers? How have his purchasing patterns changed through the years?

7. How has Lagesse's and Walker's approach to purchasing raw materials for Venetian Paradise inventory evolved? What limitations do they face in terms of inventory?

SELF-TEST

1. Purchasing activities help a firm acquire all production factors *except*
   a. merchandise for resale.
   b. raw materials.
   c. supplies.
   d. labor.

2. Which of the following is *not* a part of a firm's purchasing cycle?
   a. Receipt of purchase request
   b. Request for credit reports on customers
   c. Issuance of a purchase order
   d. Verification of receipt of goods

3. A form of partnering that enables buying and selling firms to work more closely than is usual in a contractual arrangement is called
   a. an exchange agreement.
   b. a trade-out.
   c. a strategic alliance.
   d. barter purchasing.

4. An advantage of buying rather than making component parts is that buying component parts
   a. uses otherwise idle capacity.
   b. requires less diversified managerial experience skills.
   c. protects a secret design.
   d. permits closer control of total production operations.

5. Among the chief arguments for diversifying your sources of supply is
   a. one supplier may suffer down-time and be unable to deliver what you need at the right time.
   b. you may get a better price by splitting your purchases among a number of suppliers.
   c. you're more likely to get financial help if you're in a crunch.
   d. it is not legal to purchase supplies from a single-source vendor.

6. Which of the following is *not* an inventory record-keeping system?
   a. physical inventory system
   b. cyclic counting system
   c. just-in-time inventory system
   d. perpetual inventory system

7. An advantage associated with diversifying sources of supply is that it
   a. may lead to quantity discounts.
   b. may mean special treatment in times of crisis.
   c. provides insurance against interruptions.
   d. may result in access to marketing information.

8. The inventory analysis method that reduces inventory levels to the bare minimum is called
   a. ABC inventory analysis.
   b. two-bin method.
   c. economic order quantity.
   d. just-in-time (Kanban) inventory.

9. Which of the following considerations is typically *least* important in selecting a supplier?
   a. Supplier's price quotations relative to prices of other suppliers
   b. Buyer's quality requirements and quality of supplier's product
   c. Public awareness of the supplier's name, which can be used in buyer's advertising
   d. Supplier's ability to meet delivery schedules

10. Which of the following is *not* an objective of inventory control?
    a. Securing maximum sales
    b. Getting merchandise when the market price is low
    c. Minimizing inventory investment
    d. Protection of assets

EXTEND WHAT YOU HAVE LEARNED

1. As the owner or potential owner of a small business, categorize the inventory you must carry on the chart below, according to its value. If you already have an inventory control system in place, describe it briefly and evaluate its effectiveness given the value of the items within that category. If you do not have a system in place, indicate what reasonable controls and precautions should be implemented.

_____

_____

_____

High-value Inventory (Close Control)	Less-costly Inventory (Moderate Control)	Low-cost Inventory (Loose Control)

2. Carefully consider the value of establishing a Kanban system for your business. What effect will it have on your operations? on your cash flow? on customer satisfaction?

_____

_____

_____

Lesson 21

"The Play's the Thing . . ."
The Oregon Shakespeare Festival

Management is both an art and a science. It takes special people to create the kind of environment in which others will want to work, and it takes specific, hard-nosed business skills to make it an economic success. Combining those two often distinct qualities is a difficult task for the small business owner, but the success enjoyed by many small businesses is a tribute to the fact that it *can* be done.

The task becomes even more challenging, however, when the organization's product is artistic expression. The artist's desire to stretch the limits of creativity can clash—often jarringly—with the business owner's need to protect the bottom line. So the arts organization that succeeds in reaching its creative potential, while also succeeding as an economic enterprise, offers a valuable lesson to every entrepreneur. The Oregon Shakespeare Festival is that kind of organization.

The Oregon Shakespeare Festival Looking at the ruins of the walls of the old Chautauqua theatre in Ashland, Oregon—left by a West Coast branch of the Chautauqua movement, which brought culture and entertainment to rural America in the late 1800s—Angus Bowmer had an idea. That idea would prove to be the genesis of what today is America's largest not-for-profit theatre.

The Chautauquas came to Ashland in 1893, beginning a tradition that would bring notables such as John Phillip Sousa, William Jennings Bryan, and the popular preacher Billy Sunday to the rural West Coast. For more than three decades, families traveled from southern Oregon and northern California to enjoy each program.

When the Chautauquas built a second, larger theatre in Ashland in 1917, it was designed as a round, dome-covered structure. At the time, it was the second-largest unsupported wooden dome in the world. But the building outlived the Chautauqua movement, which faded into obscurity only a few years later.

When Angus Bowmer visited the old Chautauqua site in 1935, the theatre's wooden dome had been razed, out of fears it would collapse on children who had taken to playing in the aging structure. But the legacy of the theatre's early grandeur seems to have been passed on to the Oregon Shakespeare Festival. The round shape of the old theatre walls reminded Bowmer of sketches of Shakespeare's Old Globe Theatre. And the idea was born.

Why not produce Shakespearean works for the residents of Ashland, Bowmer thought. Three performances, he decided, would give an added luster to the community's Fourth of July celebration. He convinced the city to contribute $400 to help cover his expenses, obtained donated materials from local businesses, and persuaded the federal government to provide a crew to help build the stage.

But Bowmer must have known that his 1935 festival would be more than a pleasant, one-time memory. Playbills announcing the three-day event billed it as the "First Annual Oregon Shakespearean Festival." And it was—the first in what has become a lasting American tradition.

From 1935, when Bowmer and his friends and colleagues staged a three-day festival—offering two performances of *Twelfth Night* and one staging of *The Merchant of Venice*—until today, the Oregon Shakespeare Festival has presented more than 10,000 performances to more than five million visitors. Currently, the Festival presents an eight-month season of eleven plays in its three Ashland theatres, and a five-month season of five plays in its Portland, Oregon, location.

Equalling its artistic success, the Festival also has found economic success. Its attendance ranks number one among not-for-profit professional theatres in the United States, it employs some 350 theatre professionals in Ashland alone, and it operates on a budget of nearly $10 million—75 percent of which is earned income, rather than donations.

Organizing for Artistic Success But just like any other business, the Festival must operate systematically to realize success. And it has. The short- and long-range planning processes at the Oregon Shakespeare Festival rival those of the best-run small corporations in the United States. In fact, the Festival's first five-year plan (it's on five-year plan number three now) is used as a teaching tool in Yale University's business and theatre and arts administration graduate programs.

That first five-year plan was developed in the 1970s with the help of the Ford Foundation, which at the time was providing grants to arts organizations to help stabilize them economically and improve their management. According to Festival officials, it has been the key to the organization's continued success.

What planning has done for the Festival, its managers say, is to help them identify where they're going as an organization and what they need to do to get there. That process works on a short-term as well as a long-term basis. Representatives of the organization's two major departments—the artistic unit and the administrative team—meet weekly to set plans for the following week's activities. Another group meets periodically to plan the following year's performances and decide on the staffing, technical, and administrative requirements of those performances. And the entire organization works together to develop, observe, and monitor its five-year plans—plans which take nearly a year to prepare.

The Impact of Planning According to Festival officials, the effort has paid off. "A lot of the reason we are here today," said General Manager Paul Nicholson, "is because of the planning that took place 15 years ago."

The Festival planning process encompasses the entire organization—the artistic side, the audience, facilities, finances, and organizational elements. Among the major impacts:

- Shifting from hiring people who were just beginning their careers to those with a stronger track record—a decision that propelled salary levels upward.

- Signing a contract with Actor's Equity, a move that enabled the Festival to continue attracting top-quality talent as more and more actors decided to unionize.

- Increasing theatre capacity to meet growing demand.

- Adopting a pricing philosophy that calls for small, regular price increases rather than huge occasional jumps.

- Targeting an increase in donations, from 20 to 25 percent of the operating budget, to cover increased costs once the Festival's capacity limits had been reached.

Planning has also brought people closer together, Nicholson suggested. "It's an integrated process . . . one that involves a lot of participation, a great deal of work. . . . But the payoffs are remarkable."

Among the key payoffs, he suggested, is the conscious effort to sustain the Festival's original guiding philosophy. "The Festival started," he said, "as a group of people—a group of friends—who wanted to put on plays, and in a way that's what it still is. We still try to have the concept of being friends who are putting on plays."

Staff Supports Line That philosophy could be a reason for the Festival's strong commitment to teamwork. In a statement that could be adapted to any firm with a line-staff organizational structure, Nicholson said, "We look upon ourselves, on the administrative side, as being as professional as the people on the artistic side. The approach we try to take is that we're as professionally supportive as we possibly can be."

Comments from the Festival's artistic leaders reflect the same commitment to the organization. Everyone has to work together, said Artistic Associate Kirk Boyd, if the organization is to succeed. "In most theatres, they have weekly production meetings . . . so everybody can look eyeball to eyeball and make decisions about what's happening with the play. We just don't have that kind of luxury here because everybody's working on more than one play, so we have to rely on our stage manager and staff, and they keep everybody in communication."

If that staff doesn't do its job, Boyd explained, you'll find the prop shop building a prop that already has been cut from a scene, or an actress wearing a hat to rehearsal that won't fit when she climbs through a window. Such complications, he said, could lead to personnel problems, if the organization allows them to occur. "The biggest thing is that we don't have time to take somebody's emotional value into consideration. . . . We just have to cut to the heart of the matter, make a decision and go on, `cause it just frankly moves too fast."

Having a team that is committed to the organizational mission helps prevent trouble. "One of the joys of working here," Boyd said, "is that the organization cannot be brought to its knees by one temperamental actor, or one temperamental costume designer."

Personnel Issues Balancing the potentially contradictory goals of staff longevity and the infusion of "new blood" is another issue that affects the Festival, just as it does other organizations. And Festival officials seem to have found that balance.

According to the Festival's Executive Director, Bill Patton, the organization has been able to hold onto key personnel partly because "they like living in Ashland, and it's exciting to be able to work with the theatre. I think that [longevity] has helped a great deal because in so many instances they have had such changes of artistic management in other theatres that it's caused some faltering. You need new blood, but it takes a balance, and I think we've had both here."

And, added Patton, the Festival inherited Bowmer's philosophy of helping to nurture new people coming into theatre and developing their careers. So, Patton explained, "we've not stagnated . . . I never had a feeling that we're sliding backward."

Festival leadership is careful, too, about establishing clear job responsibilities and lines of authority. While people outside of arts organizations might think they're run with a *laissez faire* attitude, it's clearly not the case at the Festival. "Every position within the company has a job description," said Nicholson. "We're very businesslike from that point of view."

When it comes to computerization, the same businesslike philosophy prevails. Ten years ago, Nicholson recalled, there wasn't a single computer in Festival offices. But now, he said, "we're probably one of the most computerized arts organizations in the country. We probably have . . . over a hundred people who can sit down at a computer terminal and make it do something that . . . makes it easier for them to do the job. Our basic philosophy," he added, "has been one of demystifying computers, trying to make them accessible to everybody . . . the production side for control of production costs, the scheduling for working on overtime of actors and things like that, a great deal of word processing . . . budgeting, long-range planning, using spreadsheets—things like that."

The Festival even created a computer hookup to an outside printing company, enabling the organization to get programs and other materials printed without having to keystroke copy twice. And in 1990, the Festival's box offices "went computer," taking technology straight to the Festival's customers.

Managing Growth Among the transitional issues with which Festival officials have had to deal over the years are issues common to every organization with entrepreneurial roots. The Festival had to deal first with making the shift from an organization run by the entrepreneur-founder and a small team of "wear-lots-of-hats" associates, to a full-fledged business enterprise with a full-time manager, employees who specialize in narrow areas of the operation, and clear-cut distinctions between line and staff units.

Next, it found itself dealing with the phased departure of the entrepreneur-founder when Angus Bowmer retired and became an organizational advisor.

And finally the Festival confronted the question, "How much growth is too much growth?" That issue forced its leaders to look down the road to determine how much growth—and what kind of growth—would be best for the organization's long-term success. Their conclusion reflected the Festival's essential artistic mission: they'd avoid becoming so big that the organization overwhelmed its own product, instead maintaining operations at their current level and working to improve the quality of that product.

By remaining true to their heritage, leaders of the Oregon Shakespeare Festival are helping to ensure the survival of an artistic institution, and demonstrating to the world that art and business can, indeed, go hand in hand.

APPLYING THE CONCEPTS FROM LESSONS 18–20

Before you watch the video program for Lesson 21, *The Play's the Thing...*, review chapters 17, 18, 19 pages 444–451, and 22 pages 520–522 from chapter 18 in the text. Then answer the following questions:

1. Angus Bowmer is said to have been a manager who readily shared leadership with others in his organization. What impact do you think that fact had on the growth and long-term survival of the Oregon Shakespeare Festival?

2. If you were starting an entrepreneurially-based theatre company, would you start it in a small, rural community? Why or why not?

3. Why do you think the Oregon Shakespeare Festival succeeded in its location?

4. List and discuss three of the ways in which the administration of an artistic organization like the Oregon Shakespeare Festival is just like that of any other business organization.

5. How can an organization balance the desire to encourage longevity among its staff with the need to infuse the organization with "new blood" from time to time?

6. How can hiring policies be designed to foster fairness and equity for both current and prospective employees of an organization?

7. What are some of the key risks to organizations in making the transition from startup to established organization?

Lesson 22

Keeping Track:
Financial Accounting

LEARNING OBJECTIVES

Upon completing your study of this lesson, you should be able to:

■ Understand the underlying importance of establishing a viable accounting system for a small business.

■ Indicate the basic requirements for maintaining records and controlling cash.

■ Describe and differentiate among the financial tools of the entrepreneur: budgets, balance sheets, income and cash flow statements, and ratio analyses.

■ Relate the importance of financial information to managerial decision-making.

■ Discuss the various methods that are used to conduct financial ratio analyses.

■ Evaluate the advantages and disadvantages of a small firm's maintaining its own accounting records versus using a bookkeeper or accounting service.

When it comes to proving the success of your organization to others in business, only one thing really matters: your financial results. It won't matter to prospective investors, lenders, or suppliers if yours is the most innovative new product, or your stores enjoy steady foot traffic, or your phone rings off the hook. What will matter is that a financial analysis shows that your organization is healthy in an economic sense.

Setting up accounting systems and understanding the various measures of financial health is our topic for this lesson.

OVERVIEW

When entrepreneurs go into business for the first time, they are far more likely to be experts at the business they've launched than they are at maintaining the necessary financial records. Of all the shortcomings of most new business owners, a lack of financial accounting experience is probably the greatest.

And, for the very small company, that shortcoming may not be crucial. If the organization is small and its work process relatively simple—a two-person service firm, for example, with no need to establish a fancy payroll system or account for product inventory—the owner can overcome his or her lack of financial knowledge. It might even be possible for the owner to do the accounting without outside help, since a sophisticated system may not be needed. But if that small organization intends to grow—even if it never produces a product that presents an inventory accounting challenge—a more formal system of accounting will be needed.

Formal System Provides Information A good accounting system will offer the business owner a wealth of information, far beyond its narrow role as pulse-taker of the firm's economic health. By analyzing information obtained through financial accounting, a business owner can do a better job of planning, controlling, and evaluating his or her operation.

A good accounting system will give the business owner a clear picture of operating results; a quick comparison of the current year's results with those of prior years; a complete financial statement for management, bankers, and potential creditors; the information needed to file government-mandated reports and tax returns; and a way to monitor employee fraud, theft, waste, or record-keeping errors.

In addition, the accounting system gives management a way to monitor accounts receivable, accounts payable, inventory, payroll, cash receipts and disbursements, and purchase and depreciation information on fixed assets. All of this information will help the owner do a better job of budgeting and running the business.

Setting Up a System As a business owner, you can opt to do all of your accounting manually, retain an outside bookkeeper or CPA to do your books for you, or purchase one of the many computer software programs that enable you to keep your own computerized books. The choice you make will depend on the amount of time you can devote to accounting, your knowledge of accounting practices and principles, the form of business organization you're operating, and the size of your firm.

The greater your level of knowledge and the simpler your organization, the more likely it is that you can keep more of the work in-house. Just be sure to leave yourself enough time to run your business if you do retain control of the accounting function. You don't want this part of the business to overwhelm the rest.

Whichever path you choose, you will need to develop systems for three key components: financial statements, ratio analyses, and budgets. We'll look in detail at both financial statements and ratio analyses in this lesson. But first, let's discuss the three major accounting decisions you'll need to make before you start jotting down figures in a ledger.

One, you must decide whether you'll use a *cash* or *accrual method* of accounting. The choice defines when your firm will "recognize" revenues and expenses—when you will declare that money has come into the firm and when it has been paid out.

In the cash method—a simpler method used more often by small businesses and by organizations with slow receivables (whose owners don't want to pay taxes on income they haven't yet received)—you record revenues once they're actually received and you record expenses only when you pay them.

In contrast, the accrual method records both revenue and expenses when they are incurred, no matter when the cash actually changes hands. So if you sign a contract to buy supplies on December 28th, you will show that expense on your books for that year, even if you don't receive the supplies until January of the following year and don't pay for them until March. Likewise, if you agree to sell something to a customer on December 28th, you will show the full amount of income on your books for that year, even if the customer buys on credit and takes a year and a half to pay.

The accrual method is more complicated than the cash method, but it measures profitability more realistically than does the cash method. And that is why most companies shift to the accrual method as they grow, even if they don't use it from the outset.

Two, you must decide on a *single-entry* or *double-entry accounting system.* This determines how you will record your business' financial transactions. Your particular information needs will help you decide which system is best for you.

Single-entry systems work satisfactorily for small businesses that do not plan to grow substantially. They create no balance sheets and generate no income statements. Simply put, a single-entry system is a checkbook system of receipts and disbursements, for which you keep sales tickets and receipts for payments you make to back up the checkbook record. Financial summaries can be prepared annually or monthly, depending on your need.

Double-entry systems require the use of journals and ledgers to record income and expenses, and they require that each transaction be recorded twice in your accounts—hence their name. There's a self-balancing characteristic to double-entry systems that makes them quite useful: if you make no math errors on either the record of income or the record of disbursements, the books will balance.

An even more attractive feature of the double-entry system is its usefulness when the time comes to prepare formal financial statements. You simply "plug in" the figures from your accounting books to those financial statements, making the task much simpler.

Once you've made these key decisions, you're ready to set up your accounting system.

Whichever type of system you choose, you should make sure that it includes *internal control*—the system of checks and balances that will protect your firm's assets from fraud or theft by insiders, as well as safeguard the accuracy and reliability of your financial statements.

To understand the concept of internal control, here are a few examples. One, the person who sells merchandise to a customer should not be the one to record transactions in your accounting ledgers. Two, you should limit access to company accounting records to those authorized to do accounting work. And three, you should control access to company computer systems.

Typical Financial Statements   The key components of accounting statements for any business are the *income statement*, which shows the results of a firm's operations over a certain period of time (usually a year); the *balance sheet*, which pinpoints the firm's financial condition at a particular moment in time; and the *cash flow statement*, which shows how cash receipts and cash payments compare with one another. We'll look at each of these in more detail here.

The *income statement* offers information on five key issues: sales, gross profit, operating income (earnings before interest and taxes), profits before taxes, and profits after taxes.

The first three sections of the income statement show the result of corporate operating decisions, concerning such matters as sales, cost of goods sold, marketing expenses, and general and administrative expenses. The result of calculations done in these sections: "operating income."

The next section takes financing costs into account, by subtracting any interest expense from the "operating income" amount calculated earlier, to arrive at the "profits before taxes" amount.

And the final section determines "profit after taxes" by subtracting tax payments from the "profits before taxes" amount identified in section four.

The *balance sheet* is a snapshot—a picture of the business' economic condition on a particular day. It distills the cumulative impact of earlier operating decisions to a single point in time. Typically, balance sheets are prepared at year-end. The basic components of a balance sheet are:

1. Current assets, such as cash, accounts receivable, and inventories.

2. Fixed or long-term assets, such as equipment, buildings, and land.

3. Any other assets used by the company.

In reporting dollar values in each of these categories, most companies report those values on a historical cost basis—what the assets cost when purchased. (Some businesses prefer to show value at whichever is lower—cost or current market value—to give a closer approximation of fair market value for the business, but most choose the historical cost basis.)

Also included on a balance sheet is a discussion of liabilities and equity, to show how the firm has financed its asset acquisitions—whether with debt, equity capital, or a combination of the two. Here, the terms "equity" and "net worth" are interchangeable, since the equity figure represents the contributions the owners or partners have made to the firm's acquisition of assets.

The *cash flow statement* shows the relationship between a company's profit and its cash flow—how and when funds move into and out of the corporate coffers. Among the types of cash flow activities that are analyzed in this statement are:

- cash flows from operations (collections from customers, payments to suppliers, marketing expenses, interest payments, and tax payments),

- cash flows from investment activities (the amount of cash used for investments on either current or fixed assets), and

- cash flows from financing activities (cash inflows or outflows to the firm's investors, excluding interest payments).

By combining the cash flows from operations, investments, and financing, a summary of cash flows is produced.

Financial Ratios Once you've produced your accounting statements, you'll want to analyze them, to see how your organization measures up financially. Professional accountants have developed a number of financial ratios, which they use to gauge the financial health of organizations; a number of these ratios are appropriate for use by small businesses to gauge their own health.

These key ratios analyze financial health in four areas: liquidity, sales, profitability, and debt.

Ratios that measure whether a firm has sufficient *capital,* and whether enough of that capital is *liquid* (available for immediate use when needed) include:

- The *current ratio*—compares level of current assets to current liabilities. Banks like to see a two-to-one ratio of assets to liabilities.

- The *acid-test (or quick) ratio*—compares current assets, excluding inventory, with current liabilities. Since inventory is less liquid than other assets, it is subtracted from total assets before the ratio is established. The minimum satisfactory ratio here is one-to-one.

Ratios that measure *sales* seek to compare sales levels with investment in various asset accounts. They include:

- *Average collection period*—determines how quickly you're being paid for merchandise or services you've sold. A two-step process, this ratio is determined by dividing total sales for the year by 360, and then dividing that figure into your receivables. The answer tells you the average number of days you are waiting to be paid by your customers. If your average collection period is longer than the industry average, you'll want to tighten up your collection procedures.

- *Accounts receivable turnover*—calculates the number of times your accounts receivable "roll over" during a year. A comparison with industry averages will tell you how we'll you're doing in this area.

- *Inventory turnover*—shows how often a firm has turned over or sold its inventory during the year, by determining the ratio of sales to inventory (carried at cost, not at the sales price). If your sales are highly seasonal, you'll want to use an average inventory figure for the year. Again, compare your ratio with the industry average.

Ratios that measure profitability show the net result of all decisions you've made—managerial, financial, and marketing. They include:

- *Operating income return on investment*—serves as a measure of operating profits relative to assets, by dividing total assets into operating income. Once more, you should compare your results with industry averages.

- *Operating profit margin*—compares net profit to dollar value of sales by dividing sales into operating income.

■ *Total asset turnover*—shows the earning power of all of your assets, also known as return on total investment. Dividing your sales by your total assets gives you a percentage of return.

■ *Fixed-asset turnover*—measures how well you're using the plant and equipment you've invested in, by dividing sales by fixed asset value. If your figure is lower than the industry average, you're not using your plant and equipment as efficiently as you should.

Ratios that consider debt position show the relationship between your borrowed funds and invested capital. If you discover that your amount of debt is high relative to your equity, your firm may be in trouble. The two key ratios here are:

■ *Debt ratio*—the percentage of total funds provided by your creditors. Divide total debts (both current and long-term) by total assets to assess this ratio.

■ *Times interest earned*—measures how far your earnings might be able to decline before your ability to meet interest costs is affected. Divide operating income by interest charges to determine this ratio, and compare your result with the industry average.

Finally, you'll want to analyze whether your investors or stockholders are receiving an adequate return on their investment. The key ratio here:

■ *Return on net worth*—measures the return on equity (ROE) that you're achieving, an important figure for your shareholders. Divide your net profit by your net worth to calculate your percentage of return on equity, and compare it with the industry average. If your ROE is lower than that average, you may want to consider additional debt, to allow you to provide more ROE to your investors.

In developing all of these ratios, three recommendations usually are offered: be conservative, be consistent, and be candid. Don't paint an overly rosy picture—use the numbers to help you develop a cautious approach. Don't use a figure one way one month, and another way the next, to improve your financial appearance. And don't try to hide a bad ratio—be open about it, so the people who need to know how your business is doing can know the truth.

ASSIGNMENTS

■ Before you watch the video program, be sure you've read through the preceding overview, familiarized yourself with the learning objectives for this lesson, and looked at the key terms below. Then read chapter 21 of Longenecker, Moore, and Petty, *Small Business Management,* "Evaluating Financial Performance." Also review pages 209-219 in Chapter 10, "Accounting Statements and Financial Requirements."

■ After completing these tasks, read the video viewing questions and watch the video program for Lesson 22, *Keeping Track.*

■ After watching the program, take time to answer the video viewing questions and evaluate your learning with the self-test which follows the key terms.

■ Extend your learning through the applications, exercises or field experiences this lesson offers.

KEY TERMS

Cash method — Accounting method that reports income when cash is received and expenses when cash is disbursed.

Accrual method — Accounting method that reports income and expenses when they are incurred, no matter when they actually are received or paid out.

Single-entry system — Accounting system that uses the checkbook to determine receipts and disbursements. It should be supported by sales tickets or invoices and by receipts for disbursements.

Double-entry system — Accounting system that uses journals and ledgers to record each transaction twice; enables user to check accuracy of records by comparing entries in journal and ledger.

Internal control — System of checks and balances that enhances the accuracy and reliability of financial statements, and guards against fraud and theft.

Income statement	Shows results of a firm's financial operations over a given period of time.
Balance sheet	Shows firm's financial condition at a particular point in time.
Equity	All owners' investments in a company, and the profits retained in the firm.
Statement of cash flow	Shows cash receipts and cash payments for the operating, financing, and investing activities of the firm; shows changes in a firm's cash position over a period of time.
Liquidity	Measurement of a firm's ability to meet debt obligations as they mature.
Current ratio	Comparison of current assets to current liabilities.
Acid-test ratio	Comparison of current assets, less inventory, to current liabilities.
Average collection period	Shows how quickly a firm is paid for goods or services delivered to buyers.
Accounts receivable turnover	Measure of the number of times accounts receivable "roll over" during a year.
Inventory turnover ratio	Measure of how quickly a firm is turning over its inventory.
Operating income return on investment	Measure of operating profits relative to assets.
Operating profit margin	Profits derived from operations divided by sales.
Total asset turnover	Measure of the efficiency with which a firm's assets are used to generate sales.
Fixed-asset turnover	Shows how efficiently plant and equipment are being used; ratio of sales to fixed assets.
Debt ratio	Shows percentage of total funds that have been provided by creditors.
Times-interest-earned	Shows how far a firm's earnings may decline before it is unable to pay interest on its debts.
Return on net worth	Measures return on equity (shareholders' investments).

Profit margin on sales	Determines profit per dollar of sales. For example, if the profit margin is 5 percent, that means for every $1.00 in sales the company had, it netted, or cleared, 5 cents.
Return on total assets	Measures return on investment in the business.

VIDEO VIEWING QUESTIONS

1. In maintaining records and controlling cash, what basic requirements must a small business fulfill?

2. How do the various financial reports described in this lesson relate to managerial decision-making?

3. As you listen to the experts talk about the advantages of using a bookkeeper or accounting service versus maintaining your own accounting records, which option seems most advantageous to you?

4. As a relatively new entrepreneur, David Hertz is having difficulty with certain financial aspects of his business, Syndesis. Describe the basis for the problem, and what advice you might give him.

5. Lee Browne is a professional, not a bookkeeper. She has an accountant, and yet she still finds herself spending hours trying to uncover mistakes in the records the accountant must use. Is her problem a personnel problem, a procedures problem, or some other kind of problem? What would you do if you were in her position?

6. Ellen Galeski freely admits that she bought the Flower Concierge, an existing business, without a clue as to how to manage the financial aspects of a business. Describe the role her accountant has played in helping her "keep track" and in developing the information she needs to expand the business.

SELF-TEST

1. Accounting records help a business owner keep track of everything *but*
   a. inventory.
   b. cash.
   c. vacation schedules.
   d. accounts receivable.

2. A small, relatively simple business operation is more likely than a large, complex organization to be able to use the
   a. accrual method of accounting.
   b. internal control method of accounting.
   c. income statement.
   d. cash method of accounting.

3. An accounting system that uses ledgers and journals, and that has a self-balancing feature is called
   a. a double-entry system.
   b. a balanced accounting system.
   c. a single-entry system.
   d. a cash flow system.

4. The financial statement which shows the results of a firm's operations over a period of time is the
   a. balance sheet.
   b. income statement.
   c. statement of cash flow.
   d. cash accounting statement.

5. The three major financial statements used by small businesses are the income statement, balance sheet, and
   a. cash flow statement.
   b. pro-forma statement.
   c. changes in financial condition statement.
   d. bank statement.

6. To see if you're being paid as quickly as others in your industry for goods or services sold, you'd compute the
   a. average collection period.
   b. total assets turnover.
   c. inventory turnover ratio.
   d. acid-test ratio.

7. To reassure your investors that their investment is doing well, you'd want to show them a satisfactory
   a. profit margin on sales.
   b. inventory turnover.
   c. debt to total assets ratio.
   d. return on equity.

8. The ability of a company to meet maturing debts is called
   a. the acid-test ratio.
   b. liquidity.
   c. the current ratio.
   d. the debt-to-equity ratio.

9. To measure operating profits relative to assets, you would calculate the
   a. inventory turnover ratio.
   b. operating profit margin.
   c. operating income return on investment.
   d. total asset turnover.

10. If you wanted to find out how much income your company must take in to meet its debt obligation, you would calculate the
    a. fixed asset turnover.
    b. debt ratio.
    c. return on equity.
    d. times-interest-earned ratio.

EXTEND WHAT YOU HAVE LEARNED

1. What kind of accounting systems have been set up for your business? (If you are not associated with a business, answer the question in terms of what kinds of systems you would establish for a business you might some-day own.) In each case, indicate why one option was selected rather than the other.

   ❑ Cash accounting

   OR _____

   ❑ Accrual accounting _____

   _____

   ❑ Cash accounting

   OR _____

   ❑ Accrual accounting _____

   _____

2. Get a copy of the most recent balance sheet and income statement for your business. Compute the following financial ratios using the data form those statement:

Current ratio = _____

(Divide current assets by current liabilities)

Acid-test ratio = _____

(Subtract inventories from current assets.
Divide your answer by current liabilities)

Rate of inventory turnover = _____

(Divide net sales by your average inventory)

Profit margin no sales = _____

(Divide net profit by net sales)

Return on total assets = _____

(Divide net profit by total assets)

If you do not have this information available to you at your place of business, secure a recent annual report from a business that is of interest to you, and calculate the ratios listed above.

Lesson 23

The Money Flow:
Management of Working Capital

LEARNING OBJECTIVES

Upon completing your study of this lesson, you should be able to:

■ Explain the concept of working capital and recognize its significance in the day-to-day management of a small business.

■ Identify ways in which a manager can use a cash budget and/or forecast to optimize the cash flow cycle.

■ Describe the life cycle of receivables, and how an aging schedule can be used to prompt the collection of past-due accounts.

■ Give examples of strategies a manager can use to monitor purchasing and inventory.

■ Indicate strategies that are important in the financial management of accounts payable.

■ Indicate the procedures a small business must establish in order to control and minimize the cost of credit.

■ Suggest some approaches a small business might use to counter financial problems that are common to small businesses: maintaining cash flow, securing funds for expansion, credit hold.

On the surface, it would seem that as long as a business has customers for its products or services, growth can readily take place. But growth costs money—whether that money is used to hire more people, obtain more inventory, or acquire more space—and the small company may lack the cash necessary to pay for that growth.

This lesson is designed to help you learn how to manage working capital so your business can grow and still meet its current financial obligations.

OVERVIEW

If Cummins Engine Company—a major player in the U.S. engine manufacturing marketplace—could find itself in a cash-flow crunch in 1990, despite spending $1 billion in the 1980s to become more competitive, it's easy to see how a cash crunch can hit any business, large or small.

Ironically, the crunch is more likely to affect the small, growing company than the larger enterprise. That's due in part to the fact that small companies tend to grow more quickly than large organizations. It's also because small companies have a harder time convincing prospective sources of financial assistance to extend credit to them.

The problem is exacerbated by the fact that a company may be profitable on paper but discover itself short of cash. Sales have been made, and the merchandise or services have been provided, but because the business extends credit to some of its customers, there's not enough cash on hand to buy additional inventory or pay another sales representative. So when the time comes to expand the business to meet growing demand, even highly profitable small companies may find themselves unable to finance growth or pay for it out of profits already realized. It's a classic case of the "growth trap" in which so many small business owners find themselves.

So what's the owner of a small company to do? First and foremost, decide if you *want* to grow. Some people make a conscious effort to keep their businesses small. Maybe they don't want the responsibility for others' livelihoods, or they don't want the more demanding work life that nurturing a small company into a major player entails. There are millions of small businesses across the land whose owners are perfectly happy being *small* business owners, or at least controlling their rate of growth.

If expansion is your objective, identify any constraints to that goal. You may not have the resources—economic, human, or physical—to sustain much growth, and acquiring those resources may simply be too costly. You may not have access to enough capital to finance your growth plans. Small businesses can have a tough time landing the credit they need for expansion. Quite simply, some people lack the ability to manage a larger business. Every business magazine in print has carried more than a few stories about the expanding small business that fell apart because the management team couldn't keep up with the new demands placed on it by its increased size.

Plan carefully. Learn all you can about working capital management and capital budgeting if you decide that growth is your goal.

What's Working Capital?   Working capital is composed of a business' current assets, which include cash, accounts receivable, and inventory. By carefully managing each of these components, as well as the business' accounts payable—what it owes to suppliers for the goods it has used in its own operations—the small business can ensure itself sufficient working capital to fund growth . . . or at least keep business rolling along at the same pace.

When we talk about *managing cash flow*—managing the cash component of your working capital—we're talking about maintaining a positive balance between the sales dollars you bring in and the expense dollars you pay out. Ideally, you want to regulate the timing of these two elements so you're always bringing in more than you're spending. This simple idea is violated by many people, with disastrous results.

To analyze your cash flow, all you need to do is look at your bank account. You wouldn't look at sales figures, because they'll include credit sales—and until a credit customer pays you, you don't have the cash from that sale. And you wouldn't look at expenses because, if you're smart, you'll be acquiring some goods and services on credit yourself and paying for them at a later date. So, by looking at your bank account records, you can study *cash receipts* and *disbursements*—the two components of cash flow.

Once you've studied that bank account history, you can begin to develop a comprehensive cash budget for your company. You'll need to first forecast your monthly sales. If you've prepared an operating budget, you can find the relevant figures there. But remember to reduce your anticipated sales figures from the operating budget by the percentage of sales you expect to make to credit customers. The resulting monthly figures are your estimated cash receipts.

Then calculate your monthly cash disbursements by adding up the cost of everything you'll need to pay for each month—raw materials, products to sell, supplies, sales and administrative expenses, rent, insurance, interest payments, fixed asset expenses, taxes—*everything*.

Comparing the two sets of figures month by month will tell you whether you should expect a positive or negative cash flow each month. Because you may have some months of negative cash flow—particularly if your product or service is seasonal—the cash budgeting process will help you determine how much extra cash you'll need to get through those months. It will also tell you when you might have extra cash on hand that can be placed into short-term investments to carry you through the leaner months.

Beyond developing a cash budget, there are other activities you can undertake to help maintain a positive cash flow over the course of the year. You can manage your accounts receivable, inventory, and accounts payable. Let's look briefly at each of those activities.

Managing Accounts Receivable By managing accounts receivable, you deterine the impact of your credit-granting decisions on the amount of working capital available to you and on your month-to-month cash flow.

Granting credit to customers is a two-edged sword. It helps you build sales by enabling people to buy something for which they may not have the available cash. On the other hand, it forces you to wait for that cash—and if you have to wait too long, or if the cash comes a month or two after you have had unusually high cash outlay requirements, the credit you granted could be the reason you have difficulty managing cash flow during that time.

If you're careful about the people to whom you extend credit, however, and careful about requiring payment on a timely basis, credit will work for you in the long run. If it didn't, business analysts wouldn't refer to it as "near cash" or identify it as a current asset.

There are three stages in the "life cycle" of a receivable: the point at which the credit sale is made, the time when the seller prepares and sends an invoice, and the time when the buyer processes and pays that invoice. Because delays can occur in that cycle, it's important to keep close tabs on your receivables, as well as to move the process along as swiftly as you can.

The owner of one small southern California service firm is, by her own description, "just about obsessive" about processing and mailing invoices for the services she provides. Invoices are prepared the last day of each month and mailed that day, with the balance due ten days later. If payment isn't received within 15 days, a reminder invoice is sent. And if payment still isn't received within 30 days, a late notice, with a 1.5 percent late fee applied to it, follows. That diligent effort has paid off for the consultant, who can count on her fingers the number of times she's had to wait more than two months for a payment—in 12 years of private practice. By establishing a routine and sticking to it, this business owner not only keeps close tabs on her accounts receivable; she also lets her clients know, in a matter-of-fact way, that she expects to be paid . . . and paid promptly.

Besides moving promptly to process and mail invoices, the small business owner should also establish clear credit-granting policies. These can help in making the decision about whether a customer's or client's credit privileges should be suspended for late or non-payment. It's wise to provide some form of incentive for prompt payment: either a discount for early payment or a service fee or interest charge for late payments.

Another tool for managing accounts receivable is the practice of "aging" receivables. As an example, that southern California consultant uses a simple system—a red "hash mark" in her ledger, to indicate each time that a late notice has been sent on a particular invoice. If more than one late notice must be sent, the second and any subsequent mailing dates are noted in the margin.

It's quite easy to see, simply by glancing at that business ledger, which clients are causing cash flow problems for the business.

Finally, if a customer or client simply won't pay, it's important to follow through, either with a collection agency, reposession, or Small Claims Court. Do whatever you can, without spending time that should be invested elsewhere, to secure payment for your goods or services.

If you need cash and can't push people to come through any more quickly with accounts receivables, consider borrowing against your receivables. There are two ways to go. First, you can simply borrow against your receivables by pledging them as loan collateral. You receive a loan from the bank or other lender, and when your receivables come in, you turn them over to the lender to pay off the loan. Second, you can "factor" your receivables, by selling them to a finance company. The company charges you a fee for the service, so you earn less on your receivables than you would if you waited for payment. But you gain access to cash sooner—and sometimes that's more important than getting every last penny.

But borrowing against your receivables *is* expensive. In a loan situation, you'll pay an interest rate that's usually several points above prime. Factors charge even more, to cover their credit checking activity and to protect themselves against any bad debts in the accounts you sell.

Managing Inventory   Not having enough inventory can hurt a business, when the lack of a product sends customers away unsatisfied. But having too much inventory can hurt a business, too. Simply put, inventory is money. Since inventory ties up some of your cash, it's critical to manage that inventory so you have what you need, and no more.

In service firms, the problem seldom arises, since virtually the only inventory items required are supplies. But for manufacturers, retailers, and wholesalers, the inventory requirements are greater—ranging from raw materials to finished products and packaging, as well as supplies.

The "right" amount of inventory will vary from one kind of company to another, even from one outlet of a chain of stores to another. The customer base—its size and its demographics—will determine how much inventory each business needs. Your primary objective in determining that "right" amount is to figure out the minimum, or base, inventory you need to carry that either will allow you to maintain production schedules or achieve a particular level of customer satisfaction. Buying that amount, and no more, allows you to free up as much cash as possible for cash flow purposes.

Once you've figured out how much inventory to keep on hand—for *every item* in your inventory—you must keep track of what you have. The days of the once-a-year inventory check are long gone. It's far easier for a business to keep track of inventory today because of the advent of the personal computer. By using a computer to monitor inventory levels, you'll be far less likely to discover a carton full of swimsuits in the middle of December—which should have been put on sale back in August and may be out of style by next spring.

Resist the temptation to stockpile extra quantities of merchandise, unless you can get it at a ridiculously low price and unless you're sure—*absolutely* sure—that you'll sell it fast. As a rule of thumb, if a vendor can offer a "great" deal today, he's likely to offer it another day, too.

Managing Accounts Payable On the other end of the cash flow management equation is the management of accounts payable—deciding when to pay your suppliers for the raw materials, merchandise, or supplies you've bought from them. By negotiating the timing of the payments you make, and by making those payments at times that maximize the economic benefit to you, you improve your firm's cash flow.

Don't be afraid to contact a creditor when you're in a crunch, either. They're almost as eager to see you stay afloat as you are, because if you go under, they're sure to lose, too. If you have a hard time meeting a payment schedule, talk to them and work out a mutually satisfactory alternative.

When your cash flow is positive and you can afford to do so, take advantage of payment incentives offered to you. Sometimes you can receive a discount by paying early. But if it costs you no more to wait till the end of a payment period before delivering your check, take advantage of that option.

ASSIGNMENTS

- Before you watch the video program, be sure you've read through the preceding overview, familiarized yourself with the learning objectives for this lesson, and looked at the key terms below. Then read chapter 22 of Longenecker, Moore, and Petty, *Small Business Management*, "Managing the Firm's Assets."

- After completing these tasks, read the video viewing questions and watch the video program for Lesson 23, *The Money Flow*.

- After watching the program, take time to answer the video viewing questions and evaluate your learning with the self-test which follows the key terms.

■ Extend your learning through the applications, exercises or field experiences this lesson offers.

KEY TERMS

Working capital   Current assets held by a firm, including its cash, inventory, and receivables, which are considered "near cash."

Working-capital management   Process of managing a business' cash, accounts receivable, inventory, and accounts payable for maximum cash flow benefit.

Working capital cycle   Day-to-day flow of resources through a firm's working-capital accounts.

Cash conversion period   Time required to convert paid-for inventories and receivables into cash.

Growth trap   Cash "crunch" that results from rapid growth.

Cash budget   Tool used to manage cash flow which analyzes when cash is likely to be received and when it must be paid out, to identify times when a firm may be cash-short or have extra cash to invest.

Accounts receivable   Payments due from customers for goods or services already received.

Pledged accounts   Accounts receivables used as collateral for a loan.

Factoring   Selling a firm's accounts receivable to a finance company to gain earlier access to the cash.

Inventory   Raw materials, merchandise, and supplies kept on hand by a business.

Accounts payable   Payments due to vendors or suppliers for goods or services already received by the business.

VIDEO VIEWING QUESTIONS

1. How does the concept of working capital relate to the day-to-day management of a small business?

2. A number of the experts who appear on the program talk about what a small business owner/manager can do to optimize cash flow. Make a list of their suggestions, and relate them to the activities of your own business.

3. How important is capital budgeting to the survival and success of most small businesses? Does the technique you use to choose among alternative investments adequately evaluate the profitability potential of each investment opportunity? If not, what procedural changes would you recommend?

4. In what ways does Ken Gootnick, owner of It's Greek to Me, attempt to minimize the costs associated with manufacturing his product? How does he deal with cash flow problems related to the large-quantity orders? Given the location of his suppliers, what other steps could he take to improve his cash flow?

5. Mike Patterson's business is not steady enough to project a predictable flow of income. What can a small business owner do to handle this sort of situation?

6. When George Olieux expanded his model train shop, he anticipated that the new lines he planned to carry would pay for the renovation, at least within a reasonable length of time. In reality, what has happened in relation to this capital expenditure? What steps is Olieux taking to ease the financial strain?

SELF-TEST

1. Profitable businesses can run out of money if they mismanage their
   a. assets.
   b. accounts payable.
   c. working capital.
   d. budgets.

2. Net cash flow is the difference between
   a. cash flow and profit.
   b. cash inflows and outflows.
   c. revenues and expenses.
   d. expenses and profits.

3. Cash budgets *do not* include
   a. payments made to suppliers for raw materials.
   b. payments made to suppliers for merchandise.
   c. cash payments for goods purchased by customers.
   d. charge payments for goods purchased by customers.

4. Accounts receivables represent
   a. the total of customer credit balances.
   b. the balance owed to suppliers.
   c. the value of cash purchases made by customers.
   d. merchandise ordered but not yet received.

5. If you need cash in your business and a number of clients owe you money, you might consider
   a. borrowing from those clients.
   b. factoring those bills.
   c. taking all non-paying customers to court.

6. Among credit-management practices you could adopt for their positive effect on cash flow are *all but*
   a. aging accounts receivable on a monthly or weekly basis to quickly identify delinquent accounts.
   b. employing effective collection methods.
   c. maximizing the time between shipping, invoicing, and sending notices on billings.
   d. reviewing credit experience to identify cash flow blockages.

7. The correct amount of inventory to have on hand is
   a. enough to get you through a full year.
   b. enough to meet last year's sales figures on a month-by-month basis.
   c. enough to meet all customer requests.
   d. enough to maintain production schedules or a pre-determined level of customer service.

8. The two key tools to use in managing accounts payable are
   a. billing and bookkeeping.
   b. negotiation and timing.
   c. cash and credit.
   d. monitoring and paying.

EXTEND WHAT YOU HAVE LEARNED

1. Many of the decisions a manager must make affect the cash position of the business. Suppose you are asked to make the following decisions within the course of the next week. How would your answer be influenced by the company's current and anticipated cash position? Explain.

Decision to be Made	Limited Cash Available		Adedquate Cash Available	
	Approve	Deny	Approve	Deny
Liberalize credit terms for customers from net 30 to net 60				
Take advantage of a cash discount offered by supplier				
Reduce the rate of inventory turnover				
Pay invoices before their due date				
Postpone payment of an invoice until next month even though it means paying a penalty				
Send "past due" notices every 15 days instead of every 30 days				
Stockpile a critical raw material				
Offer deep discounts to customers who buy items in quantity and pay cash				

_____

_____

_____

_____

_____

_____

_____

_____

2. If you are like most small business owners, there are a number of capital expenditures you would like to make. Choose one that seems particularly important to your developing business (or two if you would like to take a comparative look). Try to evaluate the advisability of the investment, using each of the following methods. (If you have a computer program available that will assist you with these calculations, take advantage of the help it can provide.)

    — payback-period method

    — return-on-investment method

    — net-present-value method

    — internal-rate-of-return method

3. Given the varied approaches, how different are your results? Are these methods helpful as decision-making tools? What influence will this activity have on your investment decision?

    _____

    _____

    _____

    _____

    _____

    _____

Lesson 24

Computers in the Small Business

LEARNING OBJECTIVES

Upon completing your study of this lesson, you should be able to:

■ Discuss the ways in which computers can be used to improve small business operations.

■ Identify the kinds of computer technology available to the small business, and determine which would be most appropriate for your new venture.

■ Understand the basics of computer hardware and systems.

■ Explain the purpose of various kinds of computer software, and discuss the types of application software that would be useful to you.

■ Consider the use of computers as a telecommunications tool.

■ Detail the ways in which computer technology can be used to enhance office, production and purchasing productivity.

■ Evaluate the various computer acquisition options, such as service bureaus, time-sharing, leasing, and purchase.

■ Discuss the steps to be taken in "going computer."

In 1990, when executives at Hyundai Motor America equipped their field sales and service force with laptop computers, one regional sales manager said that watching his team learn how to use the microcomputers was "like watching a kid learning how to play his first video game." Sales and service personnel—whether or not they had prior computer experience—took to the new technology like the proverbial duck to water.

That's how it's likely to be for any business that makes the move into the computer age. Although some employees may be reluctant participants, the productivity gains that most businesses experience make the move almost mandatory for companies that want to remain competitive. This lesson will describe standard computer systems and identify the primary uses to which a small business might successfully put computer technology.

OVERVIEW

Any time you encounter a repetitive, time-consuming, or mathematically complicated task in the work environment, and any time you encounter the need to communicate quickly and clearly to staff in remote locations or working at different hours, chances are there's a computer system and software program capable of handling your need. Not just handling it, but doing so faster, more accurately, and more economically than any manual system can.

If it makes sense for kids to learn how to use computers in elementary school, it certainly makes sense for adults in the workplace. Any business owner who expects to *get*—competitive and *stay*—competitive ought to consider the kinds of computer applications that make sense for his or her business, and then decide how to acquire the tools to handle that work. Prices for microcomputer systems—personal computers, including "laptop" or "notebook" portables—have dropped substantially in recent years, enough so that virtually any business can afford some type of computerization. It's unwise to argue simply that computers cost too much; the cost of *not*—computerizing your operations can be far greater in a competitive sense, if not just in a cost-benefit sense.

Delaying the decision because technology is changing so quickly—saying, in effect, "maybe we should wait until the `next generation' of machines is here"—is foolhardy, too. The technology always will be improving; what matters is that you find a system today that meets your current needs, and provides a degree of growing room. In all likelihood, you'll be able to upgrade that system for a number of years to come—keeping up with your needs as well as technological advances. And if you spend your computing dollars wisely, you'll recoup the expense soon enough no matter how much technology might change in the coming years.

The Magic of Computers   Far from being a simple tool for record-keeping or information processing, today's computer can be a key part of the most complex creative operations—and still be within the financial reach of virtually every organization. A wide variety of applications, from computerized design to electronic data interchange to financial planning, is available to every computer user.

In the *financial planning*—arena, a wide range of business and financial transactions can be tracked via computer. Among the most likely uses of computers in this area are:

- order entry and inventory management,

- monitoring of vendor stock availability (using telecommunications systems that connect your computer to your vendors'),

- tracking of accounts receivable and payable,

- payroll administration,

- production of financial statements, such as profit-and-loss statements and balance sheets, and

- doing credit analyses for prospective borrowers.

The *marketing*—function can also be enhanced through computer technology. Computers enable you to personalize your direct-mail appeals, set up a computerized calendar of marketing call-backs, and even tabulate and analyze market research data.

Communication—and *work coordination*—also can be facilitated through the use of computers. A *local area network*—a system that connects employees' computers to other electronic devices and to each others' computers—enables people to share information quickly and easily. And *work group software*—computer programs that help coordinate the work of different employees—make the task simpler yet.

Manufacturing—operations can be streamlined and technologically improved, too. Using *computer-aided design*—(CAD) and *computer-aided manufacturing*—(CAM), companies can simplify the design and production of new goods—and they can do so in a very cost effective manner.

The list goes on and on. Whatever your need, there's probably a way to meet it more economically and more efficiently by computerizing some or all of your operations.

Computers Hardware Computers are, to put it quite simply, machines that follow instructions to process information. Among the tasks computers can take on are recording and classifying data, handling calculations, storing information, and communicating with other computers (to allow *you*—to communicate with other individuals or organizations).

Computers are composed of four primary components: the input device (usually a keyboard); the central processing unit (the computer itself), which processes information; an output device (usually a printer); and storage equipment (hard disks, floppy diskettes, or magnetic disk drives).

Depending on the size of your organization and the complexity of the computing work you want to do, you'll need one of the following:

- *Personal computer (PC)*—Also known as a microcomputer, the PC can be stationary or portable (the terms "laptop" and "notebook" both refer to portable computers). It is designed for use by one individual, but individual PCs can be connected to other similar computers through a *network,*— creating a synergistic benefit that adds value to the microcomputer acquisition.

- *Minicomputer*—A scaled-down version of a mainframe (a large, expensive system that processes massive amounts of information in a relatively short time), the minicomputer is used by organizations that have large-scale computing needs but lack the economic resources to go to mainframe computing. The minicomputer is useful for organizations where multiple computer users need simultaneous access to a common database.

- *Client/Server Model*—A system that divides processing between clients (users working at personal computers to input or access data) and servers (where data is stored). In this model, the user's personal computer runs the application locally. This dramatically improves processing time over having users on "dumb" terminals that have to wait for a host computer that is processing data for a number of users.

Computer Software   On the software side, you'll be acquiring at least two types of software (the computer programs that run your system):

- *System software*—computer programs that control overall computer operations and link your hardware to software applications packages. This software normally comes pre-installed on a new computer.

- *Application software*—there are two classifications of application software: productivity software and customized software. In the productivity category are programs such as word processing, spreadsheets, database management, presentation graphics, desktop publishing, groupware, and project management.

   You may also need one or more of a variety of customized software. These programs allow a computer to perform functions specific to a particular business. Typical customized packages include software for payroll, ordering and billing, accounts receivable, accounts payable, general ledger, inventory management, computer-aided design (CAD), computer-aided manufacturing (CAM), and material requirement planning (MRP).

Communication Between Computers   Not only can computers help you and your employees work together more effectively, they also can help your company interact more effectively with other organizations—not to mention with co-workers based in other locations. Both inter-company and intra-company communications have become far easier and more efficient with the advent of telecommunications—the exchange of data between remote computers. Telecommuting—employees working at home or other decentralized locations—also has been facilitated by telecommunications technology.

To communicate with computers located off-premises, you will need to link your system via telephone lines to those other systems. Among the tools you will use are:

■   A *modem*—(modulate, demodulate), which converts the computer's digitally-stored information into a continuous signal for transmission across telephone lines. The computer on the receiving end uses another modem to convert the signal back to digital form.

■   A *communications control program*—to connect one microcomputer to another via telephone lines. This is the kind of program needed to link your computer to such information services as CompuServe and Prodigy.

■   For linking personal computers, in what is called a *local area network (LAN)*—you'll need a special circuit card called a network card, and one computer in the network to be designated as the file server (to store the programs and the common database).

Telecommunications Applications   Even the smallest businesses can afford the latest wonders of computer technology—such as voice mail, facsimile (fax) communications, electronic data interchange (EDI), and of course, the Internet.

Voice mail—is a computerized system that accepts telephone messages and stores them on a magnetic disk until the recipient plays them back.

Facsimile (fax) machines—allow people to transmit copies of physical documents across a conventional telephone line. A fax modem is a circuit board installed in a personal computer that allows the sender to transfer documents from his or her computer disk directly to another PC equipped with its own fax modem.

Electronic data interchange (EDI)—is the direct electronic transfer of data from one business's computer system to another. EDI can increase a firm's profits by lowering its transaction costs, although it is too costly for most small businesses.

The Internet—a worldwide network that allows users to send and receive information around the globe. The Internet has become a powerful tool for small firms, allowing them access to markets and resources, customers and suppliers, that might otherwise be out of their reach. The Internet provides even the smallest business access to e-mail, the worldwide web, and e-commerce.

- *E-mail* enables users to send messages electronically from their own computer to one or more other computers. It speeds communications and allows people to keep in touch with the office no matter where their work may take them.

- A *Web browser* is the communications software that enables users to access Internet web sites.

- *E-commerce* is conducting business through an electronic network, which put it out of the reach of most small businesses until recently. Many large companies are now moving their electronic data (EDI) business to the Internet, making them accessible to any business with a computer and web browser software. In addition to giving small businesses access to large companies, it enables a small company—by establishing a home page—to create a showcase for their product or service that anyone with a computer and web browser can access.

Intranet—A private communication system within a business that cannot be accessed by outsiders. This is another business application of the Internet and web technology. Businesses use these internal communication networks to maintain product inventories, customer profiles, and policy manuals to name a few examples. These systems enable sales staff, customer representatives, and others to have immediate access to current data, if the system is properly maintained.

Choosing the Right System   The first step in choosing a system is conducting a feasibility study, to determine just how much your business *would*—benefit from computerization. Be sure you *know*—what you want your system to do. Take a close look at the processes that you think would benefit from computerization. Talk to computer systems vendors about those particular applications. They may identify additional uses for your system.

By doing your own investigation, you'll be more certain that you're really buying what you need, and not being sold every bell and whistle in the marketplace. Do a cost-benefit analysis to determine how readily you'll recoup the cost of computerization through improved work processes. Only if your management systems are well thought out will computerization give you an edge.

Once you've decided that you should computerize, you can:

- hire a *service bureau*—(if you have just one or two simple application needs and your staff would require extensive training to do the computer work);

- *lease*—computer equipment (to avoid the initial purchase expense, minimize the impact of technological obsolescence, and gain access to consulting advice; or

- *buy*—computer equipment (to have full control over your system and gain the benefit of tax depreciation for the equipment purchase).

If you decide to buy your system, you should do a lot of looking before you make a purchase decision. Visit other businesses and learn all you can about their systems. Meet with computer vendors and ask them questions—and demand a product demonstration that shows you how a system would do the kind of work you'd need it to do. Even though this kind of investigation takes time—and time is a precious commodity to the small business owner—it will save you time and money in the long run.

When you decide what you want to buy, develop a time-table for every application you plan to use, so you can add computer capability to your organization on a carefully-designed schedule. Unless you're a very small organization, don't try to shift your entire organization to computers at one time.

Your purchase contract should specify in detail exactly what you're buying in the way of equipment, software, training, and follow-up service. The contract should specifically state what the computer system will accomplish for your organization—not just that it will provide you with "computer capability." If you're buying word processing capability, the contract should say so. This applies regardless of the application you're purchasing—spreadsheet, database, accounting, or any combination.

Before the computer system and the software arrive, brief your employees and encourage them to look at computerization as an opportunity to work smarter, not harder.

During the conversion, be sure that individual responsibilities are clearly delineated, that one individual has primary responsibility for the conversion, and that manual systems continue to operate until the last computer "bug" has been exterminated. Then—sit back, take a deep breath, and get ready to enjoy the computer age!

ASSIGNMENTS

■ Before you watch the video program, be sure you've read through the preceding overview, familiarized yourself with the learning objectives for this lesson, and looked at the key terms below. Then read chapter 20 of Longenecker, Moore, and Petty, *Small Business Management*, "Computer-Based Technology for Small Businesses."

■ There is no video program for this lesson. If you would like to know more about the productivity to be gained by the addition of computer applications to the business environment, see if your college has the video series *ComputerWorks*. The introductory program plus programs 1, 4, 7, and 11 from this 16-program series are particularly valuable for the novice.

■ Be sure to evaluate your learning with the self-test.

■ Extend your learning through the applications, exercises or field experiences this lesson offers.

KEY TERMS

Computer	A machine that follows instructions to process information more quickly than humans can.
Computer system	A combination of computer equipment (hardware) and the programs (software) that provide it with instructions.
Microcomputer	Small, single-user computers, including personal computers (PCs) and "laptop" or "notebook" portables.
Minicomputer	Scaled-down versions of mainframe computers, used by organizations with large-scale computing needs but insufficient funding for mainframes.
Network	System that links microcomputers within or between organizations.
Work group software	Computer programs that help coordinate efforts of employees working on a common project.

CAD   Computer-aided design; the use of computers to design products.

CAM   Computer-aided manufacturing; the use of computers to control machines used in a manufacturing process.

CPU   Central processing unit, the "brains" of the computer system, which processes data and instructions.

System software   Software designed to tell the computer how to work.

Application software   Software designed to be used for specific business tasks (word processing, spreadsheet preparation, etc.).

Customized software   Programs designed or adapted for specific uses by specific organizations.

Word processing   Using a computer to produce, edit, and print out text and graphics.

Telecommunications   Exchanging data between remote computers via telephone lines.

E-mail   Electronic mail; sending messages from one computer to another.

Voice mail   Computerized telephone message system.

Desktop publishing   The production of high-quality printed documents on a personal computer.

Facsimile   Fax machine; a device that sends copies of documents over telephone lines.

Service bureau   Computer firm that receives data from business customers, performs the data processing, and returns processed information to customers for a fixed fee.

SELF-TEST

1. The Internet phenomenon has been driven by *all but one* of the following. Which one has not contributed to to its growth?
   a. Faster product development cycles
   b. The availability of satellite signals to transmit data
   c. Growth opportunities created by a global economy
   d. Increasing complexity of projects involving multiple industries

2. A small company with a number of basic computing needs is likely to choose
   a. microcomputers linked by a network.
   b. minicomputers linked by a network.
   c. personal computers.
   d. a service bureau.

3. When choosing a computer system, there is always a trade-off between
   a. speed and size.
   b. speed and throughput.
   c. speed and multitasking capabilities.
   d. speed and cost.

4. Programs that perform specific business processing functions are called
   a. application software.
   b. system software.
   c. operations software.
   d. customized software.

5. To tell your computer how to operate, you use
   a. the operations manual.
   b. application instructions.
   c. system software.
   d. formatting instructions.

6. Identify the system below that utilizes "dumb" terminals, which provide no processing capabilities.
   a. minicomputers
   b. client/server systems
   c. personal computers
   d. all multi-user systems utilize "dumb" terminals.

7. Which of the following is *not* considered productivity software?

   a. word processing programs

   b. desktop publishing

   c. operating system software

   d. database management programs

8. The first step in computerizing a business is

   a. hiring a consultant.

   b. conducting a feasibility study.

   c. determining a purchase plan.

   d. performing an audit.

9. Which of the following is an advantage of using a service bureau?

   a. Quick turnaround time in receiving processed information.

   b. Variable costs.

   c. Availability of a large number of sophisticated application programs.

   d. Avoidance of the need for specialized computer personnel.

EXTEND WHAT YOU HAVE LEARNED

Chances are, your business takes advantage of some form of computerization, like word processing or basic accounting. But if you are a business owner who has held computer technology at arm's length, hesitating for any number of reasons to take the plunge, visit one or two small business operations whose products or services are similar to yours, and see how computerization has affected their businesses. Talk to both managers and employees to find answers to the following:

1. How did you go about identifying productivity needs and tasks that would be assisted by computerization?

   _____

   _____

   _____

2. Did you work with an analyst who had a breadth of knowledge regarding software and hardware options, but who also took the time to learn about your business before providing you with alternatives from which to choose?

_____

_____

_____

3. What kinds of business disruptions did you encounter in the transition to computer technology?

_____

_____

_____

4. How long did the training take? Did most of your employees adapt to the new systems?

_____

_____

_____

5. If the computer system were to be removed tomorrow, and you had the ability to save one program (such as word processing, spreadsheets, database, accounting, graphics, project management, or electronic publishing), what aspect of the system would you choose to save? Why?

_____

_____

_____

6. If you could expand your computer system, what is the next new program or peripheral you would install? Why?

_____

_____

_____

Lesson 25

Risky Business:

Risk Management

LEARNING OBJECTIVES

Upon completing your study of this lesson, you should be able to:

■ Describe the risks that small businesses commonly face within each of the following categories:

   a. property-centered risks

   b. personnel-centered risks

   c. customer-centered risks

■ Define risk management and identify the basic ways in which a small firm can cope with business risks.

■ Recognize the basic principles of a sound insurance program.

■ Indicate the requirements that must be met before an insurance company will underwrite possible losses.

■ Give examples of the variety of insurance classifications and coverages that insurance companies offer to small businesses.

Setting up a business and working to make it succeed are tough jobs. Imagine how devastating it would be to have all your hard work go down the drain because of employee fraud, a customer's lawsuit, or a natural disaster. And imagine how much worse it would be to discover later that you could have prevented the economic impact of that event—if you'd only planned for the possibility.

Learning how to minimize the impact of risk by putting together a solid, balanced risk management program is the focus of this lesson.

OVERVIEW

When we talk about risk, we're talking about any event that would create losses for a business. Those losses might involve assets (inventory, equipment, or cash), employees, damage to the organization's reputation, or a reduction in earning potential that results from another loss. For example, a fire would create an immediate loss to property and inventory, but it would also impair the organization's earning potential by forcing it to close down for a time.

Most risks are insurable, so dealing with them is a matter of deciding what kinds of insurance are needed and calculating how much coverage is appropriate. The most common risks are losses from fires, personal injury, theft, and fraud—all of which are at least partially insurable. Among the risks that may be uninsurable are product obsolescence, competition from former employees, and some "acts of God" for which insurance companies may refuse to offer protection.

In this lesson, we'll talk about risks in three categories: property-centered, personnel-centered, and customer-centered. And we'll consider three ways to deal with risk: by *controlling it* (through maintaining a safe workplace, guarding against fires, etc.), *saving for it* (self-insuring your firm against losses by putting cash aside), or *transferring it* (buying insurance to help recoup any losses you might incur).

Property-centered Risks Most property-centered risks—which include such things as fire, natural disaster, burglary, business swindles, and shoplifting—are insurable. So is the potential business interruption that may follow a fire or natural disaster. But there still are a number of things the business owner can do to minimize the risk of their occurrence. (At least for everything except a natural disaster!)

Beyond buying insurance that covers burglary losses, for example, you might install burglar alarms or hire a private security service.

Protecting against business swindles is largely a matter of personal vigilance—watching out for deals that seem too good to be true, or being careful about buying something (whether it's advertising in a community directory or an equipment-repair service contract) from individuals or organizations you've never heard of.

If you're worried about shoplifting, you can lay out your store to maximize sight lines. Keep small, easily concealed merchandise close to employee work areas, like the cash registers; keep high-priced items in locked display cases or easily-seen areas; monitor your facilities with closed-circuit television; and control access to stockrooms and other key areas. Most important, make it clear to customers—through your signage and your reactions to any shoplifting attempts—that you mean business . . . that shop-lifters *will* be prosecuted. If you make shoplifting hard to do, and convince people that they're likely to be caught and certain to be prosecuted if they do attempt to take anything, you will go a long way toward minimizing the problem.

Personnel-centered Risks When it comes to the people who work for you, you may encounter a number of risks. A lengthy illness or an injury to an employee, whether it's sustained on or off the job, may require the provision of long-term disability or medical benefits. In addition, you may be confronted with instances of employee dishonesty or competition from former employees, or even the death of a key executive. All of these could spell big trouble for your organization.

You'll want to check on the types of insurance that are available to guard against dishonesty (whether it's a case of stealing supplies, equipment, or trade secrets), or competition from a former employee who starts his or her own business or goes to work for a competitor. But you'll have to set up some system safeguards.

Small businesses can fall prey to employee dishonesty just as easily as large firms—in fact, it's probably more likely in small firms because their owners don't take the same precautions as do owners of larger organizations. So be sure to establish controls for inventory, supplies, equipment, and cash— as well as check-writing—to make it more difficult for people to steal from you. Just because you're a small, friendly organization in which people know one another on a first-name basis doesn't mean you will be immune to theft. So make it harder to do, and those who might be tempted to take from you will be less likely to try.

You can insure against the death of a key employee by purchasing life insurance with the company as the beneficiary. The value of such policies should cover the anticipated cost of replacing the person named. But an even better—and less expensive—solution is to begin grooming replacements for every key position. That solution will pay off in another situation, too. If a key executive "jumps ship" to join another firm or go out on her own, your operation won't be disrupted for long.

To make it harder for employees to take the secrets of your success to another organization, you could require each new hire to sign a non-competition or non-disclosure agreement with your organization. Such agreements don't work in every industry, but if they apply to your situation, they're a cost-free form of protection.

Customer-centered Risks Customer-centered risks are generally insurable. They include such situations as on-premises injuries suffered by customers, on- or off-premises injuries that customers claim were caused by your products, and unpaid debts.

Beyond buying liability insurance to guard against on-premises injuries, you should make it a habit to check your facilities regularly for any conditions that might create dangerous situations for your customers. Preventive maintenance is another way to guard against trouble.

In terms of product liability, it's frighteningly easy to find yourself on the receiving end of a lawsuit if your product is involved in a situation in which someone is hurt—even if your product isn't the *cause* of the accident. The arm of the law reaches a long, long way in product liability cases.

Among the protections you can build in to your business practices to help limit your liability are:

- the distribution of complete, precise directions for the use of your products and clear warnings concerning any hazards they might present;

- cautious preparation of any product advertising to ensure it doesn't weaken the instructions or warnings on your products;

- establishment of a solid customer complaint program and a comprehensive disaster plan;

- analysis of all products to decide if any are simply too risky to keep on the market, and product testing to uncover any potential problems;

- thorough employee training, to help your employees guide customers in the proper use of your products; and

- regular review of all legislation and litigation that might affect your business.

In the area of bad debt, the best first step is to set up a careful screening process to use before approving any customer for credit purchases. This may include credit applications, or it may be a simple matter of accepting only bank credit cards (so the risk is assumed by the bank instead of your firm). Whatever form it takes, establish your ground rules and stick to them.

If you do find yourself with a non-paying customer (and maybe that should read *when* rather than *if*), act promptly and firmly to recover the money owed. Be aggressive in your actions, but remain courteous. In cases where it's clear the customer is trying to take the goods without paying for them, turn over the problem to a collection agency or attorney for action. And don't wait too long. If the amount is small or the customer flat broke, you may decide not to bother going after the bad debt. But in most cases, you should make some effort to recover what you're owed.

Buying Insurance   Before you buy insurance of any kind, you should first determine what risks you'd like to cover. You may discover that some risks are too expensive to guard against with insurance—if the risk is very high, the insurance cost will be high, too. Just think about the customers Lloyds of London accepts, and you'll understand the concept completely.

To help you decide which risks to cover with insurance, think about those that would be a major expense if you had to pay for them yourself. If a risk represents a major potential loss, it's one for which you ought to consider buying insurance. (Again, that holds true only if insurance companies will sell the coverage to you for an affordable price.)

When buying insurance, you'll have an array of products from which to choose. You'll certainly want some form of *commercial property coverage* to protect against fire, explosion, vandalism, business interruption, theft, employee dishonesty, and other causes of loss. You'll also need *commercial liability insurance*, which covers both *general liability* (liability to customers injured on your premises or injured off-premises by your products) and *employer's liability or worker's compensation* claims (required in all U.S. states to protect employees). You may want to purchase *surety bonds* if it's important to protect your business against losses caused by the failure of other firms or individuals to fulfill their contracts with your organization. You may need *credit insurance* to protect yourself against bad-debt losses. This form of insurance, however, is available only to manufacturers and wholesalers. And you may want to consider *key person insurance* if it's important to insure the lives of key executives in your organization.

To cut the cost of insurance, it's sometimes possible to join an *insurance cooperative* with other business owners. You can choose to join a *risk-retention group*—an insurance company set up by a group of business owners with similar insurance needs. Or you can opt for a *purchasing group*—in which a group of business owners band together to buy insurance for all members, their objective being to obtain coverage at group, rather than individual, rates.

In considering your application, insurers must be able to verify that:

■   the risk is calculable—they can put a price on it.

■   the risk is one that exists in large numbers—they can amortize the risk over a large number of customers.

■ the property they're insuring has commercial value—they can't insure something for symbolic or sentimental value, only for its value in the marketplace.

■ you have an insurable interest in the property or person being insured—you have a right to be protected against the loss of that property or person.

ASSIGNMENTS

■ Before you watch the video program, be sure you've read through the preceding overview, familiarized yourself with the learning objectives for this lesson, and looked at the key terms below. Then, read chapter 23 of Longenecker, Moore, and Petty, *Small Business Management*, "Risk and Insurance."

■ After completing these tasks, read the video viewing questions and watch the video program for Lesson 25, *Risky Business*.

■ After watching the program, take time to answer the video viewing questions and evaluate your learning with the self-test.

■ Extend your learning through the applications, exercises, or field experiences this lesson offers.

KEY TERMS

Risk   Situation in which you might face negative circumstances; in business, your risks are associated with loss of assets or earning potential.

Risk management   A program to preserve a business's assets and earning power by minimizing the impact of the business's risks.

Self-insurance   When an organization protects itself against potential losses by saving money to cover the cost of risk.

Business interruption insurance Coverage against the cost of having to close down a business operation while still paying salaries, rent, and other ongoing expenses.

Dishonesty insurance	Coverage against the cost of employee dishonesty (fraud, theft, etc.).
Coinsurance clause	Clause in an insurance contract that requires insured to cover a certain percentage of the property value of the property being insured, in exchange for lower rates.
Surety bond	Protection against the failure of another firm or individual to fulfill a contract with the insured company.
Credit insurance	Provides financial protection against bad debt losses.
General liability insurance	A type of commercial liability insurance that covers a business's liability to customers injured on-premises, or injured (on- or off-premises) by the business's products.
Employer's liability insurance	Coverage required in all U.S. states to protect against suits brought by employees who are injured at work.
Workers' compensation insurance	Provides coverage for employees under each state's workers' compensation laws.
Key-person insurance	Life insurance coverage of key members of an organization's management team.
Risk-retention group	Insurance company formed by a group of business owners to pool self-insurance liability funds.
Purchasing group	Group of companies that form a group for the purchase of group liability insurance.

VIDEO VIEWING QUESTIONS

1. List some of the major risks faced by the small business owner that are discussed in the video. Categorize them as market-centered, property-centered, personnel-centered, or customer-centered risks.

2. What recommendations do Chellie Campbell, Gary Goldstick, and Michael Yeargin offer regarding the critical question of how a small business firm can cost effectively manage the risks it faces.

3. What opinions are put forth regarding what is an appropriate insurance program for a small business?

4. How have the three firms profiled in this program—Turbo Tek Industries, Powerhouse Gym, and Sabina's—managed the risks entailed in their specific business situations? Are there other steps you feel they should take to protect themselves?

SELF-TEST

1. Risk management covers
   a. insurable risks.
   b. uninsurable risks.
   c. both insurable and uninsurable risks.

2. An example of an uninsurable business risk is
   a. an earthquake.
   b. a product that doesn't sell well.
   c. a fire.
   d. fraud.

3. Product liability, bad debts, and on-premise injury
   a. property risks.
   b. customer risks.
   c. employee risks.
   d. market risks.

4. An example of a property risk is
   a. when demand for a product declines.
   b. when your store is burglarized.
   c. when a key executive leaves the company with your trade secret.
   d. when a customer slips on your doorstep and hurts his back.

5. Employment contracts are a good way of guarding against
   a. competition from former employees.
   b. pay disputes.
   c. employee fraud.
   d. employee lawsuits.

6. There are three ways to deal with business risks. They are
   a. risk-transfer, replacing, and self-insurance.
   b. replacing, self-insurance, and risk control.
   c. risk-transfer, self-insurance, and risk control.
   d. risk reduction, risk-transfer, and replacing.

7. One of the most important means of transferring business risks is
   a. preventive maintenance.
   b. insurance.
   c. a system of internal checks and balances.
   d. good management.

8. Businesses that need to guard against the cost of frequent acts of vandalism should buy
   a. business interruption insurance.
   b. commercial property insurance.
   c. commercial liability insurance.
   d. surety bonds.

9. To guard against losses associated with bad debts, a business can obtain
   a. surety bonds.
   b. general liability insurance.
   c. dishonesty insurance.
   d. credit insurance.

10. Self-insurance means
   a. owning an insurance company.
   b. owning stock in an insurance company.
   c. planning to have money to cover risk losses.
   d. having coverage on the owner of the business.

EXTEND WHAT YOU HAVE LEARNED

1. Incidences of fraud and embezzlement threaten the stability of any business organization, but they can be particularly devastating for a small firm in which there are close working relationships. Listed below are steps that the small business owner can take to minimize the threat of fraud and embezzlement. Expand on the suggestions listed below, indicating, in each case, the specific actions you might take to lessen your company's vulnerability.

As owner/manager, set a good example.

_____

_____

Establish a climate of accountability.

_____

_____

Maintain an adequate accounting system.

_____

_____

Establish appropriate internal and external controls.

_____

_____

2. Carefully analyze the risks your business faces by filling in the chart that is provided below. Use this as a guide for taking the actions necessary to preserve your company's assets and earning power.

Type of Risk	Degree of Liability for your Company	Preventive/Protective Actions
Property-centered Risks		
Fire hazards		
Natural disasters		
Burglary and swindles		
Shoplifting		
Personnel-centered Risks		
Employee dishonesty		
Death of key executives		
Competition from former employees		
Customer-centered Risks		
Product liability		
On-premises injury to customers		
Bad debts		

Lesson 26

Publish or Perish:
The Sun Publications Story

Running a community newspaper is much like operating a local television station. Just as the station charges nothing to its viewers but instead obtains its revenues by selling ad time, a community newspaper earns its keep by selling ad space rather than charging for subscriptions. (In fact, it's traditionally referred to as a "throwaway" or a "wraparound" because the small amount of news each one contains is simply "wrapped around" all the grocery, department store, and classified ads.) It can be a hard way to go.

Combine that fact with the characteristics of the typical community newspaper owner/editor—often someone who simply loves to write and cares about his or her community, but who possesses little or no formal business education—and you have the ingredients for financial disaster.

In such situations, overcoming a lack of formal finance and managerial training can be the key to editorial success. And that's just what the owners of Kansas City-based Sun Publications have done.

Sun Publications   More than 40 years ago, Stan Rose completed his tour of duty as a sailor on the USS *Idaho*. The University of Missouri Journalism School graduate had spent much of his free time on board the *Idaho* publishing a newspaper to help relieve the monotony for his fellow sailors.

Heading home at war's end, he looked around for work as a print journalist, and found none. So he went to work for a radio station in Emporia, Kansas. One day, he heard about a newspaper that was for sale—a small community publication in a booming new suburb of Kansas City. He and his wife scraped together the cash, and "for a couple thousand dollars, we were newspaper owners."

So began Sun Publications, today a multi-publication community newspaper company whose products serve several distinct local markets in the Kansas City area.

But Sun Publications isn't just Stan and Shirley Rose's story. It's their son's story, as well. Because Steve Rose, now president of Sun Publications, quite literally grew up with the company.

Stan remembers it this way: "When he was a little guy, he'd see me writing columns, and he'd write little books . . . and he'd come over to me and say, 'Do you like it, Dad?', and I said 'Yeah.' He said, 'Is it good enough to publish?' I kind of got an inkling that he was interested. My advice to him," Stan continued, "was to become either a nuclear physicist or a brain surgeon—and it worked."

Steve's recollections aren't far afield: "These newspapers were started in our home so I literally grew up with them. . . . I remember answering the door and taking ads and taking stories from people . . . and watching my father stay up—I don't think I ever saw him go to sleep before two or three o'clock . . . and my mom sold the ads. . . . When I was seven," Steve added, "I remember telling the people next door that I wanted to be in the newspaper business."

And it's good for Sun Publications that he is. For if Stan brought the newspaper to life, infused it with his entrepreneurial spirit and reporter's zeal; Steve has brought the company into the modern business world, struggling to meld the close-knit family atmosphere of a community publication with the hard-nosed realities of publishing in a competitive business environment.

The Financial Challenge   As Stan Rose recalls, he never thought of himself as a businessman. "I wrote well and I was a pretty darn good editor, but ... I had the feeling that I was a lousy businessman."

But a week-long analysis by a management consulting firm told him otherwise. "He stayed a week," Stan recalled, "and when he left, he said, 'You're a better businessman than you think you are, or you wouldn't be in business for 15 or 20 years.'"

But both Stan and Steve knew that even the most successful seat-of-the-pants finance and management style wouldn't suffice in later years as the business continued to grow and competition increased. Gradually, as management control shifted from Stan's entrepreneurial, "do it my way because it's always worked before" style, to Steve's teamwork-and-delegation-oriented leadership philosophy, so shifted the company's approach to financial management.

Steve's Trial by Fire   Just home from Vietnam and back in journalism school at the University of Missouri, Steve quickly found himself trying to complete his education and run the newspaper business after Stan suffered a serious heart attack. "I was 21 years old and I was running ads all across the country trying to find an editor . . . I was really thrown in before I was ready."

Because of Stan's illness, Steve's parents couldn't keep on top of the business. Steve soon discovered that "we had some cash problems—things were COD, and I learned quickly what that meant." So he set out to put the business on more solid financial ground.

"What I had learned," Steve recalled, "I learned from my father. . . . But I also realized that there were some things that neither one of us knew . . . we didn't even have a profit and loss statement when I started!"

That was okay when it was a two-person operation, with Stan heading up editorial and Shirley writing all the checks. But with a larger organization— Sun Publications numbered some 30 people when Steve took over—and with the dispersed decisionmaking that accompanies increased size, something had to change.

The biggest change, Steve reported, was the development of a management team—one that would have the freedom to make its own decisions. "We have a lot of people going in a lot of different directions . . . it's a completely different world."

Among the managers recruited to Sun Publications was a general manager-controller. "We'd done financial analyses before," Steve said, "but she's brought an entirely new perspective into this . . . the details and the kind of analysis, the kinds of comparisons and budgeting we're doing. . . ."

"I never had any training in this area," he said, "but I became an instant accountant. I understand amortization and depreciation. . . . I can talk turkey with just about anybody, because when it's your money and it's your business—by God, you'd *better* understand these things."

Financial Analysis   The financial analysis tools that Sun's new controller brought to the table enable the company to get, as Steve puts it, "a snapshot of where you are—specifically in areas where you are in line or out of line. It's amazing when you go through the process—you think you know where you're spending the money, and there right in front of you . . . suddenly you find . . . my cost of sales is two points higher than it was last year."

It's the "little things" that make the difference, he said. "A little cost per page too much in the composing room, or one percent too much newsprint waste, can cost you hundreds of thousands of dollars."

And it's the human factor. "I think it's easier to make a decision about equipment than it is about people," Steve said. "A good reporter, for example, doesn't necessarily pay for him or herself. You can't quantify that. I expect X amount of sales from a salesman, but do you need that writer or do you not need a writer—when does the quality of the product really suffer? Those are very difficult things to tell."

Formalizing the business has affected people, too. By imposing modern management on a homey, family-run business, the Roses have created a more bottom-line-oriented organization. And that doesn't always sit well with long-time employees.

No longer can the company observe the philosophy, said Steve, that "as long as there's enough . . . to pay the people well and to pay ourselves well, it really didn't matter whether the profit margins could be 30 percent more . . . the competition which we face is much tougher today. . . . If we continue to run that way, the company could be extinct in 10 or 15 years." So salary increases are sometimes smaller—and incentive programs less generous—than they used to be.

Now, he said, management must make decisions "based on actual performance rather than longevity . . . or how we may feel about an individual.... The larger the corporation or the chain, the more apt the evaluation or the analysis is going to be strictly on margins and profits and so on."

Some long-time employees may view this philosophical shift as a violation of a trust, said Steve Rose. But to him, it's "an overdue change that is required. People who really understand the business, understand the environment under which we operate today and who are good at what they do will not be . . . afraid for their own jobs and . . . will understand we did what we had to do."

The Environmental Imperative The business environment in which Sun Publications now finds itself makes those sorts of changes essential. A contracted economy means fewer ads sold, and lower revenues.

Competition from major metropolitan news organizations—which are suddenly discovering the high-readership, high-education-level audiences long considered the private province of local community papers—necessitates more aggressive news coverage and more active ad sales efforts on the part of the community press.

Then, there's the competition for advertising dollars from direct mail and "shoppers" and cable TV sales channels.

And the lower newspaper readership statistics deeply concern publishers like Steve Rose. "What will happen to newspaper readership?" he asked. "Can newspapers change to appeal to current non-readers?"

Somehow, one thinks, Steve Rose will find a way. For, as he put it, he's "not in this for the money. I don't think any entrepreneur is. There's got to be more to it than that—the challenge, the mountain-climbing . . . the thrill of getting there. . . ."

APPLYING THE CONCEPTS FROM LESSONS 22–25

Before you watch the video program for Lesson 26, *Publish or Perish*, review chapters 20–23 and 10 pages 209–219 from chapter 11 in the text. Then answer the following questions:

3. What risks are involved in running a business's finances by the "seat-of-the-pants" approach?

4. How much about accounting and finance should the business owner understand? Why?

5. What risks are involved in paying people as much as possible, without regard to margins or to salaries paid by the competition?

6. When an organization moves toward more formal financial management practices, some "old-timers" may feel threatened. Why? What can be done to ease their concerns?

7. How does a business's external environment affect its financial planning?

8. Can a financially successful business operate without regard for external economic influences? Why or why not?

Lesson 27

For Everybody's Good:
Social Responsibility

LEARNING OBJECTIVES

Upon completing your study of this lesson, you should be able to:

■ Recognize the contributions society expects from privately-owned firms, particularly in relation to their customers, the environment, and public welfare.

■ Describe the kinds of ethical issues that are prevalent in small businesses.

■ Indicate why small firms may be especially vulnerable to pressures to act unethically.

■ Suggest the ways in which a small business can provide leadership in the areas of ethics and social responsibility.

Entrepreneurs from the Milton Friedman school of thought would tell you that a business's only social responsibility lies in making a profit. Business, they argue, owes nothing more to society than that. But many business owners in the United States and around the world look at the issue of social responsibility from a much broader perspective—believing that, while companies must indeed earn a profit, they also must do so responsibly. That belief is at the core of their corporate social responsibility philosophy.

Some of what we'll term "socially responsible" corporate behavior is regulated by public agencies or mandated by law, and some of it is completely voluntary. In this lesson, we'll take a look at both areas.

OVERVIEW

Among the many areas of responsibility for businesses, whether they're large or small, making a profit must come first. A business owner may be the most kind-hearted soul in the universe, but if his business is running in the red, he won't be able to give much back to the community—at least, not for long! So clearly the profit obligation comes first.

The successful operation of a business does more than just enable its owner to give something back to the community. By running a profitable business, the owner can keep people employed, keep suppliers selling, keep tax revenues flowing to government agencies, and keep the local economy on the upswing.

Among the core expectations the public has of business are that it protect the interests of those with whom it deals (suppliers, employees, customers, and the general public), and that it act ethically in all of its business dealings. Those expectations sound simple enough, but living up to them isn't always easy. It takes the right attitude, and a commitment from top management.

It's not necessary to be a Fortune 500 company to give something to your community. The owner of a small public relations agency in Los Angeles found that out when she was approached by a nonprofit arts festival organization that was looking for PR counsel and had been referred to her by one of the major corporations for which she'd worked. The festival had been rebuffed by a number of much larger PR agencies because it lacked the financial resources to cover their overhead, much less enable them to earn a profit.

But business was booming at the small PR firm, and the owner had a special interest in the activities sponsored by the festival. So she decided to provide the festival with the services it needed, donating half of her time—something that none of the larger firms would agree to do.

Her firm took the assignment and helped a nonprofit organization bring the arts to the community (and provide food to the homeless, since the festival's only admission charge is two cans of food per guest!). The owner's justification for giving away some of her time? "I *wanted* to do the job, I *wanted* to help the festival, and I could afford to give them some time. Besides, when you give something, you often get something in return. It may not happen for a while—and it might *never* happen—but much of my business has come through referrals, so this job could do the same thing for me someday. I figured *everyone* could win this way." A long-term perspective and acceptance of the "give and you shall receive" belief are both components of the philosophy of socially-responsible organizations.

You'll see the same sort of thinking in much larger corporations. In another recent development in Los Angeles, a group of executives from major southern California corporations have banded together to establish a nonprofit organization whose sole purpose is to improve the quality of education in Los Angeles area schools.

Why, you ask, should corporations go into the business of education? Because, as the corporate executives put it, they need to be sure that the people who graduate from high school are prepared to go on to college or enter a work environment that grows more technologically demanding with each passing day. And if the public sector can't do the job—or can't afford its cost—the private sector had better do something about it, or it will find itself running its own remedial education classes for new hires. Thus corporations can be socially responsible—an altruistic notion—and do so because it also makes good economic sense.

The final justification for social responsibility lies in its profit potential. If you like the philanthropies to which a company contributes, such as McDonald's "Ronald McDonald House," you're more likely to drive through the golden arches when you're in the market for a fast-food meal. Doing good—in the eyes of your customers—can convince them to buy from you rather than from your competition.

The Environmental Movement It doesn't matter what kind of business you're in—you can contribute to the burgeoning environmental movement. If you manufacture something, you can install the best pollution control equipment, minimize the amount of packaging materials used on your products, and use no Styrofoam in your packages. If your business owns the property on which it sits, you can landscape that property so trees are added to the environment—and you can plan your landscape design to conserve water.

No matter what kind of business you run, you can always participate in recycling and energy conservation efforts. It's as simple as putting more than one trash can in every location, to separate paper, glass, aluminum and plastic items for recycling—and using equipment that is energy-efficient.

The cost of your environmental efforts may have to be passed on to your customers, unless the cost is small enough to be absorbed or the steps you take actually increase profitability. If it is necessary to raise prices and you present your case in a positive manner—and if your customers care about the environment—you may find them willing to spend a bit more to gain the knowledge that they're doing something for the environment in the process. It's all a matter of positioning your organization in a positive way.

Government is beginning to recognize that environmental regulations can sometimes have a disproportionately high economic impact on smaller firms. So the negative impact of environmental regulation may become more evenly weighted between large and small organizations. Small firms must speak out when regulation does affect them more heavily than it does larger firms.

Consumerism and Small Business When it comes to protecting consumers from unfair business practices, the small business has certain advantages over larger organizations. It's easier for small businesses to hear customers, and it's easier for them to adapt their policies to be responsive to customer concerns. When they're dealing with small firms, customers don't have to direct their messages through ten layers of corporate bureaucracy to be heard.

By the same token, it can be harder for small firms to meet customer expectations. In terms of manufacturing, it may be harder to institute the kind of quality control mechanisms that guarantee absolutely safe products. And in any kind of business, it may be harder for the small firm to avoid service blunders, since employee training may not be as comprehensive as it is in larger organizations.

It takes a high degree of concern and commitment from top management—in small organizations as well as large—to ensure that customer concerns are heard, considered, and responded to. This is often a market niche for small business.

Some consumer protection issues are regulated. A host of laws govern everything from deceptive labeling and packaging to product safety and truth-in-advertising. There are truth-in-lending laws, fair credit reporting laws, equal credit opportunity laws, consumer safety laws, investor-protection laws, restaurant sanitation regulations, professional licensing requirements—the list goes on.

No matter which regulations apply to your business, it's important to strive to live up to the spirit of those regulations—and to speak out to government officials when the impact of a proposed regulation will hit harder at small business than at larger organizations. Both efforts are important if you plan to keep your business operating successfully while honoring your ethical commitment to the public you serve.

Ethical Dilemmas No business or industry is immune from ethical challenges. You will always encounter situations in which you may be tempted to sacrifice your principles for economic or personal gain. And only you can decide what to do when those situations arise.

The most obvious area is that of taxation. Many small business owners—pressured by the competitive disadvantages they encounter in butting heads with larger firms—find it tempting to underreport income and overreport expenditures, by "skimming" cash from the business and reporting non-business-related expenses as those for which the business should pay.

If you're ever tempted to play this game, heed this warning from one small business owner who was the subject of a random IRS audit. "I wasn't cheating, but it was still a daunting experience to have to reconstitute an entire year's worth of income and expenses. The way an audit is conducted, the IRS *will* find out if you've been cheating. Let me put it this way—if you don't 'have religion' when you start the audit, you'll be a believer when you're done."

In terms of accounting practices, honesty once again is the best policy. Keeping two sets of books—one for you and one for the accountants—may give you some extra income for a while, but it may also give you a big headache someday. If you're to receive financial advice that will truly help you do a better job of managing your business finances, your financial advisors need to hear the truth.

Another area of concern is marketing—advertising claims, packaging claims, sales contracts, the bid process, and other related activities. Truth-in-advertising laws can hit hard at the company that makes advertising claims that simply don't stand up to scrutiny. Exaggeration can harm your credibility with customers, too, even if your claims aren't outrageous enough to cause someone to sue you for false advertising.

Providing clients with contracts that are easy to read and understand and that clearly spell out all terms and conditions of the purchase is an important practice, too. If you want your business to be known as above-board, fair, and candid; this is one way to reach that goal.

The same thing goes for bid situations. When you're bidding out work or purchases, make sure the bid process is open and impartial. Don't rig the system to give one company the edge—you may find yourself in legal hot water if you do. And even if no one prosecutes, you'll lose credibility, and that could cause you to lose sales.

Internally, you must make management decisions that are fair, honest, and impartial, and you must encourage open two-way communication to allow employees to let you know what *they* think about your decisions. And if you don't like what you hear, don't get mad at the employees—*think* about what they're saying!

In the end, it's up to the business owner to set the tone for each of the many ethical decisions his or her employees will have to make, some of them on a day-to-day basis. As the organization grows, the need for a code of ethics may emerge—but the best thing to do is to set the tone and establish a high standard from day one. Honest and ethical business practices can pay dividends.

ASSIGNMENTS

■ Before you watch the video program, be sure you've read through the preceding overview, familiarized yourself with the learning objectives for this lesson, and looked at the key terms below. Then, read chapter 16 of Longenecker, Moore, and Petty, *Small Business Management*, "Social and Ethical Issues."

■ After completing these tasks, read the video viewing questions and watch the video program for Lesson 27, *For Everybody's Good*.

■ After watching the program, take time to answer the video viewing questions and evaluate your learning with the self-test.

■ Extend your learning through the applications, exercises, or field experiences this lesson offers.

KEY TERMS

Social responsibilities Obligations an organization has to its customers, employees, community members, and to society at large.

Environmentalism Concern for the environment and for the role that individuals and organizations can play in preventing damage to it.

Consumerism Movement whose purpose is to protect consumers from harm, whether that harm evolves out of unfair business practices, unsafe products, or other factors over which businesses have control.

Code of ethics Statement of the principles on which a business organization and its employees will base their business practices.

Skimming Taking some cash from a business without reporting it as income for tax purposes.

Bait advertising Advertising one product at an extremely low price to lure customers to a store and then convincing them they ought to buy a different, more expensive product instead.

VIDEO VIEWING QUESTIONS

1. Are society's expectations regarding the contributions a small business "owes" its community reasonable?

2. Does a small company's responsibility in relation to the environment differ from the large corporation's obligation?

3. Describe the kinds of ethical issues that face the small businessperson. Do the experts that appear on the program feel that a small firm is particularly vulnerable to pressures to act unethically? Why or why not?

4. In what ways can small business provide leadership in the areas of ethics and social responsibility?

5. How does Paul Friedman carry out his commitment to the environment through his business, The Green House?

6. Compare the public benefit activities of Kaleidoscope Kites and Hollywood Little Red School House. What collateral advantages do businesses derive from caring about and contributing to their communities?

SELF-TEST

1. A business's social responsibilities extend to
   a. activities that can be regulated.
   b. voluntary decisions on the part of management.
   c. both regulated and voluntary activities.
   d. only those activities that impact the bottom line.

2. To most respondents, according to the text, an ethical business is one that not only treats customers and employees honestly, but also
   a. contributes to charities.
   b. acts as a good citizen in its community.
   c. provides maximum earnings to stockholders, who can decide what social issues to address.
   d. complies with social responsibilities regulated by law.

3. Meeting environmental responsibilities can be harder for small companies because
   a. they may be less able to absorb or pass on the cost of environmental efforts.
   b. they can't install the same environmental controls as larger companies can.
   c. environmental regulations are different for small companies.
   d. they feel their efforts will have little, if any, impact.

4. When it comes to consumerism, small business
   a. has a harder time meeting consumer expectations because of the costs involved.
   b. can be more flexible in responding to consumer expectations.
   c. always does a better job of producing safe products.
   d. is at a disadvantage because of the excessive regulation created by consumer legislation.

5. Small firms are vulnerable to unethical behavior because
   a. they lack management controls.
   b. their owners aren't aware of the issues involved.
   c. employees of small firms aren't as well trained or educated.
   d. their management often finds itself at a competitive disadvantage with larger firms.

6. The most glaring example of poor ethics practiced by small businesses in general is
   a. lack of pollution controls.
   b. untruthful labeling of products.
   c. lack of loyalty to employees.
   d. fraudulent reporting of income and expenses for income-tax purposes.

7. In a small business, the most important key to ethical performance is
   a. a code of ethics.
   b. the personal integrity of the founder or owner.
   c. a training program based on the code of ethics.
   d. the amount of legislation affecting the organization.

8. A code of ethics
   a. helps members of larger organizations understand the principles on which they should operate.
   b. is a good tool for small-firm management.
   c. is essential for only those companies whose products or services are controversial.
   d. is required for all businesses by the federal government.

EXTEND WHAT YOU HAVE LEARNED

1. Most small business owners are bombarded with opportunities to contribute to their community, from supporting school-related activities to sponsoring local charity events. How can a small businessperson walk the fine line between fulfilling his or her social obligation and jeopardizing the company's productivity and profits? Would you argue that such activities are *always* good business?

    _____

    _____

    _____

    _____

    _____

    _____

2. In a *Wall Street Journal* article entitled "Small Business Jungle," Michael Allen contends that walking the straight and narrow may be more difficult and costly on Main Street than it is on Wall Street. Think of the times, in recent history, when you have observed or been asked to participate in a business activity that bordered on the unethical. How did you justify your involvement . . . or, if you rejected the opportunity, how did you avoid the temptation? What tipped the balance one way or the other? How would you respond to the contention that to be successful, a small business must engage in such practices now and then in order to survive in today's tough business climate?

    _____

    _____

    _____

    _____

    _____

    _____

Lesson 28

It's the Law

LEARNING OBJECTIVES

Upon completing your study of this lesson, you should be able to:

- Recognize the role government regulation plays in the life of a small business.

- List and describe the major regulations that affect small businesses, and the legal agencies that administer these regulations at local, state, and federal levels.

- Describe the ways in which a small business can protect its intangible assets.

- Briefly explain the categories of legal agreements and relationships listed below that are part of most business operations:
  a. contracts
  b. agency relationships
  c. negotiable instruments.

- Discuss key issues concerning the taxation of small business organizations.

You don't have to go to law school to be a business owner—but it's important to understand both your rights and obligations under the law. And you need to know when it's time to call in a lawyer, so you're sure to get professional legal counsel when you need it.

In this final lesson, we'll take a look at the legal rights and regulatory obligations of business owners, and offer a few tips designed to help small business owners protect their legal interests.

OVERVIEW

Any time you enter into a business agreement with someone—whether you're agreeing to hire a new employee, sell something to a customer, or buy something from a supplier—you've entered into a contractual arrangement. Whether or not you sign a piece of paper, a contract exists between your organization and that other firm or individual.

In addition to your contractual obligations, a host of government regulations establish crucial ground rules for the nature and quality of the services or products you offer to your customers or clients. So even if you don't make a specific promise regarding your products or services, the government may require you to live up to the standards it has set for your industry.

Those regulatory requirements cover everything from product pricing (to maintain free competition) to unfair trade practices (bait and switch tactics, preferential discounts, and so on). They protect the consumer from misleading advertising claims, deceptive labeling, unsafe products, and other consumer concerns. They protect securities investors from fraudulent practices, and they promote the general public welfare in the areas of environmental protection and licensing of professionals. Many times these regulations place a particular burden on the small business owner.

So does taxation—the other big load that small business must carry. With federal, state and local governments all claiming their share of the small business' profits, taxation can sometimes become the straw that breaks the camel's back—the expense that makes it impossible for a small business to prosper. So knowledge of all applicable tax laws is crucial to the success of small businesses.

Regulation and Small Businesses Government regulation comes in all shapes and sizes, and much of it impacts American small business. According to one study, the four greatest federal regulatory burdens confronting small business in America today are the 1989 minimum wage increase, the 1990 Americans With Disabilities Act, the 1990 amendments to the Clean Air Act, and the 1991 Civil Rights Act.

Business opposition to, or discomfort with, these regulations is seldom a result of indifference or hostility to the rights of other Americans. Most business owners understand why such measures may be necessary, and most are likely to support them in principle; but for many business owners, these regulations have increased their cost of doing business. And that affects their ability to compete.

Fortunately, the federal government has recognized the disproportionate impact regulation may have on small businesses, and it has passed several acts to help alleviate that impact. They are:

- *The Regulatory Flexibility Act of 1980*, which requires federal agencies to measure the impact of proposed regulations on small business, reduce their paperwork requirements, simplify rules, and exempt small businesses whenever possible.

- *The Paperwork Reduction Act of 1980*, which created the Office of Information and Regulatory Affairs in the Office of Management and Budget. (A 1990 Supreme Court decision reduced this act's power significantly, however.)

- *The Equal Access to Justice Act of 1980*, strengthened in 1985, which requires the federal government to reimburse court costs for small firms that win cases against regulatory agencies.

Regulation and the Marketplace Marketplace regulations have targeted a number of issues over the years, including free competition, consumer protection, investor protection, safeguarding the public welfare, employee protection, and protection of a business' intangible assets. We'll look briefly at the key legal and regulatory actions in each area.

Opening up the marketplace to *free competition* has long been a goal of U.S. legislators, starting with the Sherman Antitrust Act of 1890 and the Clayton Act of 1914. Both measures were designed to promote competition by eliminating artificial trade restraints, and to help small business compete on an even footing with larger enterprises. Although neither guarantees equal opportunity, the two acts have done much to help small businesses in America succeed.

Price discrimination, which once enabled larger companies to outmaneuver smaller firms by obtaining supplies or merchandise at preferential prices, was banned by the Robinson-Patman Act of 1936, an amendment to the Clayton Act.

And the Women's Business Ownership Act of 1988 was created to offer fair opportunities to women business owners to compete in the free enterprise system, and to access capital sources as easily as their male counterparts.

The second key area of marketplace regulation aims at *protecting consumers* from unfair market practices or unsafe products. A number of acts covering consumer protection issues have been passed, among them:

- *The Wheeler-Lea Act of 1938*, which gave the Federal Trade Commission the right to attack unfair or deceptive marketing practices or actions. Its regulations cover labeling, product safety, packaging, product advertising, truth-in-lending, fair credit reporting, equal credit opportunity, and more. Similar laws exist in the states, as well.

■ *The Consumer Product Safety Act of 1972*, which authorized the Consumer Product Safety Commission to set safety standards for toys and other consumer goods and to ban those the CPSC deems unsafe.

■ *The Nutrition Labeling and Education Act of 1990*, which established regulations for listing information about calories, fat, salt and nutrients on food products; and the use of product claims such as "low salt" or "low fat" on those products.

■ *The Telephone Consumer Protection Act of 1991*, which seeks to protect consumers from unethical practices in the telemarketing industry.

In the area of *investor protection*, both federal and state regulations are designed to protect investors from fraudulent schemes for the issuance and public sale of securities. Federal regulations in this area include the Securities Act of 1933 and the Securities Exchange Act of 1934.

Small businesses usually are exempt from SEC regulation, but they are subject to state-by-state *blue-sky laws*, which cover the registration of new securities within the state, as well as the licensing of dealers, brokers or salespeople, and prosecution of those who might engage in the fraudulent sale of stocks and bonds.

Even if you decide to conduct a private offering of your company's stock to raise operating capital, you must observe certain SEC rules. Although private placements are exempt from SEC registration requirements, they still must use a uniform notice of sales form, and they must observe specific rules that apply to offerings of various amounts ($500,000 or less, between $500,000 and $5 million, and over $5 million).

To promote the *public welfare*, myriad laws and regulations have been passed on the local, state and federal levels, covering everything from sanitation in local restaurants to business zoning requirements to environmental protection. Among the major federal regulations in this area are:

■ *The Federal Clean Air Act of 1970* and its 1990 amendments, which set standards for vehicle emission testing, freon removal and other concerns.

■ *The Americans With Disabilities Act of 1990*, which forbids discrimination in the employment of or the provision of service to people with disabilities. Regulations in this act have been tailored to businesses of various sizes, to blunt the economic impact on small business; and some of the costs business must incur to adhere to those regulations are tax-deductible.

In addition, state licensing of specific professions or businesses and state permitting of certain types of companies serve to offer additional safeguards to the public interest.

Employee protection is yet another area of concern in the marketplace. The key federal legislation in this area includes the Age Discrimination Act of 1967, the Occupational Safety and Health Act of 1970, the Civil Rights Act of 1991 (a major amendment of the 1964 act), and the Family and Medical Leave Act of 1993. Again, the government has sought when possible to protect small business from the more economically burdensome regulations included in these acts, by exempting businesses under a certain size (in dollar value or number of employees).

Finally, *protection of a firm's intangible assets* has been safeguarded by regulation in four areas: trademarks, patents, copyrights, and trade dress. These regulations help the business owner protect his or her investment in such things as a product name or logo, a product design or manufacturing process, a creative work, or even the "look" of one's place of business.

To protect your products or their trade name or logo from copycat marketers, you can *trademark* them. Trademarks can be acquired for products, words, figures, or any other symbols of a particular manufacturer or merchant.

Before choosing your trademark, you must conduct a careful search to be sure no one else is using it. Firms that provide trademark search services can help. Once you've determined that the trademark is original, you can claim ownership of it by adding the TM symbol to the item being trademarked, and you can register the trademark with the U.S. Patent and Trademark Office for extra protection. Trademark registration lasts for ten years, and it can be renewed for ten-year periods.

Patents establish the registered right of an inventor to make, use, and sell something he or she has invented. If you want to protect a new process or the function of a new product, you should apply for a utility patent, which is good for 17 years. If you want to protect the appearance of a product as well as all of its components, you should apply for a design patent, which lasts for 14 years. And, if you develop a new plant, there's a specialized plant patent to guard your creation.

The patent application process is long and expensive, and you're wise to retain an experienced patent attorney to guide you through the regulatory maze. And patent infringement suits are costly as well, so work hard to avoid the possibility—and think hard before taking on someone else for patent infringement.

If you're involved in a creative business—writing, composing, graphic design, or the creative arts, for example—you may want to copyright your work, to prevent others from copying it without your permission. The only copying which people may do of copyrighted work is limited copying for research purposes. According to the terms of the Copyright Act of 1976, copyrighted work is protected for the life of its creator plus 50 years. Copyrights are registered in the Copyright Office of the Library of Congress.

Finally, there's the question of trade dress protection—protecting your firm's operating image (the look of its stores, your employees' uniforms, and so on) from copying. Trade dress protection enables you to challenge others who attempt to copy your look so potential customers may think they're buying from you when they're really buying from an imitator.

Business Agreements   Whenever you enter into a business agreement, you must try to ensure its validity. Whether you sign a contract, enter what is called an "agency agreement," or accept a negotiable instrument (a check, promissory note or other instrument) as payment for your products or services, you want to be sure that the agreement can be enforced. Here's how to protect your rights in these areas.

Contracts create mutual legal obligations. In exchange for giving their time to you and performing certain specified tasks, you agree to pay your employees a certain wage. In exchange for providing a product or service to your customers, they agree to pay you a certain price. And, in exchange for supplying raw materials or merchandise to you, you agree to pay your vendors a specified price for their goods. That is, if the contract is valid. In order for a contract to be valid, it must:

- be voluntary on the part of both parties;
- be agreed upon by two parties, both of which are competent (of proper age, not intellectually impaired, etc.) to enter into a contract;
- be legal; and
- offer something of value to the seller.

If the contract is oral, there must be some way to prove its existence—for example, through work records that show a person worked a certain number of hours for a certain number of weeks and was paid a certain amount of money. If that work pattern were established, even if the employer and employee never signed a written contract, it could be argued that a work agreement existed.

There are three situations in which a written contract must be prepared: when a transaction is valued at $500 or more, when it's a real estate transaction, and when the agreement covers a period of one year or more.

If either party to a contract doesn't live up to the terms of that contract, the "injured party"—the one which has met all contract terms—can try to force the issue by asking a court to require performance. The injured part may also cancel the contract or seek money damages in the amount that would have been received had the contract been honored by the other party.

To guard against the non-performance of a contract, you may benefit from one of several forms of protection. If you're repairing something that belongs to someone else, you can use the mechanic's lien, which enables you to place a lien against the property on which you're working, to cover the cost of labor or materials if the property owner fails to pay you. Bulk sales laws prevent business owners who owe money to others from secretly selling the business before paying off their creditors. They are required to notify all creditors in writing of their plans to sell the business, so creditors have an opportunity to claim some of the sale proceeds. But creditors must observe any statute of limitations laws, which set a time limit for them to file claims of non-payment.

Agency relationships—when one person or organization represents another in a business transaction—create some special contract conditions.

If you retain an agent (for example, a real estate broker to sell your business, an attorney to represent your business in a contract negotiation, or a branch office of a CPA firm), that agent must carry out your instructions, act in good faith, and exercise care in discharging its duties on your behalf.

You, in turn, are liable to the third party with which your agency negotiates for the performance of any contracts negotiated on your behalf, and you're liable for any fraud, negligence, or wrongful acts performed by the agent.

Clearly, then, it's important to choose agents carefully, and to give clear, precise instructions to your agent concerning the work you want the agency to do.

You must be equally careful in accepting negotiable instruments rather than cash as payment for goods or services you provide to others. Whether it's a promissory note, a draft, a trade acceptance, or a bank check, your acceptance of the instrument makes you the holder in due course—making it your job to ensure that the instrument is negotiable. To be negotiable, an instrument must:

- have a written, signed, unconditional promise or order to pay;

- indicate the specific amount that is due;

- provide for payment on demand, payment at a definite time, or payment at a determinable time; and

- be payable to the bearer or to the order of a person or organization.

Taxation and the Small Business No one likes paying taxes, but doing so is inherent to good business operation. The best advice you'll ever get in this area: pay all taxes that are required of you, attempt to follow the rules (which can sometimes be nearly impossible to understand), and work with a competent tax professional to make sure you're meeting your tax obligations.

Among the federal taxes for which small businesses are responsible are income tax, self-employment tax (for the sole proprietor), estimated taxes, annual return of income taxes (for partners), Social Security, Medicare (FICA), and unemployment tax (FUTA). Even if your business doesn't show a profit in a given year, you still will be required to meet your tax obligations to the federal government—as well as to any state or local agencies to which you are obligated.

You should learn all you can, too, about the federal income tax regulations that affect small businesses. They cover such issues as the proper accounting period to be reported, acceptable accounting methods, the amortization or deduction of "going into business" costs, property depreciation, and the deduction of business expenses.

A wide variety of software packages, designed for use on personal computers, can help you meet your responsibilities in this area. But the advice and counsel of a qualified tax professional can be invaluable, by protecting you against costly errors or legally damaging omissions.

ASSIGNMENTS

■ Before you watch the video program, be sure you've read through the preceding overview, familiarized yourself with the learning objectives for this lesson, and looked at the key terms below. Then read chapter 26, "Working Within the Law," of Longenecker, Moore, and Petty, *Small Business Management*, 10th edition, which is included as Appendix B of this Telecourse Guide.

■ After completing these tasks, read the video viewing questions and watch the video program for Lesson 28, *It's the Law*.

■ After watching the program, take time to answer the video viewing questions and evaluate your learning with the self-test.

■ Extend your learning through the applications, exercises or field experiences this lesson offers.

KEY TERMS

Blue-sky laws	State laws regulating the sale of securities, designed to protect investors from unethical securities sales practices.
Trademark	Word, figure, or other symbol that identifies a product sold by one merchant or manufacturer; can be protected by trademark registration.
Patent	Registered right of an inventor to make, use and sell an invention.
Utility patent	Patent that covers a new process and the function of a product.
Design patent	Patent that covers the appearance of a product and its parts.
Plant patent	Patent that protects a new, distinct plant variety.
Copyright	Registered right of a creator (writer, composer, designer, or artist) to reproduce, publish, and sell a creative work.
Trade dress	The "look" of a company, one of its intangible assets that is protected by trade dress laws.
Contract	Agreement between two parties in which each party agrees to do something for the other (one party works for the other party, and the second party pays the first for that work).
Statute of frauds	Law which requires a written contract for sales of $500 or more, real estate sales, or agreements that extend for one year or longer.
Mechanic's lien	Lien against property being repaired, to protect repairer against non-payment by the property owner.
Bulk sales laws	Laws which prevent the sale of a company without prior written notification to the company's creditors.

Statute of limitations	Time limitation within which a creditor must make a claim for non-payment.
Agency	Relationship in which one party (the agent) agrees to represent another party in a contractual agreement with a third party.
Negotiable instrument	Credit instrument that can be transferred from one party to another in lieu of cash; it is up to the receiver to ensure that the instrument is negotiable.
Holder in due course	Person or firm that has accepted a negotiable instrument and is responsible for its negotiability.

VIDEO VIEWING QUESTIONS

1. What advice do the experts who appear in this program provide small business owners who are inundated, confused, or frustrated by the maze of governmental regulations that affect their firms?

2. How much must a small business owner really know about business law, particularly contracts, agency relationships, and negotiable instruments?

3. What strategies can a company use to protect itself from legal entanglements?

4. Earl Rider, owner of Rider's Automotive Maintenance, indicates that it's getting more and more difficult to deal with all the regulations imposed upon his business. At what point does the benefit derived from such requirements exact too great a cost in terms of the survival of small automotive service firms?

5. Describe the challenges Jon McLeod faces in keeping his business within legal boundaries. How does his situation compare to that which Rider has encountered?

6. What actions did Irma Pons, owner of Free Bird, Inc., take when she suspected that the papers some of her employees presented to prove their immigrant status were bogus?

SELF-TEST

1. Government regulations
   a. only apply to large businesses.
   b. rarely affect the ways in which a small business operates.
   c. impact small businesses at state, but not federal, levels.
   d. often impose a real hardship on small firms.

2. Which of the following is not an attempt to alleviate the burden of small-business regulation?
   a. Women's Business Ownership Act.
   b. Regulatory Flexibility Act.
   c. Paperwork Reduction Act.
   d. Equal Access to Justice Act.

3. If you verbally agree to hire someone who is 14 years old and lacks a work permit, you haven't entered into a valid contract because
   a. all employees must have work permits.
   b. the contract wasn't written.
   c. the prospective employee wasn't competent to enter into a contract.
   d. work permits are not legally enforceable.

4. If you agree to pay someone $800 to paint your house, your contract with the painter
   a. must include information on the kind of paint to be used.
   b. must be written.
   c. is proof of an agency relationship.
   d. is negotiable.

5. Blue-sky laws
   a. are federal legislation regulating air pollutants.
   b. are state laws regulating air pollutants.
   c. are federal regulations protecting investors from securities fraud.
   d. are state laws protecting investors from securities fraud.

6. A broker who buys stock for you from a company is
   a. your registered representative.
   b. your investment partner.
   c. your agent.
   d. violating securities laws.

7. If you accept a promissory note as a form of payment, you are
   a. the holder in due course.
   b. liable for any losses the payer suffers.
   c. the customer's agent.
   d. not obligated to provide products or services until the note is paid in full.

8. To distinguish a product as one sold by your company exclusively, you should apply for
   a. a product identification permit.
   b. a copyright.
   c. a patent.
   d. a trademark.

9. If you write a song, you can protect it with a
   a. full and complete title.
   b. copyright.
   c. patent.
   d. trademark.

10. Creators of a new process to dry-clean carpeting should protect their interest in the process with a
    a. copyright.
    b. design patent.
    c. utility patent.
    d. process patent.

EXTEND WHAT YOU HAVE LEARNED

The legal questions and problems faced by small businesses cover a broad range of subjects, from contract law to negotiable instruments and agency. Answer the questions below, explaining your decision in each case with information you have gained from this lesson.

1. A local department store offers a name-brand suit for the sale price of $149. A customer calls and asks if the suit is available in size 8 in dark gray. When the clerk finds that the right size and color are available, the customer asks her to set the suit aside. If the color is the right shade of gray, she states, she will take the suit. Does a valid contract exist?

   _____

   _____

   _____

2. A customer tells the owner of an appliance store that he will buy a $595 refrigerator as soon as the model he wants is received from the wholesaler. When the refrigerator arrives a week later, the customer tells the store owner that he has changed his mind, and that the contract was invalid because it was not in writing. Did a valid contract exist according to the law in most states?

_____

_____

_____

3. Jim Spencer, 17 years old, agrees to purchase a $400 shotgun from The Gun Shop. Before making the first payment, he changes his mind. Does a valid contract exist?

_____

_____

_____

4. A prospective entrepreneur, in talking with a realtor and the owner of a business site, agrees to purchase the property for a specified sum. No contract was signed, however. During the next 24 hours, the prospective buyer changes his mind and decides to look for another site. Is he bound by his promise of the previous day?

_____

_____

_____

5. A furniture retailer purchases a shipment of furniture and signs a promissory note which the furniture manufacturer sells to a finance company. The retailer finds the furniture to be defective. Can he decline to pay the note?

_____

_____

_____

6. The owner of a small service business who has been leasing office space finds an ideal location available for purchase. She gives the owner of the site a check for $500 pending the development of a written agreement. Later that day, the property owner receives a higher bid for the property and accepts it. Can the service firm owner force the property owner to sell the site to her?

_____

_____

_____

_____

7. The owner of an accounting service rents an office space consisting of three separate rooms, and proceeds to have an air conditioner and ducts installed. At the expiration of the lease three years later, the landlord objects to the removal of the air-conditioning system. The lease did not address the matter. To whom does the air-conditioning system belong?

_____

_____

_____

_____

Appendix A

The Entrepreneur's Quiz[1]

ANALYSIS

The percentages are the answers to the survey as given by the 2,500 members of CEM.

8. How were your parents employed?
   a. Both worked and were self-employed for most of their working lives. (4%)
   b. Both worked and were self-employed for some part of their working lives. (10%)
   c. One parent was self-employed for most of his or her working life. (36%)
   d. One parent was self-employed at some point in his or her working life. (16%)
   e. Neither parent was ever self-employed. (34%)

   The independent way of life is not so much genetic as it is learned, and the first school for any entrepreneur is the home. More than a third of our respondents came from homes where one parent had been self-employed for most of his or her working life, and two-thirds came from homes where a parent had tried to go it alone in business at least once.

9. Have you ever been fired from a job?
   a. Yes, more than once. (17%)
   b. Yes, once. (34%)
   c. No. (49%)

   This question is tricky because the independent-thinking entrepreneur will very often quit a job instead of waiting around to get fired. However,

1. Copyright © 1983 Joe Mancuso.
   Reprinted with permission of Joseph R. Mancuso, The Center for Entrepreneurial Management Inc., 180 Varick Street—Penthouse, New York, NY 10014, (212) 633-0060.

the dynamics of the situation are the same; the impasse results from the entrepreneur's brashness and his almost compulsive need to be right. Steven Jobs and Steven Wozniak went ahead with Apple Computer when their project was rejected by their respective employers, Atari and Hewlett-Packard. And when Thomas Watson was fired by National Cash Register in 1913, he joined up with the Computer-Tabulating-Recording Company and ran it until a month before his death in 1956. He also changed the company's name to IBM. The need to be right very often turns rejection into courage and courage into authority.

10. Are you an immigrant, or were your parents or grandparents immigrants?

    a. I was born outside of the United States. (7%)

    b. One or both of my parents were born outside of the
        United States. (10%)

    c. At least one of my grandparents was born outside of the
        United States. (36%)

    d. Does not apply. (47%)

America is still the land of opportunity and a hotbed for entrepreneurship. The distanced people who arrive on our shores (and at our airports) every day, be they Cuban, Korean, or Vietnamese, can still turn hard work and enthusiasm into successful business enterprises. Our surveys have shown that, though it is far from a necessary ingredient for entrepreneurship, the need to succeed is often greater among those whose backgrounds contain an extra struggle to fit into society.

11. Your work career has been:

    a. Primarily in small business (under 100 employees). (62%)

    b. Primarily in medium-sized business (100 to 500 employees). (15%)

    c. Primarily in big business (over 500 employees). (23%)

Small business management isn't just a scaled-down version of big business management. The skills needed to run a big business are quite different from those needed to orchestrate an entrepreneurial venture. While the professional manager is skilled at protecting resources, the entrepreneurial manager is skilled at creating them. An entrepreneur is at his best when he can still control all aspects of his company. That's why so many successful entrepreneurs have been kicked out of the top spot when their companies outgrew their talents. Of course, this isn't always a tragedy. For many, it offers the opportunity (and the capital) to start all over again.

12. Did you operate any businesses before you were twenty?
    a. Many. (24%)
    b. A few. (49%)
    c. None. (27%)

The enterprising adult first appears as the enterprising child. Coin and stamp collecting, mowing lawns, shoveling snow, promoting dances and rock concerts, are all common examples of early business ventures. The paper route of today could be the Federal Express of tomorrow.

13. What is your present age?
    a. 21–30. (18%)
    b. 31–40. (38%)
    c. 41–50 (26%)
    d. 51 or over. (18%)

The average age of entrepreneurs has been steadily shifting downward since the late '50s and early '60s, when it was found to be between 40 and 45. Our data puts the highest concentration of entrepreneurs in their thirties, but people like Jobs and Wozniak of Apple Computer, Ed DeCastro and Herb Richman of Data General, and Fred Smith of Federal Express all got their businesses off the ground while they were still in their twenties. We look for the average age to stabilize right around 30.

14. You are the _____ child in the family.
    a. Oldest. (59%)
    b. Middle. (19%)
    c. Youngest. (19%)
    d. Other. (3%)

There is no doubt about this answer. All studies agree that entrepreneurs are most commonly the oldest children in their families. With an average of 2.5 children per American family, the chances of being a first child are about 40%. However, entrepreneurs tend to be the oldest children nearly 60% of the time.

15. You are:
    a. Married. (76%)
    b. Divorced. (14%)
    c. Single. (10%)

Our research concluded that the vast majority of entrepreneurs are married. But then, most men in their 30s are married, so this alone is not a significant finding. However, follow-up studies showed that most successful entrepreneurs have exceptionally supportive wives.(While our results do not provide conclusive results on female entrepreneurs, we suspect that their husbands would have to be doubly supportive.) A supportive mate provides the love and stability necessary to balance the insecurity and stress of the job. A strained marriage, the pressures of a divorce, or a strained love life will simply add too much pressure to an already strained business life.

16. Your highest level of formal education is:
    a. Some high school.   (1%)
    b. High school diploma.   (17%)
    c. Bachelor's degree.   (43%)
    d. Master's degree.   (30%)
    e. Doctor's degree.   (9%)

The question of formal education among entrepreneurs has always been controversial. Studies in the '50s and '60s showed that many entrepreneurs had failed to finish high school, let alone college. W.Clement Stone is the classic example. And Polaroid's founder, Edwin Land, has long typified the "entrepreneur in a hurry" who concludes that the most common educational level achieved by entrepreneurs is the bachelor's degree, and the trend seems headed toward the MBA. Just the same, few entrepreneurs have the time or the patience to earn a doctorate. Notable exceptions include Robert Noyce and Gordon Moore of Intel, An Wang of Wang Laboratories, and Robert Collings of Data Terminal Systems.

17. What is your primary motivation in starting a business?
    a. To make money.   (34%)
    b. I don't like working for someone else.   (56%)
    c. To be famous.   (4%)
    d. As an outlet for excess energy.   (6%)

The answer here is pretty conclusive. Entrepreneurs don't like working for anyone but themselves. While money is always a consideration, there are easier ways to make money than by going it alone. More often than not, money is a byproduct (albeit a welcome one) of an entrepreneur's motivation rather than the motivation itself.

18. Your relationship to the parent who provided most of the family's income was:
    a. Strained.   (29%)
    b. Comfortable.   (53%)
    c. Competitive.   (9%)
    d. Non-existent.   (9%)

These results really surprised us because past studies, including our own, have always emphasized the strained or competitive relationship between the entrepreneur and the income-producing parent (usually the father). The entrepreneur has traditionally been out to "pick up the pieces" for the family, or to "show the old man," while at the same time, always seeking his grudging praise. However, our latest results show that half of the entrepreneurs we questioned had what they considered comfortable relationships with the income-producing parent. How do we explain this shift? To a large extent, we think it's directly related to the changing ages and educational backgrounds of the new entrepreneurs. The new entrepreneurs are children of the fifties and sixties, not children of the Depression. In most cases they've been afforded the luxury of a college education, not forced to drop out of high school to help support the family. We think that the entrepreneur's innate independence has not come into such dramatic conflict with the father as it might have in the past. We still feel that a strained or competitive relationship best fits the entrepreneurial profile, although the nature of this relationship is no longer so black and white.

19. If you could choose between working hard and working smart, you would:
    a. Work hard. (0%)
    b. Work smart. (47%)
    c. Both. (53%)

The difference between the hard worker and the smart worker is the difference between the hired hand and the boss. What's more, the entrepreneur usually enjoys what he's doing so much that he rarely notices how hard he's really working.

20. On whom do you rely for critical management advice?
    a. Internal management teams. (13%)
    b. External management professionals. (43%)
    c. External financial professionals. (15%)
    d. No one except myself. (29%)

Entrepreneurs seldom rely on internal people for major policy decisions because employees very often have pet projects to protect or personal axes to grind. What's more, internal management people will seldom offer conflicting opinions on big decisions, and in the end the entrepreneur makes the decision on his own.

Outside financial sources are also infrequent sounding boards when it comes to big decisions because they simply lack the imagination that characterizes most entrepreneurs. The most notable ambition of most bankers and accountants is to maintain the status quo.

When it comes to really critical decisions, entrepreneurs most often rely on outside management consultants and other entrepreneurs. In fact, our follow-up work has shown that outside management professionals have played a role in *every* successful business we've studied, which wasn't the case when it came to unsuccessful ventures.

21. If you were at the racetrack, which of these would you bet on?
    a. The daily double—a chance to make a killing. (22%)
    b. a 10-to-one shot. (23%)
    c. A 3-to-1 shot. (40%)
    d. The 2-to-1 favorite. (15%)

Contrary to popular belief, entrepreneurs are not high risk takers. They tend to set realistic goals. While they do take risks, these are usually calculated risks. They know their limits, but are willing to bet on their skills. For instance, they'll seldom buy lottery tickets or bet on spectator sports, but they are not reluctant to gamble on games involving their own skills such as tennis or golf.

22. The only ingredient that is both necessary and sufficient for starting a business is:
    a. Money. (3%)
    b. Customers. (44%)
    c. An idea or product. (25%)
    d. Motivation and hard work. (28%)

All businesses begin with orders and orders can only come from customers. You might think you're in business when you've developed a prototype, or after you've raised capital, but bankers and venture capitalists only buy potential. It takes customers to buy a product.

23. If you were an advanced tennis player and had a chance to play a top pro like Jimmy Connors, you would:
    a. Turn it down because he could easily beat you. (4%)
    b. Accept the challenge, but not bet any money on it. (78%)
    c. Bet a week's pay that you would win. (14%)
    d. Get odds, bet a fortune, and try for an upset. (4%)

This question narrows the focus on the risk-taking concept and the results emphasize what we have already stated: entrepreneurs are not high rollers. What is interesting about this response is that more than three-quarters of our respondents would accept the challenge, not so much on the off-chance of winning, but for the experience, and experience is what entrepreneurs parlay into success.

24. You tend to "fall in love" too quickly with:
    a.   New product ideas.   (40%)
    b.   New employees.   (10%)
    c.   New manufacturing ideas.   (4%)
    d.   New financial plans.   (13%)
    e.   All of the above.   (33%)

One of the biggest weaknesses that entrepreneurs face is their tendency to "fall in love" too easily. They go wild over new employees, products, suppliers, machines, methods, and financial plans. Anything new excites them. But these "love affairs" usually don't last long; many of them are over almost as suddenly as they begin. The problem is that during these affairs, entrepreneurs can quite easily alienate their staffs, become stubborn about listening to opposing views, and lose their objectivity.

25. Which of the following personality types is best suited to be your right-hand person?
    a.   Bright and energetic.   (81%)
    b.   Bright and lazy.   (19%)
    c.   Dumb and energetic.   (0%)

The best answer isn't always the right answer. "Bright and energetic" is the best answer, but "bright and lazy" is the right answer. But why is that and why do entrepreneurs consistently answer this question wrong? Because the natural inclination is to choose "bright and energetic" because that describes a personality like your own. But stop and think a minute. You're the boss. Would you be happy, or for that matter efficient, as someone else's right-hand man? Probably not. And you don't want to hire an entrepreneur to do a hired hand's job.

That's why the "bright and lazy" personality makes the best assistant. He's not out to prove himself, so he won't be butting heads with the entrepreneur at every turn. And while he's relieved at not having to make critical decisions, he's a whiz when it comes to implementing them. Why? Because, unlike the entrepreneur, he's good at delegating responsibilities. Getting other people to do the work for him is his specialty!

26. You accomplish tasks better because:
    a.   You are always on time.   (24%)
    b.   You are super-organized.   (46%)
    c.   You keep good records.   (32%)

Organization is the key to an entrepreneur's success. This is the fundamental principle on which all entrepreneurial ventures are based. Without it, no other principles matter. Organizational systems may differ, but you'll never find an entrepreneur who's without one. Some keep lists on their desks, always crossing things off from the top and adding to the bottom. Others keep notecards, keeping a file in their jacket pockets. And still others will keep notes on scraps of paper, shuffling them from pocket to pocket in an elaborate filing and priority system. But it doesn't matter how you do it, just as long as it works.

27. You hate to discuss:
    a. Problems involving employees. (37%)
    b. Signing expense accounts. (52%)
    c. New management practices. (8%)
    d. The future of the business. (3%)

The only thing an entrepreneur likes less than discussing employee problems is discussing petty cash slips and expense accounts. Solving problems is what an entrepreneur does best, but problems involving employees seldom require his intervention, so discussing them is just an irritating distraction. Expense accounts are even worse. What an entrepreneur wants to know is how much his sales people are selling, not how much they're padding their expense accounts. Unless it's a matter of outright theft, the sales manager should be able to handle it.

28. Given a choice, you would prefer:
    a. Rolling dice with a 1-in-3 chance of winning. (8%)
    b. Working on a problem with a 1-in-3 chance of solving it in the allocated time. (92%)

Entrepreneurs are participants, not observers; players, not fans. And to be an entrepreneur is to be an optimist; to believe, that with the right amount of time and the right amount of money, you can do anything. Of course, chance plays a part in anyone's career—being in the right place at the right time; but entrepreneurs have a tendency to make their own choices.

29. If you could choose between the following competitive professions, it would be:
    a. Professional golf. (15%)
    b. Sales. (56%)
    c. Personnel counseling. (8%)
    d. Teaching. (21%)

Sales give instant feedback on your performance; it's the easiest job of all for measuring success. How does a personnel counselor or a teacher ever know if he's winning or losing? Entrepreneurs need immediate feedback and are always capable of adjusting their strategies in order to win.

30. If you had to choose between working with a partner who is a close friend, and working with a stranger who is an expert in your field, you would choose:
    a. The close friend. (13%)
    b. The expert. (87%)

    While friends are important, solving problems is clearly more important. Oftentimes the best thing an entrepreneur can do for a friendship is to spare it the extra strain of a working relationship.

31. You enjoy being with people:
    a. When you have something meaningful to do. (32%)
    b. When you can do something new and different. (25%)
    c. Even when you have nothing planned. (43%)

    Contrary to popular belief, entrepreneurs are not bores. They enjoy people and they enjoy being with people. They're extroverts—doers. To the entrepreneur there is no such thing as "nothing to do," so not having plans doesn't mean not having anything to do.

32. In business situations that demand action, clarifying who is in charge will help produce results.
    a. Agree. (66%)
    b. Agree, with reservations. (27%)
    c. Disagree. (7%)

    Everyone knows that a camel is a horse that was designed by a committee, and unless it's clear that one person is in charge, decisions are bound to suffer with a committee mentality.

33. In playing a competitive game, you are concerned with:
    a. How well you play. (19%)
    b. Winning or losing. (10%)
    c. Both of the above. (66%)
    d. Neither of the above. (5%)

    Vince Lombardi is famous for saying, "Winning isn't everything, it's the only thing." But a lesser known quote of his is closer to the entrepreneur's philosophy. Looking back at a season, Lombardi was hard to remark, "We didn't lose any games last season, we just ran out of time twice."

    Entrepreneuring is a competitive game and an entrepreneur has to be prepared to run out of time occasionally. Walt Disney, Henry Ford, and Milton Hershey all experienced bankruptcy before experiencing success. The right answer to this question is *c*, but the best answer is the game itself.

YOUR ENTREPRENEURIAL PROFILE

235 – 285	Successful Entrepreneur*
200 – 234	Entrepreneur
185 – 199	Latent Entrepreneur
170 – 184	Potential Entrepreneur
155 – 169	Borderline Entrepreneur
Below 154	Hired Hand

*The average CEM member profile is 239.

Appendix B

Chapter 26

Working Within the Law[1]

After studying this chapter, you should be able to:

1. Discuss the regulatory environment within which small firms must operate.
2. Describe how the legal system protects the marketplace.
3. Explain the importance of making sound legal agreements with other parties.
4. Point out several issues related to federal income taxation.

Chapter 25 presented several social and ethical issues confronting small firms and discussed how small businesses might deal with these challenges. However, observance of social responsibilities and ethical standards is not left entirely to the discretion of those in business. Federal laws, as well as state laws and local ordinances, regulate business activity in the public interest. Therefore, this chapter examines the legal framework of regulation within which business firms operate.

GOVERNMENT REGULATION AND SMALL BUSINESS OPPORTUNITY

Not all entrepreneurs can or want to be lawyers. Nevertheless, they must have some knowledge of the law in order to appreciate how the legal system safeguards the marketplace and to make wise business decisions.

---

1. This is a text-only excerpt from Chapter 26 of *Small Business Management*, 10th Edition by Longenecker, Moore, and Petty, published by South-Western College Publishing of Cincinnati, Ohio, copyright © 1997. Used with permission of the publisher.

The Burden of Regulation Government regulation has grown to the point at which it imposes a real hardship on small firms, both domestically and abroad. To some extent, problems arise from the seemingly inevitable red tape and bureaucratic procedures of governments. However, the sheer magnitude of regulation is a major problem.

An interesting perspective on the situation is offered by a recent president of the National Federation of Independent Business in the introduction to a book entitled *Small Business Under Siege*:

> *In America, the growing belief in a government fix for every problem is leading quickly to a system in which individuals who have never started or run a business are issuing regulation after regulation telling small business owners whom they can hire and what they must be paid. These same elected officials and bureaucrats—most of whom have never met a payroll—are piling on mandatory employee benefits, employment guidelines, workplace regulations and compliance paper-work overload.*
>
> *This belief in a government fix for every problem has created a web of regulations and accompanying regulatory bureaucracy which often frightens the owners of even the fairest, safest and healthiest work-places. It has created a system that can destroy jobs and family businesses in order to save drainage ditches and obscure fish.*
>
> *This belief in a government fix for every problem has led us to a society in which the majority of American people, when asked, say without considering the broader implications that, yes, the government should require employers to provide this or that new benefit. (The misinformed assumption, of course, is that employers can provide these benefits with no impact on jobs or the salaries of current employees.)*
>
> *In the end, this belief in a government fix for every problem is leading our nation to the ultimate choice between government dictates and the free market.*[2]

The results of two recent studies point out the strong feelings of small business owners regarding government regulations:

> *[The] 1993 Survey of Mid-Sized Businesses by National Small Business United (NSBU) and the Arthur Andersen Enterprise Group shows busi-*

---

2. Jack Faris, ed., *Small Business Under Siege* (Nashville, TN: Hammock Publishing, 1994), pp.4–5.

ness owners rank regulatory burdens and federal taxes third and fourth out of the 10 biggest challenges to future growth.[3]

In a 1993 survey of 250 midsized manufacturers, Chicago-based Grant Thornton Accountants and Management Consultants found that 81 percent listed "reduced regulation" as the change that would be most beneficial to their companies.[4]

Another study published in *Small Business Reports* found that from 1989 to 1992 the government tax and regulatory burden per worker increased 34 percent while the business profit per worker declined 22 percent. The authors of this study name four specific regulations as the major contributors to the increased burden: the 1989 minimum-wage increase, the 1990 Americans with Disabilities Act, the 1990 amendments to the Clean Air Act, and the 1991 Civil Rights Act. The study concluded, "Federal government policies since 1989 amount to nothing less than economic crib death, suffocating jobs in the cradle of small business."[5] Other spokespersons for small business agree with this assessment. "The current level of regulation is so high, and so complicated, and so intrusive that it's strangling business and suppressing productivity," according to Brink Lindsey, director of regulatory studies for the Cato Institute in Washington, D.C.[6]

Thomas D. Hopkins, of the Rochester Institute of Technology in Rochester, New York, estimates that in 1991 federal regulations cost taxpayers over $400 billion—more than $4,200 per household.[7] Since regulation also occurs at state and local levels, the total cost of regulation is even greater than this figure suggests. Regulatory costs at the state and local levels are virtually impossible to estimate. Nevertheless, it is important to recognize that states are extremely active in establishing regulatory policies.

Another burden imposed on small businesses by the government is taxes. Taxes have a direct impact on small business cash flow and, therefore, represent a costly drain on the financial health of small firms. The federal income tax is the most publicized, but certainly not the only tax facing small firms. States raise funds from citizens and businesses through the use of state income taxes, sales taxes, and other forms of revenue production.

3. Erika Kotite, "Call to Action," *Entrepreneur*, Vol. 22, No. 7 (July 1994), p. 95.
4. Jane Easter Bahls, "Seeing Red," *Entrepreneur*, Vol. 22, No. 6 (June 1994), p. 106.
5. Reported in "Crippling Regulations," *Small Business Reports*, Vol. 18, No. 4 (April 1993), p. 5.
6. David Warner, "Regulations' Staggering Costs," *Small Business Reports*, Vol. 80, No. 6 (June 1992), p. 50.
7. David Warner, "How Do Federal Rules Affect You?" *Nation's Business*, Vol. 80, No. 5 (May 1992), p. 56.

A small firm must work within state laws if it is to avoid legal problems. Major differences among state regulations compound the difficulty of this task. Consider the following state sales tax rules:

Tennessee imposes a sales tax on mandatory tips added to a customer's bill. Minnesota taxes the preparation of a floral arrangement by a florist or nursery. Maryland now applies its sales tax to cellular telephones, telephone answering machines, pay-per-view television, newspapers, and prescribed cat and dog food; Missouri considers trophy fees charged to guests at a wild game ranch taxable, and North Carolina deems water- treatment equipment subject to sales tax.[8]

It is difficult for an entrepreneur to stay abreast of state laws. Fortunately, state chambers of commerce are able to provide small firms with regulatory information. The U.S. Chamber of Commerce offers a publication entitled *Staff Directory—State Chambers of Commerce and Associations of Commerce and Industry,* which provides the addresses of all state chambers of commerce. Also, the newly formed National Resource Center for State Laws and Regulations has a 50-state network to help firms respond to proposed new taxes, laws, and regulations.

One strategy to escape the burden of regulation is to stay small, since very small firms are frequently exempt from regulations. However, the fact that our system of laws and regulations restricts business growth seems anti-American to many observers.

Not all laws are detrimental to small business. We will now briefly examine some of the beneficial aspects of regulation.

Benefits from Regulations   Regulation of small business activity is not all bad. A business world without some degree of regulation would surely be chaotic, and some degree of regulation is of general social value. Therefore, small firms should recognize the value of regulatory policies and show some willingness to shoulder the burden. Eugene Kimmelman, legislative director of the Consumer Federation of America, says, "It's hypocritical for small business to seek tax relief and loans from the government to boost their position in the marketplace and then to decry any costs imposed on them to protect the health, safety, and other needs of their employees and customers."[9]

Some entrepreneurs acknowledge that government regulation can occasionally create profit-making opportunities. New regulations sometimes

8.   Timothy D. Schellhardt, "Tax Changes by States Vex Small Concerns," *The Wall Street Journal,* June 17, 1992, p. B2.
9.   Jeanne Saddler, "Small Businesses Complain That Jungle of Regulations Threatens Their Futures," *The Wall Street Journal,* June 11, 1992, p. B1.

spawn a market niche for a new product. For example, when the Environmental Protection Agency announced standards for automobile replacement-market catalytic converters, Perfection Automotive Products, in Livonia, Michigan, saw an opportunity to expand its product mix. Perfection's management says, "The new legislation created a market for replacement models that could be made more cheaply because they wouldn't have to last as long in aging vehicles.... [The company's sales have] significantly increased because of the catalytic-converter market."[10]

Finally, consider the new service of Clean Duds franchisees, which are actively pursuing new clients after the Occupational Safety and Health Administration issued a new rule requiring medical professionals to clean their uniforms more thoroughly. Under the rule, dental and medical offices, blood banks, ambulance services, mortuaries, and other similar businesses must clean apparel that could transmit blood-borne diseases. Philip Akin, CEO of Clean Duds, says the new business has been extremely profitable.[11]

Very small firms may find that they are exempt from some regulations—a situation that creates a favorable competitive situation for them. (Recall the strategy of the firm featured in this chapter's opening.) However, size requirements to qualify for exempt status vary from law to law.

Government Reaction to Regulatory Criticism   Recognition of the burdensome nature of small business regulation at the federal level has led to a number of legislative attempts to alleviate the problem. The **Regulatory Flexibility Act** of 1980, for example, requires federal agencies to assess the impact of proposed regulations on small businesses. These agencies are required to reduce paperwork requirements and to exempt small firms or simplify rules whenever possible. Somewhat similar legislation was enacted with the **Paperwork Reduction Act** of 1980. This act created the Office of Information and Regulatory Affairs (OIRA), which is overseen by the Office of Management and Budget. Unfortunately, in 1990, a U.S. Supreme Court decision drastically reduced the power of the act.

Another law recognizing the regulatory plight of small firms is the **Equal Access to Justice Act** of 1980. Strengthened in 1985, this law mandates the federal government to reimburse court costs to small firms that win cases against regulatory agencies. Incorporated and unincorporated businesses, partnerships, and organizations having a net worth of less than $7 million are eligible for recovery of attorneys' fees.

---

10. Jeffrey A. Tannenbaum, "Government Red Tape Puts Entrepreneurs in the Black," *The Wall Street Journal*, June 12, 1992, p. B2.
11. Michael Selz, "Medical-Apparel Rule is Boon for Laundries," *The Wall Street Journal*, August 14, 1992, p. B1.

The immediate concern for small businesses is knowing what laws they must obey and how they can operate within these laws. Therefore, the remaining sections of this chapter cover laws that influence small business operations. Although only a sampling of laws and legal issues is possible in a single chapter, we have attempted to include both old and new legislation that impact small businesses.

Figure 26-1 summarizes the legal issues selected for inclusion here. The regulatory areas are represented symbolically as hurdles facing the five entrepreneurs as they run the business race. Also, note that the starter—representing federal, state, and local regulatory agencies—is on the sidelines watching the race to be sure it is run legally. Although regulatory agencies are not discussed specifically in this chapter, they are important to a small firm's efforts to function within the law.

GOVERNMENT REGULATION AND PROTECTION OF THE MARKETPLACE

The types of regulation are endless, affecting the ways in which small firms pay their employees, advertise, bid on contracts, dispose of waste, promote safety, and care for the public welfare. Of necessity, the discussion here will be limited to a few key areas of regulation.

This section emphasizes broad areas of government regulation of the marketplace—regulation of competition, protection of consumers, protection of investors, and promotion of public welfare—and includes discussions concerning regulation of employee rights and protection of a firm's intangible assets. The last two sections of the chapter look at business agreements and the issue of taxation. Because government regulation can be overwhelming, all small firms should seek guidance through the regulatory maze from professional legal counsel.

Regulation of Competition   A fully competitive economic system presumably benefits consumers, who can buy products and services from those firms that best satisfy their needs. Of the various laws intended to maintain a competitive economy, perhaps the best known are the federal antitrust laws, especially the Sherman Antitrust Act of 1890 and the Clayton Act of 1914. Both acts were designed to promote competition by eliminating artificial restraints on trade.

Although the purpose of federal and state antitrust laws is noble, the results leave much to be desired. One would be naive to think that small business need no longer fear the power of oligopolists that would control markets.

Antitrust laws prevent some mergers and eliminate some unfair practices, but giant business firms continue to dominate many industries.

To some extent, at least, antitrust laws offer protection to small firms. The Robinson-Patman Act of 1936, an amendment to the Clayton Act, prohibits price discrimination by manufacturers and wholesalers in dealing with other business firms. In particular, the law is designed to protect independent retailers and wholesalers in competition with large chains. Quantity discounts may still be offered to large buyers, but the amount of the discounts must be justified financially by the seller on the basis of actual costs. Vendors are also forbidden to grant disproportionate advertising allowances to large retailers. The objective of this act is to prevent large purchasers from obtaining unreasonable discounts and other concessions merely because of their superior size and bargaining power.

The effectiveness of the Robinson-Patman Act and its benefits to small businesses have been debated. Some experts have argued that it discourages both large and small firms from cutting prices. Others say that this act makes it harder to expand into new markets and to pass on to customers the cost savings on large orders.

Since women-owned business firms have become a growing part of the economy, the federal government has recognized the possibility of discriminatory barriers. Therefore, Congress has created legislation such as the **Women's Business Ownership Act** of 1988 to encourage fair opportunities for women owners in the free enterprise system. Programs initiated under the authority of this act are intended to promote the interests of women-owned small businesses, in part by removing discriminatory barriers to obtaining capital.

The **Foreign Corrupt Practices Act** and later amendments to the act impact competitive practices internationally by restricting payments to foreign officials that may be interpreted as bribes. Some argue that this act places U.S. entrepreneurs at a disadvantage.

Protection of Consumers Consumers benefit indirectly from the freedom of competition provided by the laws just discussed. In addition, consumers are given various forms of more direct protection by federal, state, and local legislation.

The Wheeler-Lea Act of 1938 gave the Federal Trade Commission (FTC) a broad mandate to attack unfair or deceptive practices in commerce. The FTC's original focus on antitrust practices has been expanded through the years to cover a wide range of business activities: labeling, safety, packaging, and advertising of products; truth-in-lending; fair credit reporting; equal credit opportunity; and many others. States have also enacted laws and created consumer protection agencies to deal with unfair or deceptive practices. A few examples of the types of trade practices scrutinized by the Federal Trade Commission are the labeling of goods as "free" or "handmade," misleading advertising that offers "bargains" by pretending to reduce unused regular prices, and bait and switch advertising.

The passage of the **Telephone Consumer Protection Act** in 1991 was another effort to protect consumers. The problem addressed by this legislation is unrestricted telemarketing, which many individuals feel is an invasion of privacy. The act places restrictions on the use of automated telephone equipment in telemarketing.

The **Nutrition Labeling and Education Act** of 1990 is an example of federal labeling regulation. Every food product covered by the law must have a standard nutrition label, listing the amounts of calories, fat, salt, and nutrients. The law also addresses the veracity of advertising claims such as "low salt" or "fiber prevents cancer." Some experts estimate the labeling costs at thousands of dollars per product.

As still another measure to protect the public against unreasonable risk of injury, the federal government enacted the Consumer Product Safety Act of 1972. This act created the Consumer Product Safety Commission to set safety standards for toys and other consumer products and to ban those goods that are exceptionally hazardous.

Protection of Investors   To protect the investing public against fraudulent activities in the sale of stocks and bonds, both federal and state laws regulate the issuance and public sale of securities. To this end, the federal government enacted the Securities Act of 1933 and the Securities Exchange Act of 1934. The Securities Exchange Act established the powerful Securities and Exchange Commission to enforce the regulations implemented by both acts.

Most small businesses are excluded from extensive regulation under federal law because of the private nature of much of their financing and the small amounts involved. However, they are subject to state **blue-sky laws**, which cover registration of new securities; licensing of dealers, brokers, and salespersons; and prosecution of individuals charged with fraud in connection with the sale of stocks and bonds.

Promotion of Public Welfare   Other laws are designed to benefit the welfare of the public. Local ordinances, for example, establish minimum standards of sanitation for restaurants to protect the health of patrons. Zoning ordinances protect communities from unplanned development.

Environmental protection legislation—at federal, state, and local levels—deals with air pollution, water pollution, solid waste disposal, and handling of toxic substances. As discussed earlier, environmental laws adversely affect some small firms, although they occasionally provide opportunities for others.

The decade of the 1990s is shaping up as a period of strong emphasis on environmental protection. The 1990 amendments to the federal **Clean Air Act** of 1970, for example, put pressure on states to develop better systems for vehicle emissions testing. This, in turn, has required small service stations to make additional investments in testing equipment. The Clean Air Act requires that Freon—a contributor to the destruction of the earth's ozone layer—be recycled from automobile and business air-conditioning systems.

The **Americans with Disabilities Act** (ADA) was passed by Congress in 1990 to bar discrimination against people with disabilities. The act is enforced by the Equal Employment Opportunity Commission. Its provisions bar discrimination against qualified job applicants with disabilities. Businesses with as few as 15 employees must comply with the act's hiring, firing, and promotion policies. The act also requires reasonable accommodation for a disabled person to perform the job; "public accommodation" is also required of all businesses regardless of size.

State governments restrict entry into numerous professions and types of businesses by establishing licensing procedures. For example, physicians, barbers, pharmacists, accountants, lawyers, and real estate salespersons must be licensed. Insurance companies, banks, and public utilities must seek entry permits from state officials. Although licensing protects the public interest, it also tends to restrict the number of professionals and firms in such a way as to reduce competition and increase prices paid by consumers.

Note that there is a difference between licensing that involves a routine application and licensing that prescribes rigid entry standards and screening procedures. The fact that the impetus for much licensing comes from within the affected industry suggests a need for careful scrutiny of licensing proposals to avoid merely protecting a private interest and restricting entry into a field of business. In fact, a case can be made for the regulation of almost any business. However, failure to limit such regulation to the most essential issues undermines freedom of opportunity to enter a business and thereby provide an economic service to the community.

Protection of Employee Rights Business employees are U.S. citizens first and employees second. Therefore, employees are afforded protection from robbery, assault, and other crime at work just as they are at home. In addition, some laws—for example, the Occupational Safety and Health Act of 1970, the Civil Rights Act of 1991, and the Family and Medical Leave Act of 1993—have been designed primarily for employees and potential employees.

The **Occupational Safety and Health Act** of 1970 created the Occupational Safety and Health Administration (OSHA) to ensure safe workplaces and work practices. OSHA continues, through a structured procedure, to establish additional health and safety standards as it deems necessary.

The **Civil Rights Act** of 1964, amended by the Civil Rights Act of 1991, prohibits employment discrimination based on race, color, sex, religion, or national origin. The 1991 Civil Rights Act allows employers to be tried by juries in employment discrimination cases. Workers may now recover punitive damages in sexual harassment cases involving intentional discrimination. Those workers who win a civil rights suit can receive punitive awards ranging from $50,000 (from employers with 100 or fewer employees) to $300,000 (from employers with over 500 employees).[12] The act does exempt firms with fewer than 15 employees. Some entrepreneurs may limit their firms' growth to maintain exempt status.

The **Family and Medical Leave Act** of 1993 was passed and signed into law by President Clinton in February 1993. The law applies to firms with 50 or more employees and requires such firms to allow workers as much as 12 weeks of unpaid leave for adoption of a child, childbirth, or other specified family needs. The worker must have been employed by the firm for 12 months and have worked at least 1,250 hours. Furthermore, the employer must continue health-care coverage during the leave and guarantee that the employee can return to the same or a comparable job. During the first year of this law's application, Labor Department officials reported that approximately 90 percent of employee complaints of noncompliance were resolved with a simple phone call to employers.[13]

Protection of a Firm's Intangible Assets In addition to managing and protecting its physical assets, a business must protect its intangible assets, which include trademarks, patents, copyrights, and trade dress. These four assets are portrayed in Figure 26-2.

TRADEMARKS A **trademark** is a word, name, symbol, device, slogan, or any combination thereof that is used to distinguish a product sold by one manufacturer or merchant. In some cases, a color or scent also can be part of a trademark.[14] Small manufacturers, in particular, often find it desirable to feature an identifying trademark in advertising.

---

12. "Here Comes the Fallout," *Independent Business*, Vol. 3, No. 7 (January–February 1992), p. 44.

13. Laura M. Litvan, "Family Leave Rules Issued," *Nation's Business*, Vol. 83, No. 2 (February 1995), p. 40.

14. See Junda Woo, "Trademark Law Protects Colors, Court Rules," *The Wall Street Journal*, February 25, 1993, p. B1; Junda Woo, "Product's Color Alone Can't Get Trademark Protection," *The Wall Street Journal*, January 5, 1994, p. B2; and Paul M. Barrett, "Color in the Court: Can Tints be Trademarked?" *The Wall Street Journal*, January 5, 1995, p. B1.

Since names that refer to products are trademarks, potential names should be investigated carefully to ensure that they are not already in use. Given the complexity of this task, many entrepreneurs seek the advice of specialized attorneys who are experienced in trademark registration.

Some entrepreneurs may conduct the trademark search personally by using the Trademark Search Library of the U.S. Patent and Trademark Office (PTO) in Arlington, Virginia. The PTO provides its depository libraries with CD-ROMs containing the database of registered and pending marks. It also publishes a booklet entitled *Basic Facts About Registering a Trademark*, which is available at no cost by calling 703-308-HELP. Such publications can also be accessed through the Internet.

Common law recognizes a property right in the ownership of trademarks. However, reliance on common-law rights is not always adequate. For example, Microsoft Corporation, the major supplier of personal computer software, claimed it had common-law rights to the trademark *Windows* because of the enormous industry recognition given the product. Nevertheless, when Microsoft filed a trademark application in 1990 seeking to gain exclusive rights to the name *Windows,* the U.S. Patent and Trademark Office rejected the bid, claiming that the word was a generic term and therefore in the public domain.[15]

Registration of trademarks is permitted under the federal Lanham Trademark Act, making protection easier if infringement is attempted. The act was revised in November 1989 and now allows trademark rights to begin with merely an "intent to use," along with the filing of an application and the payment of fees. Prior to this revision, a firm had to have already used the mark on goods shipped or sold. A trademark registration remains effective for 10 years and may be renewed for additional 10-year periods. Application for such registration can be made to the U.S. Patent and Trademark Office.

A small business must use a trademark properly in order to protect it. Two rules can help. One rule is to make every effort to see that the trade name is not carelessly used in place of the generic name. For example, the Xerox company never wants people to say that they are "xeroxing" something when they are using one of its competitors' copiers. Second, the business should inform the public that the trademark *is* a trademark by labeling it with the symbol ™. If the trademark is registered, the symbol ® or the phrase "Registered in U.S. Patent and Trademark Office" should be used.

PATENTS A patent is the registered, exclusive right of an inventor to make, use, or sell an invention. The two primary types of patents are utility patents and design patents. A **utility patent** covers a new process or protects the function of a product. A **design patent** covers the appearance of a product and ev-

---

15. G. Pascal Zachary, "Microsoft Loses Bid for a Trademark on the Word *Windows* for PC Software," *The Wall Street Journal*, February 25, 1993, p. B9.

erything that is an inseparable part of the product. Utility patents are granted for a period of 17 years, while design patents are effective for 14 years. Patent law also provides for **plant patents**, which cover any distinct and new variety of plants.

Items that may be patented include machines and products, improvements on machines and products, and original designs. Some small manufacturers have patented items that constitute the major part of their product line. Indeed, some businesses such as Polaroid and IBM can trace their origins to a patented invention. Small business owners preparing a patent application often retain a patent attorney to act for them.

Figure 26-3 is a patent description appearing in the government publication *The Official Gazette of the U.S. Patent & Trademark Office*. As you can see, the advertising cap nameplate received its patent on April 2, 1991. This is a very simple idea and not necessarily one that will be profitable for the inventor—but it might be.

Lawsuits concerning patent infringements are costly and should be avoided, if possible. Finding the money and legal talent with which to enforce this legal right is one of the major problems of patent protection in small business. Monetary damages and injunctions are available, however, if an infringement can be proved.

For many years, patent infringement decisions were appealed to 12 circuit courts. Each court had its own interpretation of patent law, resulting in much confusion about what was and was not legal. However, in 1982, the U.S. Court of Appeals for the Federal Circuit was formed, and all patent appeals are now directed to this court, which has "often demonstrated a heavy bent in favor of the rights of patent owners and has put teeth into patent laws in reinterpreting them."[16]

COPYRIGHTS A **copyright** is the exclusive right of a creator (author, composer, designer, or artist) to reproduce, publish, perform, display, or sell work that is the product of that person's intelligence and skill. According to the Copyright Act of 1976, the creator of an original work receives copyright protection for the duration of the creator's life plus 50 years. A "work made for hire" is protected for 100 years from its creation or 75 years from publication, whichever is shorter. Copyrights are registered in the Copyright Office of the Library of Congress.

Under the Copyright Act of 1976, copyrightable works are automatically protected from the moment of their creation. However, any work distributed to the public should contain a copyright notice. The notice consists of three elements (which can also be found on the copyright page of this book):

1. The symbol ©

---

16. Steven D. Glazer, "Patents: A Stake in the Future," *Nation's Business*, Vol. 82, No. 3 (March 1994), p. 36.

2. The year the work was published
3. The copyright owner's name

The law provides that copyrighted work cannot be reproduced by another person or persons without authorization. Even photocopying of such work is prohibited, although an individual may copy a limited amount of material for such purposes as research, criticism, comment, and scholarship. A copyright holder can sue a violator of her or his copyright for damages.

TRADE DRESS A small business may also possess a valuable intangible asset called trade dress. **Trade dress** describes those elements of a firm's distinctive operating image not specifically protected under a trademark, patent, or copyright. Trade dress is the "look" that a firm creates to establish its marketing advantage. For example, if the employees of a pizza retailer dress as prison guards and prisoners, a "jailhouse" image could become uniquely associated with this business and, over time, become its trade dress. One court has defined trade dress as "the total image of a product, including features such as size, shape, color or color combinations, texture, graphics, or even particular sales techniques."[17] Although there are currently no statutes covering trade dress, the courts are beginning to recognize the value of this asset.

BUSINESS AGREEMENTS AND THE LAW

An entrepreneur should be careful in structuring agreements with individuals and businesses. Because today's society seems to encourage lawsuits and legal action toward others, entrepreneurs must understand such basic elements of law as contracts, agency relationships, and negotiable instruments, just to name a few (see Figure 26-4).

Contracts Managers of small firms frequently make agreements with employees, customers, suppliers, and others. If the agreements are legally enforceable, they are called **contracts.** For a valid contract to exist, the following five requirements must be met:

1. *Voluntary agreement.* A genuine offer must be accepted unconditionally by the buyer.
2. *Competent contracting parties.* Contracts with parties who are under legal age, insane, seriously intoxicated, or otherwise unable to understand the nature of the transaction are typically voidable.

17. Maxine Lans Retsky, "The ABCs of Protecting Your Package," *Marketing News* (October 98, 1995), p. 12.

3. *Legal act.* The subject of the agreement must not be in conflict with public policy, as it would be in a contract to sell an illegal product.

4. *Consideration.* The parties must exchange something of value, known in legal terms as *consideration*.

5. *Form of contract consistent with content.* Contracts may be written or oral, but under the **statute of frauds** contracts for the following must be in written form: sales transactions of $500 or more, sales of real estate, and actions that cannot be performed within one year after the contract is made. The existence of an oral contract must be demonstrable in some way; otherwise, it may prove difficult to establish.

If one party to a contract fails to perform in accordance with the contract, the injured party may have recourse to certain remedies. Occasionally, a court will require specific performance of a contract when money damages are not adequate. However, courts are generally reluctant to rule in this manner. In other cases, the injured party has the right to rescind, or cancel, the contract. The most frequently used remedy takes the form of money damages, which are intended to put the injured party in the same condition that he or she would have been in had the contract been performed.

Agency Relationships An **agency relationship** is an arrangement whereby one party—the agent—represents another party—the principal—in contracting with a third person. Examples of agents are the manager of a branch office who acts as an agent of the firm, a partner who acts as an agent for the partnership, and a real estate agent who represents a buyer or seller.

Agents differ in the scope of their authority. The manager of a branch office is a general agent with broad authority. A real estate agent, however, is a special agent with authority to act only in a particular transaction.

The principal is liable to a third party for the performance of contracts made by the agent acting within the scope of his or her authority. The principal is also liable for fraudulent, negligent, and other wrongful acts of an agent that are executed within the scope of the agency relationship.

An agent has certain obligations to the principal. In general, the agent must accept the orders and instructions of the principal, act in good faith, and use prudence and care in the discharge of agency duties. Moreover, the agent is liable if he or she exceeds stipulated authority and causes damage to the third party as a result. An exception occurs when the principal ratifies, or approves, the act, whereupon the principal becomes liable.

It is apparent that the powers of agents can make the agency relationship a potentially dangerous one. For this reason, small firms should exercise care in selecting agents and clearly stipulate their authority and responsibility.

Negotiable Instruments Credit documents that can be transferred from one party to another in place of money are known as **negotiable instruments.** Examples of negotiable instruments are promissory notes, drafts, trade acceptances, and ordinary checks. When a negotiable instrument is in the possession of an individual known as a holder in due course, it is not subject to many of the challenges possible in the case of ordinary contracts. For this reason, a small firm should secure instruments that are prepared in such a way as to make them negotiable. In general, the requirements for a negotiable instrument are as follows:

- There must be a written, signed, unconditional promise or order to pay.
- The amount to be paid in money must be specified.
- The instrument must provide for payment on demand, at a definite time, or at a determinable time.
- The instrument must be payable to the bearer or to the order of someone.

THE CHALLENGE OF TAXATION

Tax evasion accounts for a big part of underpaid federal income taxes, but some underpayment is unintentional and due to the complexity of tax laws. Even an honest mistake can bring the IRS to your business. "Nothing strikes the fear of God in people like receiving a letter from the IRS," says Thomas Sherman, a tax partner in the Coopers & Lybrand firm.[18] Most audits are triggered by IRS computers using a special "score" that is based on relationships of various items on the tax return. Also, certain deductions may be scrutinized in some years because of related court decisions. For example, a 1993 Supreme Court decision restricted the types of business activity that can qualify for home-office deductions. This will likely call attention to these expenses in future audit analyses. Because small firms are often accused of being major tax offenders, they need professional tax advice to ensure that all taxes are paid properly.[19]

Many issues have arisen since the passage of the Tax Reform Act of 1986 and, more recently, the Budget Reconciliation Act of 1993. A complete presentation of tax issues involving small firms would fill several books. The federal government provides Publication 334 each year as a tax guide for small businesses—a document that exceeds 200 pages in length!

---

18. Rick Wartzman, "Don't Wave a Red Flag at the IRS," *The Wall Street Journal*, February 24, 1993, p. C1.
19. Cary Henrie, "Notes from the Underground Economy," *Business Week* (February 15, 1993), p. 99.

Figure 26-5 summarizes the various federal taxes for which a small firm may be liable. It also indicates what type of business organization is liable for each tax, the numbers of the necessary forms, and the filing dates. It's easy to see how all these filing requirements can tend to depress and confuse a small business manager! In March 1994, the Commissioner of the Internal Revenue Service established the IRS Office of Small Business Affairs to serve as the national IRS contact with small businesses, to recommend changes to regulations and administrative practices that cause undue burden or inequity, and to address issues that are important to both small businesses and the IRS.

Table 26-1 summarizes selected federal tax regulations relating to small business issues. The issues chosen for inclusion here are those that have been significantly impacted by the Tax Reform Act of 1986 and subsequent rulings.

Several personal computer tax-preparation software packages, such as *TurboTax*, are available to assist entrepreneurs who choose to prepare their own tax returns. These programs can be tremendously helpful to small business owners as they make their way through the complicated IRS forms.[20] They virtually eliminate the math errors commonly associated with tax preparation. Most of these programs also allow taxpayers to file returns electronically.

We have discussed only the tax burden on a small firm that results from federal taxation. Of course, state, county, and local governments also have taxing authority. In many situations, these taxes are more troublesome than the federal income tax. Even when a small firm has no taxable income, it will usually have taxes to pay. For example, each of the following taxes or fees is levied by a nonfederal agency:

- Sales taxes
- School property taxes
- Motor fuel taxes
- Incorporation fees
- Business license fees
- State income taxes

Despite its laws and tax regulations, there is still no place like the United States for the entrepreneurial spirit. We expect you to be a part of that spirit. Best of luck.

---

20. A good discussion of two of these software programs is found in Walter S. Mossberg, "These Two Programs Offer Some Relief in Taxing Situations," *The Wall Street Journal*, March 11, 1993, p. B1.

Answer Key for Self-Test Questions[1]

Lesson 1 – Small Business in a Big World

1.	a	TV
2.	c	TV
3.	d	page 14
4.	a	page 16
5.	c	page 17
6.	d	TG
7.	d	page 15
8.	a	TV
9.	b	TV
10.	a	TV

Lesson 2 – On Your Own?

1.	b	page 6
2.	d	page 8
3.	c	pages 8–9
4.	d	pages 9–10
5.	b	page 20
6.	c	page 12
7.	c	pages 19–20
8.	d	page 12
9.	c	page 10
10.	d	pages 6–8

1. All page references are to the *Small Business Management* text; TV = television program; TG = telecourse guide.

Lesson 3 – Finding a Niche: Determining Business Potential

1.   c   page 98
2.   d   page 105
3.   a   page 101
4.   d   page 98
5.   a   TV
6.   c   pages 104–105
7.   c   page 113
8.   b   pages 104–105
9.   d   page 109
10.   b   pages 111–112

Lesson 4 – New or Used? Buying a Firm or Starting Your Own

1.   d   page 75
2.   c   page 74
3.   b   page 74
4.   d   pages 81–82
5.   a   page 83
6.   b   page 82
7.   a   page 84
8.   c   pages 85–86
9.   b   pages 86–87
10.   d   pages 89–90

Lesson 5 – The Ties that Bind: Franchising Opportunities

1.   b   page 50
2.   a   page 50
3.   d   page 30
4.   c   page 52
5.   a   pages 53–55
6.   c   pages 55–56
7.   b   pages 63–64
8.   d   pages 58–60
9.   c   pages 55–58
10.   a   pages 58–60

Lesson 6 – A Different Look: The Nicole Miller Story

There is no self–test for this lesson

Lesson 7 – The Business Plan

1.	d	pages 121–122
2.	c	pages 123–125
3.	d	page 131
4.	b	pages 126–127
5.	a	pages 134–135
6.	c	page 135
7.	c	page 132
8.	d	page 135
9.	a	page 128

Lesson 8 – Taking Aim: The Marketing Plan

1.	b	page 145
2.	c	page 145
3.	a	pages 146–147
4.	b	page 147
5.	d	page 147
6.	c	pages 148–152
7.	a	pages 149–150
8.	d	pages 150–151
9.	b	page 155
10.	c	page 156

Lesson 9 – Where to Hang the Sign

1.	d	page 190
2.	d	page 190
3.	b	page 193
4.	b	page 193
5.	c	page 195
6.	a	page 198
7.	d	page 194
8.	b	pages 200–202

Lesson 10 – The Buck Starts Here: Startup Capital

1. d page 222
2. b pages 212–213
3. d pages 215–216
4. c page 213
5. a pages 213, 222–223
6. c page 226
7. b page 226
8. c pages 248
9. a page 247–248
10. c page 246

Lesson 11 – Making it Legal

1. b pages 169–170
2. c pages 176–177
3. a pages 172–173
4. d page 170
5. c page 170
6. b page 172
7. a page 172
8. c page 173
9. d pages 174–176
10. b page 182

Lesson 12 – From the Ground Up: RAW Architectvre

There is no self–test for this lesson

Lesson 13 – The Right Mix: Product/Service Strategies

1. a pages 271–273
2. a pages 274–276
3. d page 276
4. b page 276
5. c pages 273–274
6. a page 278

7.   b   page 284
8.   b   pages 278–279
9.   d   pages 279–282
10.   b   pages 284–286

Lesson 14 – What the Market Will Bear: Pricing Products and Services

1.   b   page 298
2.   e   page 299
3.   a   page 301
4.   d   page 301
5.   c   page 300
6.   d   page 305
7.   a   page 305
8.   b   pages 304–305
9.   c   pages 309–310
10.   b   page 312

Lesson 15 – Out From the Crowd: Promotional Strategies

1.   b   page 324
2.   c   page 325
3.   c   page 324
4.   a   page 324
5.   b   page 333
6.   d   page 327
7.   d   page 327
8.   a   page 327–328
9.   d   page 331
10.   b   page 334

Lesson 16 – Going Places: Distribution Channels and International Marketing

1.   c   page 344
2.   b   page 345
3.   d   page 345
4.   a   page 345

5.	b	pages 346–347
6.	c	pages 347–349
7.	a	page 349
8.	d	page 353

Lesson 17 – A Vintage Blend: The Foris Vineyard Story

There is no self–test for this lesson

Lesson 18 – Making the Pieces Fit: Managing a Small Business

1.	b	page 385
2.	d	pages 386–387
3.	a	pages 386–387
4.	c	page 384
5.	a	page 399
6.	d	page 398
7.	c	page 389
8.	b	page 389
9.	a	pages 391–392
10.	c	page 393
11.	b	page 393

Lesson 19 – The Human Factor: Individuals in the Organization

1.	a	page 411
2.	c	page 413
3.	d	pages 413–414
4.	b	page 414
5.	b	page 422
6.	a	page 416
7.	d	pages 421–422
8.	b	pages 417–419
9.	a	page 419
10.	c	page 420

Lesson 20 – Taking Stock: Purchasing and Inventory Control

1.	d	page 444
2.	b	TG
3.	c	page 448
4.	b	page 445
5.	a	page 446
6.	c	page 451
7.	c	page 446
8.	d	pages 448–450
9.	c	page 447
10.	b	page 448

Lesson 21 – "The Play's the Thing . . ."
The Oregon Shakespeare Festival

There is no self–test for this lesson

Lesson 22 – Keeping Track: Financial Accounting

1.	c	page 484
2.	d	page 485
3.	a	page 485
4.	b	page 209
5.	a	page 209
6.	a	pages 491–492
7.	d	pages 498–500
8.	b	page 489
9.	c	page 493
10.	d	page 497

Lesson 23 – The Money Flow: Management of Working Capital

1.	c	page 507
2.	b	page 514
3.	d	pages 516–517
4.	a	page 519
5.	b	page 520

6.   c   page 519
7.   d   page 521
8.   b   page 522

Lesson 24 – Computers in the Small Business

1.   b   page 458
2.   a   page 460
3.   d   459
4.   a   pages 460–461
5.   c   page 460
6.   a   pages 458–460
7.   c   pages 460–461
8.   b   page 475
9.   d   page 476

Lesson 25 – Risky Business: Risk Management

1.   c   page 544
2.   b   pages 543–544
3.   b   pages 547, 550—551
4.   b   pages 546–548
5.   a   page 550
6.   c   pages 544–545
7.   b   page 545
8.   b   page 554
9.   d   page 555
10. c   page 545

Lesson 26 – Publish or Perish: The Sun Publications Story

There is no self–test for this lesson

Lesson 27 – For Everybody's Good: Social Responsibility

1.   c   page 365
2.   b   page 365
3.   a   page 368

4.	b	page 369
5.	d	page 373–374
6.	d	page 370
7.	b	pages 375–376
8.	a	page 377

Lesson 28 – It's the Law

1.	d	TG Appendix B
2.	a	TG Appendix B
3.	c	TG Appendix B
4.	b	TG Appendix B
5.	d	TG Appendix B
6.	c	TG Appendix B
7.	a	TG Appendix B
8.	d	TG Appendix B
9.	b	TG Appendix B
10.	c	TG Appendix B